The Ultimat

Carol O'Connor,
Sue Stockdale,
Clive Steeper and
Martin Manser

The Teach Yourself series has been trusted around the world for over 75 years. This book is designed to help people at all levels and around the world to further their careers. Learn, from one book, what the experts learn in a lifetime.

Dr Carol O'Connor has more than 30 years' experience teaching leadership. She's worked on five continents for businesses, governments, charities and professional firms with people from every level of management. She believes that anyone can be a leader as long as there is the willingness to step up and take responsibility on the day.

Sue Stockdale is a motivational speaker, executive coach and leadership specialist. She works with leaders and teams in some of Europe's top companies, helping them to achieve exceptional performance. As a highly motivated individual, Sue has represented Scotland in athletics and was the first British woman to ski to the North Pole. Her advice on motivation and business regularly appears in the media. www.suestockdale.com

Clive Steeper has been a business leader running high-growth companies for over 25 years including roles as Managing Director in the UK, USA and Asia. Central to Clive's success has been his ability to motivate people and teams to achieve more than they imagined possible. He now works as an executive coach, consultant and facilitator. In his spare time Clive is a keen motorsports competitor and instructor. www.clivesteeper.com

Martin Manser is a professional reference book editor. His major management experience has been in managing people and projects, including leading a team of nearly 100 people on one of the few twentieth-century study bibles to be originated in the UK (*The Thematic Reference Bible*, Hodder & Stoughton, 1996). He has also led teams to manage the award-winning *Collins Bible Companion* (HarperCollins, 2009) and the best-selling *Macmillan Student's Dictionary* (Macmillan, 2nd edition, 1996). Since 2001 Martin has been a Language Trainer and Consultant with national and international companies and organizations, leading courses on business communications, report writing, project management and time management. www.martinmanser.co.uk

Teach Yourself®

The Ultimate Leadership Book

Inspire Others; Make Smart Decisions; Make a Difference

Carol O'Connor,
Sue Stockdale,
Clive Steeper and
Martin Manser

First published in Great Britain in 2020 by Teach Yourself, an imprint of John Murray Press, a division of Hodder and Stoughton Ltd. An Hachette UK company.

Based on original material from *Leadership In A Week; Motivating People In A Week; Business Communication In A Week; Decision Making In A Week*

British Library Cataloguing in Publication Data: a catalogue record for this title is available from the British Library.

Library of Congress Catalog Card Number: on file.

Paperback ISBN: 978 1 473 68857 5

Ebook ISBN: 978 1 473 68854 4

1

Typeset by Cenveo® Publisher Services.

Printed and bound in Great Britain by CPI Group (UK) Ltd., Croydon, CR0 4YY.

John Murray Press policy is to use papers that are natural, renewable and recyclable products and made from wood grown in sustainable forests. The logging and manufacturing processes are expected to conform to the environmental regulations of the country of origin.

Carmelite House
50 Victoria Embankment
London EC4Y 0DZ
www.hodder.co.uk

Contents

Part 4: Your Decision Making Masterclass

PART 1
Your Leadership Masterclass

Introduction

World events in business and politics reveal the importance of leadership. When it is absent, things fall apart. When it inspires, things improve. The purpose of this book is to encourage good people to become leaders by presenting the basics. Using a step-by-step approach, it shows the way to gain skill through training and effort.

Anyone can be a leader, even if modesty, lack of experience or self-doubt get in the way. This first Part guides readers to identify their strengths and build upon them. It also helps them to focus on their weaknesses in order to manage them better.

The central theme is **self-awareness.** Its importance underlies every activity, idea and suggestion. People often surprise themselves when they begin to explore their inner resources and discover that they have untapped leadership qualities. The result is personal growth as well as their leadership development.

However, taking charge is never easy. Each chapter in this Part features the challenges as well as the benefits of leadership. Among these is the need to inspire other people and gain their support. Leaders must also set priorities, give direction and make decisions, often under pressure of both time and resources.

CHAPTER 1

Self-awareness

The first step to successful leadership is developing **self-awareness**. Leaders who lack personal insight are like tone-deaf musicians. Even if they gain technical skills through drill and practice, they begin each performance at a great disadvantage. They don't know if the notes they play are sweet or sour until their audience reacts.

Leaders need to cut the risk of striking the wrong note by adjusting their actions immediately. Self-awareness shows them how. Four topics support developing awareness:

- Leadership essentials
- Assessing strengths and weaknesses
- Following the leader
- Personal development.

Leadership essentials

There are three commonly held ideas about leadership:

1 Leadership is hereditary, and leaders are born to their role.
2 Character traits make a leader, including ambition, charisma, confidence, intelligence, initiative and independence, among many others.
3 Leaders emerge when special situations require them to accept leadership responsibility.

For many years, businesses, universities and the military have all debated the true nature of leadership. These ideas are still discussed around the world, and each idea has such firm support that this discussion could go on for ever.

However, everyone does agree on one point. It is clear that leaders must have the **support of their followers** because only this gives them the authority to act. When leaders lose this support, it is only a matter of time before they also lose their position as leader.

James MacGregor Burns wrote in the 1970s that leaders and followers need each other. He said that, when leaders represent their followers fairly, and followers loyally support their leaders, they create a virtuous circle. Also, if leaders later fail to respect their followers, then this circle breaks down, and the followers withdraw their support.

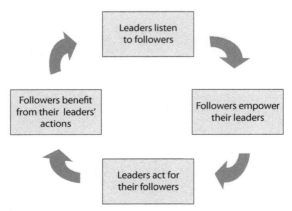

The virtuous circle of leadership

Respect is earned, and a leader's primary task is to convince people that they are worthy of receiving their support. Without followers, leadership exists only in the imagination of the would-be leader. The relationship between leaders and followers is crucial and far more important than birthright, personal qualities, a specific situation or any combination of these.

Any definition of leadership should include the idea of both leaders and followers needing each other. Here is a good definition:

> **'Leadership is the ability to present a vision so that others want to achieve it. Leaders need the skill to work with other people as well as the belief that they can make a difference.'**

People who have different backgrounds can work well together when they have a common purpose and shared goals. It's the leader's task to:

- focus everyone's attention on identifying these goals
- encourage discussion and debate until the goals are fully understood by all
- inspire action so that the goals are achieved.

All of this takes self-confidence and many would-be leaders have doubts about their abilities. There are many quiet heroes who question their own leadership ability but choose to accept responsibility anyway. This means they face self-doubt and then find the necessary confidence to take action. Therefore a first step towards leadership excellence is to gain **confidence.**

It's interesting that those who already believe in themselves and their own inner worth seem naturally to receive respect and recognition from others, while those who need to develop a sense of self-worth often receive little approval from others.

The process of gaining **respect** can begin in everyday life, when potential leaders make an effort to understand other peoples' difficulties. Mutual appreciation begins when colleagues notice other people's problems as well as their own. This is the basis for giving and receiving respect.

There are leaders who gain power through bullying or manipulation. History and news stories about politics and business show repeatedly that this kind of behaviour works for the short term only.

Those leaders who inspire, build, create and encourage others to succeed have **long-term success** and are remembered well into the future. Those who undermine, destroy, cheat and belittle others are avoided or destroyed as soon as their power weakens – as it always does.

Assessing strengths and weaknesses

Leaders need to know their strengths and weaknesses. This gives them a starting point to improve their leadership performance. One source of information about leadership effectiveness is **feedback** from other people. Asking colleagues what they think can be a valuable exercise. Occasionally, however, other people's ideas are biased, imprecise or lack perception.

So how can leaders know which comments are going to be helpful and which are not? Also, how can they avoid being defensive when they hear negative comments? They only make things worse if they try to explain away their behaviour or make excuses for themselves. They can also resent those who risked making a candid remark.

A good solution for dealing with negative comments is for leaders first to assess their own behaviour before asking anyone else for feedback. This **self-assessment** gives them a baseline against which their colleagues' comments can be considered carefully.

An honest self-image, clear goals for personal development and newly set performance standards can help a leader to decide whether colleagues' comments are helpful and appropriate, or signal the need for a further change of behaviour.

Self-assessment requires strict honesty. It is a waste of time and opportunity to create a fictional self-image. It is also self-defeating. Leaders need to see the difference between who they are now and who they want to be. They need to distinguish between their **current skills** and their **future hopes.** Honest self-assessment can produce goals for personal development and a plan of action to achieve them. Questions they can ask themselves include:

- Am I fair?
- Do I take responsibility?
- Do I listen?
- Do I care about other people?
- Am I honest?
- Am I willing to debate?
- Do my colleagues trust me?

Following the leader

Improved leadership is based on a careful study of *actual* behaviour. The first challenge is to ask: Would I follow a leader like myself? If not, then this is the starting point for discovering how to become the kind of leader that people want to follow.

It helps to think of a recent leadership experience and then focus on its details. Begin the process by **listing five positive and five negative examples** of your own actual and current leadership behaviour.

If there are fewer than ten examples, or if there are more positive than negative examples, this can signal a need for developing greater self-awareness. Concentrate and try to add one more example to each category before attempting the activity below.

However, fewer than ten examples could also mean a lack of leadership experience. If this is the case, then use the shorter list. After finishing the whole book, return to this section and repeat this activity until there are at least ten items.

After identifying examples of positive and negative leadership behaviour, it's time to include colleagues' opinions and beliefs. This new list should include their *honest opinions* about your

leadership behaviour. However, if it really isn't possible to ask colleagues directly, think about their reactions to you. Try to see yourself through other people's eyes.

Once again, make two lists. The first should include *positive* comments made by colleagues about your leadership behaviour or an estimate of their opinion about you. The second should include their *negative* comments or a best guess for this.

The following activity uses both your self-assessed and colleagues' lists in order to improve self-awareness.

Activity

Compare the two lists: your *self-assessment* and your *colleagues' ideas*.

- Are they the same throughout?
- If not, what are the differences?
- How can you increase your awareness of how other people see you?
- How can you increase self-awareness of your own behaviour?

Personal development

Identifying positive and negative leadership behaviour supports self-improvement. However, **behavioural change** should always build on qualities that a leader already has so that changes enrich natural personality. Everyone has a unique blend of qualities, such as courage, patience, faith, ambition and honesty. It's the unique mixture of **core qualities** that are the source of leadership success.

When leaders identify and accept their core qualities, then they can draw on these with greater confidence. It also helps them to discover what other qualities they need but may lack. This **self-audit** is a good first step to improving their leadership performance in future.

For example, an inability to give clear directions is a negative leadership behaviour. But there are a variety of potential causes for this, including a lack of confidence or decision-making skills, or even a need for clearer thinking or determination.

Therefore the same problem of 'an inability to give clear directions' could require a *different* solution depending upon each person's blend of qualities and their personal make-up. Improved leadership depends upon discovering what causes the negative leadership behaviour.

Positive behaviour

So how can leaders discover what qualities they already have and what qualities they need to develop? The two lists of positive leadership behaviour you compiled earlier in this chapter offer a way to begin this process. Each item from the two lists can help you to identify **personal qualities.**

For example, a positive item could read: 'remained calm during a crisis'. This behaviour could result from a variety of qualities such as courage, steadiness and trust. The task is to identify the quality that is the source of *remaining calm during a crisis.* When leaders know which qualities they already possess, they can actively draw upon them when the occasion requires it.

This insight has the direct benefit of improving self-confidence. 'I am calm in a crisis because I have courage' is a thought that obviously enhances self-image. Once a quality is identified for each item on the list, this can be written next to the item. Some qualities may be repeated and some may offer a surprise. The point of this activity is to discover qualities that underlie each example of positive behaviour.

This can be challenging if any qualities on the list are not normally associated with leadership, such as gentleness or humility. As a result, it can be tempting to ignore these qualities. However, many great leaders are guided by qualities like these and they are valuable features of any leader's personality. The challenge is learning how and when to express the less obvious leadership qualities so that they enhance leadership behaviour.

This is always possible, and the process begins with self-acceptance and the wish to discover how to express each quality in a strong and positive way. Personal development means **building on existing strengths** and **managing any weaknesses.** Masking or hiding personal qualities creates good actors, not good leaders.

Negative behaviour

The two lists of **negative leadership behaviour** you compiled earlier also offer learning opportunities. For example, if a comment on the list refers to using humour when presenting official company business, this creates an opportunity for choice, including:

- deciding that humour is an inappropriate leadership quality
- ignoring any criticism by showing increased clowning behaviour
- learning from the comment and deciding when, where and how a leader should use humour.

Rather than react blindly to negative comments, the leader can *analyse* them instead. On hearing a negative comment, a leader should ask the following questions.

- Did I really do what this person says I did?
- Does this person have all the facts?
- On reflection, do I truly believe that my behaviour was appropriate to all three essentials: time, place and audience?
- If not, when, where and how is it appropriate to express this quality in this way?

Changing behaviour

Both positive and negative feedback helps leaders see how their behaviour has an impact on other people. Positive comments are useful for identifying personal qualities. Negative feedback offers an opportunity to change behaviour.

In general, personal development can be organized into three areas: skills, knowledge and experience. Both positive and negative behaviour can offer ideas for improvement.

It may help to review the lists of behaviour you compiled once again, both positive and negative. Choose just one item and decide *three* goals for that item:

1 a goal for developing a **new skill**
2 a goal for gaining **new knowledge**
3 a goal for having **new experience.**

After achieving all of the goals for that item, proceed to choose another item from the lists. Set three goals for that item to improve skills, knowledge and experience.

Solutions for self-doubt

Self-awareness supports leadership because it shows what skills and qualities can be developed. Here are examples of issues, both physical and emotional, that many people argue make them unfit to lead. If this is what they truly believe, then so be it. But if they feel even a small flicker of a wish to lead and to make a difference as a leader, then they should explore this.

They may discover that there is an antidote to resolve the issue that they believe is holding them back. In fact, there is always an antidote. There is always a way forward. There is always a solution. *Always*. The leader's job is to find it.

Issue	Solution
High, squeaky voice	Singing lessons
Confused thinking	Learn to play chess
Weak physical presence	Martial arts or fencing
Poor stamina	Swimming
Fear of public speaking	Join Toastmasters™
Indecisiveness	Video gaming

Summary

Self-awareness is the single most important leadership quality. Leaders need to examine their behaviour regularly to continue their growth and improve their self-knowledge.

Here is a checklist to help you review your leadership performance during any work week.

1 What qualities did you express consistently throughout the week?

2 What attention did you give to creating positive relationships with your colleagues?

3 List three strengths in the way you dealt with your colleagues.

4 How can you build on these strengths next week?

5 List three weaknesses in the way you dealt with your colleagues.

6 What quality or qualities do you need to develop in order to improve on these weaknesses?

Fact-check (answers at the back)

1. How should leaders react to negative comments?
   a) By changing behaviour ❏
   b) By ignoring them ❏
   c) By analysing them ❏
   d) By defending themselves ❏

2. What should be key to any definition of leadership?
   a) Dignity ❏
   b) Status ❏
   c) Charisma ❏
   d) Supporters ❏

3. What is the first step to assessing your strengths and weaknesses?
   a) Ask a close friend ❏
   b) Study yourself ❏
   c) Ask your boss ❏
   d) List future goals ❏

4. How is leadership improved?
   a) With new skills ❏
   b) With hope ❏
   c) With ambition ❏
   d) By adventures ❏

5. What is the most important thing leaders need?
   a) Mentors ❏
   b) Self-awareness ❏
   c) Allies ❏
   d) Risks ❏

6. What use is negative feedback?
   a) To reveal enemies ❏
   b) No use: it should be ignored ❏
   c) To support development ❏
   d) To punish people ❏

7. If someone feels unfit to lead, what should they do?
   a) Find an antidote ❏
   b) Give up ❏
   c) Blame their boss ❏
   d) Change jobs ❏

8. Confidence can be what?
   a) Faked ❏
   b) Developed ❏
   c) Trouble ❏
   d) The same as arrogance ❏

9. Which of their qualities should leaders know and build on?
   a) The interesting ones ❏
   b) The funny ones ❏
   c) The worthy ones ❏
   d) The core ones ❏

10. What kind of relationships do leaders need with their supporters?
    a) Positive ❏
    b) Temporary ❏
    c) Complex ❏
    d) Difficult ❏

CHAPTER 2

Understanding people

Leaders can use a one-size-fits-all approach only if everyone is actually the same size, and this is never going to be the case. There are as many different personalities in the world as there are people.

It's this diversity that makes life interesting. It generates new ideas and lively debate. Leaders who can attract a wide range of people enrich their business. However, they also need to understand people and be able to allow them to be different.

And it's an acceptance of differences that makes relationships strong. This chapter includes three topics that help leaders understand people better. They are:

- motivation and drives
- what people need
- rewards and values.

Motivation and drives

Leaders who recognize that everyone is different can encourage other people to be themselves and express their individual skills and qualities. This produces better work in the long term, although it may cause short-term frustration and frazzled tempers. It takes time to develop understanding when people are very different, but it is well worth the effort.

Fearful leaders try to squash individual difference, often because they are either unwilling or unable to understand those who are unlike themselves. This behaviour is unfortunate because these leaders lose an opportunity to see the world through other people's eyes. This insight could draw new customers or create new products or innovative services.

Although everyone is different, everyone is also the same. Scientific research says that, around the world and across cultures, people are motivated by the same things and in the same way. Motivation is like an internal engine driving people to get up in the morning, have breakfast and start their day's activities.

However, motivation works in two different ways. Some people are motivated only when they feel pressure from outside themselves to take action. An example would be a person who dislikes their job but needs the money that work provides. This is called **external motivation**, and the need for money is one example of an external motivator.

Other people get satisfaction from their jobs and enjoy going to work. Of course, they want and need to be paid, but their motivation comes from inside themselves. This is called **internal motivation.** Getting things done takes much less energy when motivation comes from within.

There will always be occasions when the pressure to achieve a goal or do a task comes from outside. When this happens, there's the risk of unwilling workers needing to be prodded and pushed, or reluctant leaders who grouch at everyone and are very difficult to follow.

However, each person can choose to control how they react to bad news or unpleasant work. People who make a habit of being internally motivated also give themselves the option of seeing unpleasant work as part of their own bigger plan. They will see themselves as the choosers, even when circumstances seemingly force them to accept.

At times, pressure from outside increases so gradually that leaders fail to see it happening. To avoid a sudden feeling of being overwhelmed or burned out, it's best to check daily on personal reactions to work and to colleagues. The outside pressure will still be there, but taking its measure allows people to pace themselves.

Leaders have to **ask what other people need,** and not assume that they know what is best for them without asking. Everyone needs different things at each stage of their lives. For example, a young person of 20 has different priorities and family needs from someone of 50. Also, what a middle-aged boss needs in terms of working hours, salary or holiday time may be very different from the junior manager who wants to travel or have a busy social life.

What people need

Abraham Maslow, a leading psychologist in the twentieth century, pioneered the study of healthy motivation. He said that people have five levels of need. The first level is the need to survive, the second level is the need to feel safe and secure, the third is the need to belong, the fourth is the need to be respected, and at the top is the need to have a sense of purpose.

The 'Hierarchy of Needs', according to Abraham Maslow

Maslow defined each need as follows:

- **survival** – the drive to stay alive
- **security** – the need for stability, health and safety
- **belonging** – the wish to feel part of the social group
- **respect** – the need to be valued and respected
- **growth** – the need for purpose and meaning in life.

He said that satisfaction at each level allows a person to move naturally to the next level. For example, an infant is entirely dependent upon others for food, warmth and protection – that is, its survival. When this need is fulfilled, the infant must ensure that its next level of need is also fulfilled – that is, that its survival carries forward to the next day and then the next.

Babies learn at an early age how to get the attention they need: some scream while others smile and babble. Whatever tactic they use, their aim is first for survival and then security. When these needs are met, they are then able to relax into caring relationships. This is the level of belonging, and it is here that they discover who deserves their affection and how this should be shown.

Children who in their early years are denied safety and security may get stuck at this level. Their lack of family life, a secure home or a caring group may block their ability to fulfil their need to belong. If this happens, then in later life they will rarely feel fully relaxed in a social group. They are always on the lookout for danger and as a result question other people's motives.

This is because their attention is still on their need to satisfy survival and security needs. Even when they already have enough money, a home and a good job, they feel that something is missing and that they never have enough. Their pursuit of security can even get in the way of happy and healthy relationships.

Alternatively, when people are able to satisfy the first two levels of need, survival and security, they naturally focus on finding their place in the group. Even when rejected, their sense of security helps them to accept this so that they either find another group or try again to join the same group. They tend to see social rejection as a relatively minor issue.

According to Dr Maslow, healthy growth is based on satisfying each level of need in turn. Therefore, when the first three levels of need are satisfied, people naturally move to the two higher needs – that is, gaining respect and having a purpose and meaning in life.

Essentially, this means that people who are hungry and homeless always want to satisfy survival and safety needs before they feel ready to discuss philosophy. This also means that unsatisfied needs dominate behaviour. People who are under stress about money or are in poor health have less energy for team relationships.

Although business leaders are not expected to be psychologists, the **Hierarchy of Needs** is a valuable tool for understanding what motivates other people as well as themselves. They can ask if there are special circumstances influencing their colleagues. Even if they cannot help, their interest will have a positive effect.

Leaders should recognize the **impact of needs on motivation and performance.** This is the key to playing to people's strengths and also helping them to overcome their weaknesses. Motivation is never uniform or consistent within a group of people. Leaders can discover each person's starting point and build on this.

Leaders who want to support motivation can start by learning more about where their colleagues are blocked on the hierarchy. Whenever someone shows consistent frustration or anger about a level of need, this may mean they are fixed on satisfying the needs of the level below it.

That level may have trapped them so that they just can't understand the level above. Understanding people's frustration and limitations shows a leader **how to present a vision so that others want to achieve it.**

Activity

Think of a colleague at work.
What does this person talk about most often:
- physical comforts?
- job security?
- money and spending habits?
- friends, family, social events?
- job satisfaction, status, recognition?
- values, principles, quality work?

Are there any needs that they never discuss?
What are they?
Are there any needs that cause them to show impatience or anger when mentioned?

For example, when presenting an idea for a quality improvement programme – this is a level-four or -five need – to people who fear losing their jobs, it is less effective to talk about quality for its own sake. Describe instead what is in it for them and their job security.

Rewards and values

Some scientists say there are **three basic personality types** that result in three different kinds of behaviour. These can be summarized as:

1 ambitious and assertive
2 analytical and cautious
3 caring and supportive.

However, a person who is ambitious and assertive can also be caring, supportive, analytical or cautious whenever they make that choice or when the occasion requires it. Leaders with self-awareness widen their range of choice. When people think clearly about what they are doing, they will be more effective at achieving their goals.

These personality types are like habits. For example, when people are faced with similar choices every day, they develop a routine and habitual way of choosing what they do. Leaders can improve their performance by:

● identifying their personality type
● becoming aware of any habits and routines that limit their choices.

Ambitious and assertive

Ambitious and assertive types often have more ideas than there are hours in the day to achieve them. They are driven by a need to make their mark on the world and to influence other people. They very much dislike being ignored or refused access to important events and people.

Unsurprisingly, they like to be rewarded for their efforts. They want to be paid well, but primarily because this symbolizes their status. They also feel well rewarded by a large workspace or if they are praised often in public.

Although this type of person is very challenging for leaders, nothing stops this type when they are motivated to complete a task. It's also interesting that ambitious and assertive types don't mind being criticized. They have a rhinoceros hide. Instead of being hurt or embarrassed, they very likely will defend themselves or treat the criticism as a joke. Confident leaders who can accept debate are able to draw the best out of this kind of person.

Analytical and cautious

This personality type is committed to problem solving for its own sake. They are happiest when working alone and enjoy the solitude, the opportunity to concentrate, and the independence this gives them. Completing a task for them is very rewarding. For example, this kind of person genuinely feels burdened when expected to attend an office party because it interferes with their work.

Keeping their eyes down, they focus exclusively on what they are doing. They can be a big asset to the group because they bring depth to problem solving and enjoy studying complex issues.

However, the leader must be aware of this type's need for privacy. They are not shy; they just like to be alone and dislike offers of help from a caring and supportive type. They also resent the demanding behaviour of the ambitious and assertive type.

Caring and supportive

This personality type is happiest when offering care and support, and is naturally warm and friendly to all. Such people are a positive force in any group because they consider the needs of others and are generous and kind.

They feel most rewarded when their help is accepted. These are genuine virtues, but occasionally their support arises from a desire to please and be liked.

The leader's task is to guide this kind of person towards greater independence because too much people-focus can create deference to others when they should take more initiative.

Caring and supportive types can be intimidated by outspoken ambitious and assertive types because they interpret direct and bold feedback as harsh criticism. They also will need reassurance when analytical and cautious types, the loners in the group, refuse their support or even tell them to go away.

1 Using the list that follows, create a 'bank' of positive and negative words that you believe apply to yourself.

Also, create another list of any words you've heard others say more than twice in relation to yourself.

Do the words you circled show an obvious preference for one of the three kinds of behaviour?

2 Look at the descriptions of the three personality types. Do any of these descriptions match your behaviour?

Do you have any habits that could get in the way of your ability to lead? What are they?

Can you imagine what it would be like to be a different personality type?

Ambitious and assertive	
Positive features	*Negative features*
● confident	● arrogant
● dynamic	● pushy
● risk-taking	● gambling
● spontaneous	● impulsive
● directing	● dictatorial
● entrepreneurial	● unco-operative
● resourceful	● calculating
Caring and supportive	
Positive features	*Negative features*
● sensitive	● highly strung
● devoted	● doormat
● idealistic	● deluded
● friendly	● naive
● tolerant	● blind
● patient	● passive
● understanding	● submissive

Analytical and cautious	
Positive features	*Negative features*
● practical	● narrow-minded
● independent	● self-serving
● fair	● impersonal
● thorough	● obsessive
● reserved	● isolated
● methodical	● slow
● principled	● rigid

There are leaders who believe they need to appear special, more brilliant and somehow better than others. Even 50 years ago this would have been considered conventional leadership behaviour. However, this approach doesn't really work any more. People are better educated and more confident about asking questions and checking facts. The Internet, social networking, Twitter-type communication and blogging make information instantly available. As a result, leaders need real skill to inspire others.

Leaders who are willing to ask people what they value and then listen to the answers are likely to gain their attention. **Understanding other people** can lead to being better understood in turn.

Activity

Think of one occasion during the day when you took the lead.

Describe this occasion in one or two sentences. Then answer the following questions:

● What did you want to achieve as leader?

● What personal needs did you satisfy by leading?

● Were you aware of what motivated the people you were leading?

● Did you consider their needs?

● Was your behaviour 'ambitious and assertive', 'analytical and cautious' or 'caring and supportive'?

Summary

Successful leaders speak directly to people's needs, hopes and dreams. Recognizing and respecting these will create bonds of loyalty and trust between leaders and followers. It's also important to know what motivates people and what makes them feel rewarded.

Here is a checklist as a reminder that understanding people is a lifelong task. Use it to review leadership behaviour at the end of this book and also in the future.

1 Were you able to identify with your colleagues during the week?
2 How did people react when you asked them to do something or give you something?
3 Have any of the people you met merged into an indistinct group?
4 If you had taken time, could you have learned more about other people this week?
5 List three of your strengths for the way you learn about other people.
6 How can you build on these strengths?
7 List three weaknesses in the way you learn about other people.
8 What behaviour do you need to change to improve on these weaknesses?

Fact-check (answers at the back)

1. What are externally motivated people driven by?
   a) Outside pressure ❏
   b) Information ❏
   c) Gossip ❏
   d) Changes in the weather ❏

2. What are internally motivated people driven by?
   a) Power ❏
   b) Friendship ❏
   c) Choice ❏
   d) Money ❏

3. Which of the following is *not* included in Dr Maslow's hierarchy?
   a) Growth ❏
   b) Power ❏
   c) Survival ❏
   d) Security ❏

4. When colleagues are afraid of taking risks, what should you do?
   a) Ignore them ❏
   b) Ridicule them ❏
   c) Force them ❏
   d) Respect them ❏

5. What has an impact on motivation?
   a) Family ❏
   b) Fulfilling needs ❏
   c) Travel ❏
   d) Education ❏

6. Which of the following do ambitious and assertive types want?
   a) Influence ❏
   b) Isolation ❏
   c) Affection ❏
   d) Fairness ❏

7. Which of the following do caring and supportive types want?
   a) Caution ❏
   b) Arguments ❏
   c) Harmony ❏
   d) Power ❏

8. Which of the following do analytical and cautious types want?
   a) To take risks ❏
   b) Privacy ❏
   c) Teamwork ❏
   d) Friendship ❏

9. How can you demotivate ambitious and assertive types?
   a) With a high salary ❏
   b) With a big office ❏
   c) With anger ❏
   d) By neglect ❏

10. How can you demotivate caring and supportive types?
    a) With criticism ❏
    b) With parties ❏
    c) With friendship ❏
    d) With praise ❏

CHAPTER 3

Communication

Communication is the glue that holds people together. It's the way they share ideas and feelings, and the means they use to bond and form groups. Its importance is most obvious when it breaks down. Almost immediately, disagreements, quarrels and misunderstandings occur.

For all that, communication skills are frequently taken for granted. People assume that only time, effort and sincerity are necessary to communicate successfully. This optimistic view ignores the importance of emotion, motivation, intelligence, risk-taking and feelings of competition, among many other issues.

Therefore communication is the third step for improving leadership, and this chapter features the topics of:

- listening and speaking
- making an impression
- group discussion.

Listening and speaking

In its simplest form, communication is an exchange of information. This happens most often through speaking and listening, two activities that require complex skills and draw upon a person's lifetime of experience.

Even a brief encounter consisting of a casual greeting results from years of practice. Through trial and error, people create a personal style and adapt their behaviour to meet the changing needs of each situation. However, these exchanges happen so quickly and occur so often that people rarely consider whether they are any good at just saying hello.

It is important, however, for leaders to get this right because a greeting sets the tone of the exchange and shows the degree of respect that people share. The way a leader makes eye contact, gestures and chooses words invites people either to listen to the main portion of the conversation or, alternatively, turns them off.

Listening

This skill requires a leader to be aware of three things: bias, visual signs and vocal signals.

1 Bias Everyone's point of view includes some bias, even if this is not entirely conscious. Bias, by definition, is a way of thinking that colours a point of view about a person, an event or an idea. For leaders, bias can influence and even undermine the ability to understand and interpret what they see and hear. The main challenge is to identify when bias weakens judgement and reduces understanding about what is said.

Bias is a problem when it distorts understanding. It actually becomes dangerous when a leader doesn't know it is happening or even denies its existence. Bias can cause a leader to ignore essential data – for example, when the information source is unattractive or in some way different from the leader.

Indicators of bias include:

- extreme reactions to people or situations, either in favour or against
- paying attention only to that part of a presentation that is already understood
- assuming there is an understanding of what is being said even before a statement is finished.

2 Visual signs These refer to a speaker's gestures and movements, what is often called **body language.** There are numerous books, courses, podcasts and videos about this topic that interpret commonly used gestures and signs. These often are a sincere effort to improve understanding.

However, in a world that brings together different cultures through media and transportation links, leaders have to remind themselves constantly that gestures can mean different things to people from different societies.

This is because people interpret body language according to their own backgrounds. Any population including more than one nationality will lack a single meaning for hand gestures or facial expressions. So it's better to avoid thinking that there is only one meaning for body language as if there were a universal code available.

Gestures add a layer of meaning to what's being said with words. They enrich communication and alert a listener to subtleties within the message. For example, gestures and expressions show when the speaker is being funny, ironic, dramatic or sad, and a range of other emotions. They can also show intensity of feeling. Visual signs make it easier for listeners to understand what the speaker really means.

Emoticons are a substitute for physical gestures when speakers use the written word. These are icons showing facial expressions that are made using punctuation marks. When using instant messaging, email, text or online posts of any kind, emoticons show emotion and mood. Emoticons came into being in response to the increased dependence on electronic text-based communication. Their emergence recognizes that it's a mistake to assume automatically that people will understand a writer's intentions or feelings. They alert readers to be aware of emotional content whenever there may be room for doubt. Crucially, they serve to remove emotional ambiguity from whatever is being written.

3 Vocal signals Listening to the sound and tone of a speaker's voice improves understanding. Speakers can express their ideas and add deeper and richer meaning by raising and lowering the volume of their voice, changing its tone or pitch or by varying their speed of delivery. They can signal their emotional state as well as their attitude towards the audience through their voice.

At times, it's more important to hear these subtle, vocal messages than the content of what is being said. If a speaker's tone of voice contrasts with the content of their message, then it's necessary to ask for clarification. This requires tact, but it improves understanding.

Speaking

Some leaders like to let their words flow freely and their ideas emerge spontaneously without any internal editing. This is fine for the naturally eloquent, the vivid raconteur or the disciplined presenter. It also works for everyday conversation or lightweight social chat. However, if speakers suffer from confused thinking, ramble around their topic, or enjoy the sound of their own voice, then they have a problem.

A challenging business conversation requires an ordered and logical presentation of ideas. Leaders must also be aware of managing their time and respecting other people's. Clear and direct delivery encourages listening.

Effective speakers use three techniques to make listening easier. These are headlining, pacing and summarizing.

1 Headlining This is a brief opening statement that catches the listener's attention. It is comparable to a news headline that signals a story's main idea. Speakers can organize what they want to say in a series of headlines. This helps listeners identify the key points and also helps speakers avoid a rambling or wordy presentation.

2 Pacing Good speakers watch their audience and pace their delivery to meet their listeners' needs. This could mean that they pause to invite their listeners to comment. Their listeners can then answer the speaker or offer their own new headline. However, some speakers believe that their turn is over only once they have used up every one of their own ideas. This can exhaust an audience.

Pacing also refers to changing the speed of delivery as well as pausing before or after key ideas to create dramatic interest. An unwavering tone of voice and rhythm is often boring.

3 Summarizing 'I tell them what I plan to say; then I tell them; then I tell them what I just said.' This is an age-old saying for report writing and public speaking, but isn't really suitable for everyday conversation. It does contain a gem of wisdom, however.

Summarizing is a good way for speakers to end each topic by repeating the headline and then listing, bullet-point fashion, whatever has been discussed or agreed. The speaker then asks whether everyone understands.

Activity

During three conversations, practise these techniques.

Conversation 1: Headlining

- Before you begin speaking, think of headlines for your main thoughts.
- Begin by stating your first headline.
- Speak so that you expand only on this first headline.
- Move to the next headline after your listener responds.
- Be aware of when you move to the next headline.

Conversation 2: Pacing

- Listen carefully to the pace used by the other speaker.
- Then, when you speak, notice if your pace is different.
- If so, alter your pace to match that of the other person.
- Watch for signals that the other person has finished.
- Identify the signals you use to let others know you have finished speaking.

Conversation 3: Summarizing

- When you finish a headline, paraphrase what you said.
- After several contributions by both speakers, highlight the key points that were covered.
- When the discussion slows, clearly state the conclusions reached so far.
- At the end of the conversation, list all the headlines that were covered.

Making an impression

Communication also includes the impression people make. There are speakers who make an audience feel uneasy, and others who create a relaxed atmosphere. People may not know exactly why they trust someone or, alternatively, want to back away from someone else. They may just sense that something is wrong.

For example, there are those who smile with their mouths, but glare with their eyes. People notice and then decide not to trust that speaker. Another source of discomfort can be a mismatch with appearance. For example, a speaker wearing an expensive suit can raise alarm bells if listeners also see scuffed shoes, dirty hair and chewed fingernails.

The overall impression these speakers make is one of disharmony. This can be accidental and occur because speakers don't know that they are sending out contradictory signals. Their goal should be to use gestures, facial expressions, language and style of dress so that these are in harmony with the content of what they are saying. The six actions leaders can take to create a single and harmonious impression are:

1 have a goal
2 check your appearance
3 manage your emotions
4 choose time and place
5 keep it simple
6 control yourself.

Have a goal

A discussion is more satisfying when everyone believes time is well used, progress is being made and that learning is taking place. This is easier when there is a clear purpose for the communication. This purpose decides choice of words and brings confidence to their delivery.

Check your appearance

Look in the mirror and ask yourself: Would I trust or believe me? If the answer is no, then ask why. This often requires humility. Ensuring that style of dress matches the situation helps listeners accept what is being said.

Manage your emotions

Leaders need a delivery style that will work in a variety of situations. For example, when doctors give bad news to their patients, they know that this requires gravity and a serious manner. But consider the situation of the doctor who just moments before seeing a patient receives very good news.

Professionals train themselves to match their own facial expressions to the needs of the situation. To do this, they must know how they are feeling themselves and then keep this in check.

Choose time and place

This means planning when and where a message should be delivered. The question to ask before speaking is this: How would I react to hearing this information at this time and in this place? Whatever the answer, act in line with it.

Keep it simple

Decide the main points and phrase these into headlines. Avoid using leadership as an excuse to share your every thought and feeling. The task is to get a message across in a memorable, but simple, way.

Control yourself

This refers to self-discipline. For example, when people disagree or express their anger, stay calm at all times. Anyone can react emotionally or in a mindless way. Leaders should not.

Even if the situation seems to demand shouting, banging the desk or even running away, the leader stays calm. Why? Because that is part of the job of being leader.

Let's summarize:

Group discussion

It's the leader's responsibility to open a debate, encourage everyone to participate, and guide the discussion towards agreement. Group discussion, when managed well, supports unity and understanding. This can be a challenge when difficult issues are raised and there is little or no agreement at the start.

Some leaders give up at the first sign of dissent or confusion and order silence. They fear loss of control. This is a mistake. It's better not to open a debate or encourage people to share opinions if they are later told they may not disagree.

This is unwise for three reasons:

1 because people will express disagreement only when the leader is absent
2 because avoiding conflict makes a leader look weak and panic-stricken, not strong
3 because it is rude to ask for opinions and then change direction and say be quiet – colleagues are unlikely to share their opinions in future as a result.

It takes courage to listen to opposing views and also to insist that a debate is respectful to all. Leaders who are committed to creating understanding demonstrate this by setting a tone of tolerance to other people's views. It's already been said that respect generates respect, and the discussion leader has the power to begin this process.

45

The main challenges are to encourage **active participation** while avoiding an opinion free-for-all or allowing the group show-off to talk until everyone is asleep. Genuine unity emerges when differences are accepted. It helps when the group has ground rules to ensure that everyone gets a fair hearing. The leader can then maintain those rules.

When a group lacks ground rules, the leader has to get the group itself to create them. **Ground rules** should include: attentive listening, no interruptions, taking turns to speak, and waiting to be acknowledged before speaking.

Formal meetings may require using the organization's in-house guidelines or legal reporting standards. There are reference books describing how a meeting moderator should behave when leading formal meetings. This next section, however, offers ideas for leading *informal* discussions.

In informal discussions, leadership needs to have the skills of:

- guiding
- paraphrasing
- intervention.

Guiding

The first task for discussion leaders is to state the purpose of the discussion, the amount of time available and a reminder of the ground rules. Once the discussion is under way, the leader gently guides participants so that they stay on track, and ensures that no single person dominates the debate. In practice, this means that no one speaks until they are called upon to do so.

The leader must be scrupulously fair because people soon lose interest when some people take too long to make their point or when others are repeatedly called upon. The situation worsens when people begin talking over those who have been speaking for too long. If speaking in turn is a ground rule (and it should be), then it's the leader's job to maintain this.

It takes courage to insist that forceful people wait their turn because leaders become unpopular with those who like to dominate. Leaders have to be firm when anyone interrupts.

Their job is to point out that interruptions are not allowed and that everyone must wait their turn.

The leadership qualities that support effective group discussion include tact, a good memory for what's been said and who has spoken, a sense of humour, firmness and a commitment to timekeeping.

Helpful phrases

'That's an interruption. Please allow the speaker to finish.'

'I've got to ask everyone not to interrupt.'

'Let each speaker have their say.'

'That's an interesting contribution but someone else is speaking. Please wait your turn.'

'Your enthusiasm is great, but we need to hear as many different views as time allows.'

Paraphrasing

When a discussion wanders from the main point, paraphrasing allows the leader to bring it back on track. This is achieved by summarizing what was said during the digression, and then linking it – if at all possible – back to the main discussion topic. This has to be done in a non-judgemental manner.

When leaders catch digression quickly, it's easier to reaffirm the main topic without obvious strain on people's time and attention. The person who began the digression can also be invited to add the topic to the next meeting's agenda.

Helpful phrases

'This is interesting but we've left the main topic.'

'This covers some good points and they link to our main topic in this way.'

'Let's summarize this side topic's points so far. We can return to it later in this meeting or put it on the agenda for next time.'

Intervention

When two people are locked in a dispute, the leader has to intervene or their disagreement will dominate an entire meeting. This situation occurs most often when there are strong factions in a group. A spokesperson for one faction speaks forcefully and then the spokesperson for the opposition answers. It's just like a tennis match, but with a conversational ball going back and forth.

The leader must step in immediately and point out that two opinions have been presented, and now other members of the group should comment. If the same people ask to speak again, the leader has to insist that they've had their say and now others need a chance to speak.

Helpful phrases

'Thanks for your views. Now, what do others in the group think?

'You two, please, take a back seat while someone who agrees with each of you paraphrases.'

'Let's avoid a dialogue between just two people. Who else wants to comment?'

Summary

Communication skills benefit all aspects of life, not just leadership development. Although they are often taken for granted, these skills are essential. Listening and speaking are foundation stones. Also important is the impression a leader makes. This can be managed by thinking about six actions to make a positive impression.

Here is a checklist to review communication behaviour:

1 How would you describe your communication behaviour during the past week?

2 What did you like and not like about this, and how can you improve?

3 Did you prepare for any important meetings by thinking about the impression you would make?

4 List three strengths for your listening skills. How can you build on these strengths?

5 List three weaknesses for your listening skills. How can you manage these weaknesses?

6 Now list three strengths for your speaking skills. How can you build on these strengths?

7 List three weaknesses for your speaking skills. How can you manage these weaknesses?

8 Did you lead a group discussion this week? If so, what did you like and not like about the way you led this?

Fact-check (answers at the back)

1. Which word best describes bias?
    a) Distortion ❏
    b) Clarity ❏
    c) Seeing ❏
    d) Honesty ❏

2. What are emoticons?
    a) Important speeches ❏
    b) Football chants ❏
    c) Radio signals ❏
    d) Punctuation marks ❏

3. What does a 'single and harmonious impression' lead to?
    a) Expensive clothes ❏
    b) Good manners ❏
    c) Trust ❏
    d) A clearer voice ❏

4. Which of these helps make a positive impression when speaking?
    a) Staring ❏
    b) Forcefulness ❏
    c) Ambition ❏
    d) Timing ❏

5. Which of these supports group discussion?
    a) Ground rules ❏
    b) Dominant speakers ❏
    c) Bias ❏
    d) Emotion ❏

6. When listening, which of these needs your attention?
    a) Content ❏
    b) Bias ❏
    c) Cleanliness ❏
    d) Pacing ❏

7. When speaking, what do gestures add?
    a) Confusion ❏
    b) Sound ❏
    c) Meaning ❏
    d) Distance ❏

8. When speaking, what do headlines signal?
    a) Urgency ❏
    b) The core idea ❏
    c) News ❏
    d) Timing ❏

9. What does paraphrasing help the leader manage?
    a) Anger ❏
    b) Laziness ❏
    c) Writing ❏
    d) Digression ❏

10. What does group discussion lead to?
    a) Unity ❏
    b) Fear ❏
    c) Wasted time ❏
    d) Egotism ❏

CHAPTER 4

Authority and power

For many people, the words 'authority' and 'power' are menacing and negative. This is because bad leaders from both history and recent times have made them their own. But there are many more leaders who have integrity than those who want the role for glory, power or to satisfy their greed.

The best leaders use authority and power wisely and have the confidence to encourage debate. Different opinions interest them and they can listen to others without feeling threatened. This chapter features five topics that support using authority and power effectively. They are:

- styles of leadership
- four kinds of power
- using power
- adapting to events
- delegation.

What is authority?

Having the title 'Leader' doesn't automatically mean that a person has the authority to lead. A job title is just the starting point. It is the leader's behaviour that encourages people to give their support or discourages them from doing so. In practice, appointed leaders can even be ignored or bypassed.

These are leaders in name only who believe that they must use threats or coercion to get people to obey them. This approach requires an enormous outlay of their energy. It would actually be much easier for them to behave in a way that inspires confidence and makes people want to follow. However, this does take skill.

Discussion, feedback sessions and debate are essential for leaders to learn what their followers want and need. Therefore part of a leader's job is to encourage this. Repressing, ignoring or discouraging different opinions in the group is the sign of a weak and frightened leader who is hiding behind a role in order to stay in control.

Here's a definition of authority:

'Authority is the legitimate and justified claim to exercise power. It is granted by others and can be based on a set of rules, established traditions, or the emerging needs of a situation.'

Confidence, curiosity and **tolerance** are qualities of strong leadership. Inevitably, leaders who possess these also want to include other people in discussions. They willingly share the limelight whenever it is appropriate.

Every leader potentially can be undermined, manipulated or overthrown. However, this results more often when leaders refuse to allow other people to express different points of view. An open attitude and a willingness to listen create a bond between leader and follower. This is because people like those who listen to them and who show an interest in their ideas.

Styles of leadership

Authority is expressed through leadership style. Research shows that there are three basic styles. These are:

- democratic
- autocratic
- permissive.

Democratic

A democratic style is based on mutual respect among colleagues, regardless of role or status. When these leaders discover their colleagues lack skills or experience, they create opportunities for them to grow and develop. The strength of this style is the positive atmosphere it creates and the belief that innovation will be rewarded and new ideas tested and explored.

People learn from one another when leaders use this style, and everyone gains, including the leaders. There are few more satisfying leadership experiences than to start with a group of moderately skilled people who then work and grow together so that they emerge as a skilled and powerful team.

In contrast, there are leaders who feel frustrated because they believe themselves surrounded by witless underlings rather than peers. Even when they hire intelligent and talented new people, these new ones also gradually prove themselves unsatisfactory. These leaders have a serious problem because they cannot see that their leadership is to blame. When the whole world looks consistently wrong, it is time to improve the viewer – not the viewed.

Autocratic

During times of turbulence and chaos, the autocratic leadership style appeals to those who long for a strong boss who will to tell them what to do. Certainly, there are enough historic examples of dictators that were invited into power to show that autocratic leaders can be valued.

However, there is strong research which suggests that groups with a single, command-giving leader suffer poorer productivity over the long term, and are far less profitable than those that are democratically led.

When leaders are too frightened, too proud or too conceited to listen to their colleagues, they weaken their own authority. In contrast, it's a show of personal strength to open a discussion. It shows confidence in their authority, good judgement and their willingness to learn.

Permissive

The permissive style is often a misguided attempt at being democratic. These leaders are reluctant to impose their will on other people. This may result from a dislike of being bossed themselves, a lack of interest in their work, self-doubt or even laziness.

Whatever the reason for their refusal to take responsibility for leadership, these leaders are infuriating to other people whose work requires co-ordination, active support and direction.

People need and want a plain-speaking leader to remind them of their goals, keep them on track, focus their discussions, challenge performance and act as their champion. Permissive leaders fail to realize that this is part of their job.

Although colleagues may *like* these seemingly nice-guy leaders – both male and female – they also describe them as weak, spineless and incompetent, and regret the day they began working for them. Sadly, if or when these leaders discover what other people think about them, they are shocked, hurt and disappointed.

However, permissive leadership may be beneficial when leading highly creative people or those with professional or technical expertise. A leader using the permissive style allows these types of people to digress and explore while encouraging them to work together and produce results. This style depends on vision and sharing inspiring ideas on a regular basis.

All three leadership styles can both help and harm a situation and leaders need to decide when to use each style. We can sum this up as follows:

Benefits

Democratic: These leaders encourage everyone to use their skills and talents so that more work of a higher quality gets done.

Autocratic: These leaders offer speed, single-mindedness and clarity when firm direction is needed. There are occasions when people do gain from being told exactly what to do.

Permissive: These leaders are best when taking responsibility for highly creative people who flourish in a loosely structured environment. This style is useful when little co-ordination is needed.

Frustrations

Democratic: These leaders drive impatient colleagues crazy because discussion takes time and slows progress.

Autocratic: These leaders are so one-sided that they frustrate colleagues who want to contribute ideas and offer new information.

Permissive: These leaders force their colleagues to accept inactivity through their avoidance of giving direction and taking action themselves.

Four kinds of power

There are four kinds of power used in most organizations. Leaders can use all of them or just one. The four are:

1 designated
2 expert
3 charismatic
4 information.

Designated power

This kind of power is linked to a specific job or role. Leaders with this power are officially appointed to act on behalf of their organization. When leaders leave their role, they also give up the power that went with that role.

This means that the department head who vacates a position no longer has the power to lead that department. This power passes to the next person taking that role. Although a loss of role-related power can seem obvious, there are people who refuse to give it up or to accept that someone else has taken their former role. People create bad feeling when they refuse to step aside gracefully.

Expert power

This kind of power results from the personal talents, skills and experience of the people who possess it. They have this power regardless of the role they fill. When they move to another job, their expertise goes with them. This power is acquired through study, training and learning new skills.

When a person has both *designated* and *expert* power, they are in a very strong position. However, those who really enjoy the technical aspects of their work often find their designated role gets in the way of using their expertise. This causes some experts to avoid designated roles.

Expert power is often used informally. Leaders who have a designated role as their only source of power benefit everyone when they support the experts in the group.

Charismatic power

Those with charismatic power have both a blessing and a curse. They are frequently wild cards in an organization. Historically, the highly charismatic are those leaders who end up dead, in disgrace, alone, in prison or in Holly- or Bollywood.

Charismatic leaders can truly inspire their colleagues to do their best. The downside is that it is this very ability that can then tempt these leaders to depend upon charisma as their sole source of influence. This is less than wise. To ensure that they have substance along with charm and dazzle, these leaders should develop and draw upon other sources of power as well.

Information power

Digital technology enables storage of vast amounts of information. People who know how to organize data and then access it as usable knowledge are now crucial to organizations. Regardless of job title or placement within the hierarchy, knowledge workers are truly powerful.

In the past, it was the long-serving members of staff who had information power. They would be called upon to remember where items were stored, or when an event occurred. Databases replace human memory, and those managing the data now have this power.

Using power

Exercising authority is easier when the leader's source of power is obvious and easily recognized. Designated power is the only one that is given to a leader by others. Expert power results from study and experience. Charisma is an internal quality that attracts and fascinates other people. And information power, like expertise, is acquired and is based on data-management skills

On rare occasions, a leader has all four kinds of power. This strengthens their leadership position, but can also be dangerous because people avoid questioning them. These leaders risk surrounding themselves with yes-saying admirers. Although this can also happen to those with just one kind of power, it is more likely when a leader has several.

Adapting to events

Effective leaders are flexible when deciding which leadership style is best at any given time. They do this by identifying the stage of development of their group. This is called the **Situational Leadership Model.** It says that groups develop in four stages, and that leaders should adapt their style to match the group's needs at each stage.

- The **first stage** starts when the group forms. The leader's role at this point should be directive to ensure that the work gets under way. This means telling people what to do at first to get things moving. Once group members understand their assignments, the leader encourages them.
- The **second stage** is coaching, where the leader explains why the task is important and supports group members to gain skill and confidence.
- The **third stage** encourages strong relationships so that group members can better support each other. This is the participating stage and the leader asks everyone to offer ideas and solutions to improve the task.
- At the **fourth stage,** the leader delegates work decisions to group members who take responsibility themselves for the work.

Groups that go through all four stages are said to be **mature.** This four-stage model helps leaders decide what leadership style best serves their group's needs. It also explains why groups on occasion benefit from being told what to do and at other times resent this same behaviour.

Delegation

Delegation skills help leaders move the group forward. They are particularly useful at the *coaching* and *participating* stages of development because delegation encourages group members to learn new skills and gain more experience. This supports their accepting more responsibility within the group. There are four steps to effective delegation:

1 define the task
2 explain why it is important
3 describe expectations
4 evaluate results when the task is finished.

1 Define the task

This step can seem so obvious that some leaders don't give it any attention. Instead, they hand out assignments and assume people will guess what is needed and by when. Leaders who want to ensure reliable results need to do two things:

● take time to decide what they want
● ask the person being delegated how they think the task should be done.

Asking to hear the delegatee's ideas at the very start reveals their level of knowledge and understanding. It also raises their level of interest and commitment to getting the job done. This is called **empowerment** because it encourages the person who will do the task to take responsibility for its completion and success.

2 Explain why it is important

Many people do their best when they know the purpose of a task. They want to see how it fits into their work overall and why it is important.

This information also makes their deadlines more meaningful and helps them set priorities, organize steps, and fit their work into what their colleagues are doing on the same project. This reduces mistakes and duplicated effort.

3 Describe expectations

People want to know what is expected of them; otherwise their work is a guessing game. This should include budget limits, quality standards and any required procedures or processes. Some leaders give delegatees little information of this kind, arguing that they want to give the delegatee complete freedom to decide what to do. However, their colleagues are not mind-readers. Unless they have done the same task before, the delegator should explain what is required.

Making colleagues guess also undermines motivation because they do not know where they stand. This is power hoarding and negative leadership behaviour. Even when a leader is rushed, under stress or has an optimistic belief in a colleague's abilities, expectations should be explained.

4 Evaluate results when the task is finished

This step builds on the previous one. Fully explained expectations give clear performance goals towards which everyone can work. Some leaders share criteria for success only after the task is complete. This often causes unnecessary disappointment when a task is evaluated. It's also unfair because guessing a goal and getting it right is almost impossible.

Activity

- Describe an episode during the day when you were a leader.
- What kind of power did you use?
- Could you have used any other kind(s) of power?
- Which style of leadership did you use? Were you happy with this choice?
- What stage of development would you estimate your group has achieved?

Summary

The best leaders want to take charge in order to make a positive impact on the world. This means they need to have both authority and power. This chapter focused on leaders being confident enough to invite challenges, questions and comments from other people.

Use the following checklist to review the way you use power now. You can also use these questions to examine your use of authority and power in future as well.

1 Do you feel good about how you express power and authority?

2 If yes, what do you like? If no, what do you dislike and how can you change this?

3 Are you aware of using different kinds of power?

4 Are you better at using one kind over the others?

5 Are you happy with your leadership style?

6 What do you like and not like about your style?

7 How can you improve?

Fact-check (answers at the back)

1. What is authority?
   a) Automatic ❏
   b) Power ❏
   c) Harmful ❏
   d) Threatening ❏

2. Which word refers to a kind of power?
   a) Expert ❏
   b) Dictator ❏
   c) Helpless ❏
   d) Absolute ❏

3. When is the permissive leadership style best?
   a) When people are frightened ❏
   b) When people are creative ❏
   c) When people are lazy ❏
   d) When people are focused ❏

4. When is the autocratic leadership style best?
   a) During discussion ❏
   b) During periods of inaction ❏
   c) During a debate ❏
   d) During a crisis ❏

5. Which is a step in the delegation process?
   a) Guessing ❏
   b) Awareness ❏
   c) Evaluation ❏
   d) Coaching ❏

6. What do democratic leaders want their colleagues to be?
   a) Strong ❏
   b) Obedient ❏
   c) Frightened ❏
   d) Silent ❏

7. What is charismatic power similar to?
   a) Aggression ❏
   b) Trouble ❏
   c) Resentment ❏
   d) Charm ❏

8. Democratic leaders frustrate people who are what?
   a) Attentive ❏
   b) Impatient ❏
   c) Debaters ❏
   d) Talented ❏

9. Autocratic leadership can lead to what?
   a) Peace ❏
   b) Freedom ❏
   c) Weakness ❏
   d) Success ❏

10. Which of the following is a stage in the Situational Leadership Model?
    a) Coaching ❏
    b) Expert ❏
    c) Designated ❏
    d) Information ❏

CHAPTER 5

Making decisions

There are two approaches to decision making: rational (step by step) and creative (intuition driven). Leaders who can draw on both approaches make better decisions.

This chapter, however, focuses on rational decision making. It is useful for leaders who are required to make fast decisions when under pressure. It also helps leaders develop their analytical skills, forcing them to think clearly when faced with a sea of information. The three core topics for rational decision making are:

- setting priorities
- clarifying goals
- a step-by-step method.

Setting priorities

Leaders often have to make several decisions at once and juggle different streams of information at the same time. They also suffer distraction when their decisions have an impact on other matters. When this happens, they need to identify just how much interdependence exists across a variety of issues.

Setting priorities is therefore an essential skill. This takes discipline because some decisions demand attention even though they lack genuine urgency or importance. Alternatively, other truly vital matters can be ignored because they lack glamour or a noisy advocate pressing for their attention.

The first step is to recognize that there are two aspects to every priority: **urgency** and **importance.** For example, assigning a staff member to give a group of schoolchildren a tour of the building has limited business importance. It becomes urgent when the children are standing in the cold while waiting to be invited inside.

The leader's task is to identify these two aspects and then act upon them.

Urgent and important

It takes skill to put decisions into these two categories, a skill that is usually developed through trial and error. There is no golden rulebook to guide a leader to see what is crucial, nor are there right and wrong answers. Over time and with practice, leaders learn to balance urgency with importance.

The main challenge arises when some decisions appear to fit into neither category while others fit both. Also, there are decisions that are only urgent because they have deadlines and provide the basis for future decisions. For example, an organization may want to add an extension to its building and it therefore decides to file a request with the town council. Meeting the council's deadline for this filing has urgency, although the actual building work is scheduled for the next year.

Setting priorities begins by making a list of all the decisions currently under review. To illustrate this, let's imagine that the manager of a ten-person accounts department decides to review all of the upcoming decisions and issues.

He begins by making his list: office decoration, holiday schedules, allocation of staff to new projects and a new health insurance package proposed by the company's personnel office. Each of these decisions includes sub-issues that contribute to making the main decision.

However, the manager wants to avoid getting drawn into the details of each decision before deciding their urgency and importance. His time is particularly tight and so he wants clarity about deadlines as well as an idea about workload so that he can manage day-to-day business and meet future goals.

After the manager lists all the decisions, each can be assessed for urgency and importance. Another list could include all of the sub-issues under each main decision.

List of items	Urgent	Important
Office decoration	No	No
Holiday schedules	Yes	No
Staff project allocation	Yes	Yes
Health insurance	No	Yes

On the list shown here of the main items only, the manager believes that office decoration is neither urgent nor important for the business. Although money is budgeted and there has been much discussion about colours and materials, the proposal originated from their company headquarters 300 miles away.

The staff are enthusiastic, but also happy with their office as it is. This is also the department's busiest season and everyone feels highly pressured by work. The manager decides to send a short email to the person taking charge of this project to ask for an update on progress.

The next item, holiday schedules, is an urgent matter for the short term because people need to make holiday plans with their families. The actual schedule isn't important as long as everyone receives a fair amount of holiday. He decides to send an email to everyone saying that he's posting a holiday sign-up sheet on the office notice board.

Staff allocation for new project work is both urgent and important for the success of the department. The decision is urgent because several projects are just finishing and new assignments must be made to allow people to prepare and make a smooth transition to their new work.

It's also important because skilful scheduling of the right people to the right work directly impacts the department's productivity and therefore its overall budget. The manager likes to meet one to one with staff when each project ends. This gives him an opportunity to ask everyone for their highs and lows on the project and also what they learned. During these meetings, he writes a bullet-point summary for reference during annual reviews and to support future decisions about training.

The decision about health insurance isn't due for weeks, and staff received all the information months ago. However, it's very unlikely that everyone has read this material as yet. They must do this because their decision will lock them into a health plan for an indefinite period. The manager decides to email everyone a reminder using a joke he likes about a doctor attending the wrong patient.

Activity

1 List all the decisions you have to make right now.

2 Identify which are main decisions and which are sub-tasks that contribute to the main decisions.

3 Put a star next to each main decision and then group all of the sub-tasks under each of their main headings.

4 Add another two columns next to the listed items. Label these columns urgent and important.

5 Decide urgency and importance for each item.

6 Make a timeline by drawing a line on a piece of paper and writing the item with the most distant deadline at the bottom of the line, and the item with the most urgent deadline at the top.

7 Next, put any items on the timeline which are important but do not have deadlines. Estimate where they belong relative to the items with deadlines.

8 Finally, put the items that are neither urgent nor important on the line, placing them relative to all the other items.

Drawing a timeline (item 6 in the Activity box) gets things started, but each decision on the list may need further refinement. To illustrate this, the office decoration item can be interpreted in a variety of ways.

For some, it has sub-tasks that include choosing a colour scheme, painting the walls, buying new furniture and creating a layout. For others, the sub-tasks could mean tearing up the floor to upgrade the computer system. So items 1 and 2 in the Activity box need to be clarified.

Clarifying goals

Misunderstandings about goals can disrupt a project at the very start. The office decoration decision is an example. Those in the group who believe that the goal is to improve the office environment will make suggestions that reflect this. Those who think the decision is about upgrading the computer system will neither understand nor be happy with these ideas. There can be much cross-talk and even argument before they all realize that they've interpreted the decision's goal in different ways.

The successful outcome for any decision starts with a **clearly stated goal.** Time is wasted when people lack a shared view of what needs to be done. Alternatively, when goals are clarified, the actions needed to achieve them are undertaken more efficiently.

A goal is a realistic target for achievement. In decision making, it makes explicit the desired end result and the requirements for the decision's success.

The process of setting goals helps decision makers discuss fully what they think should be the end result of the decision. With a shared goal in mind, they can plan a course of action to achieve that goal.

Goals also give decision makers a standard against which they can evaluate their options. They can improve their course of action in order to serve their goal best.

Defining goals

Here are three business situations that require a decision. They each illustrate the importance of how a **goal statement** is phrased:

1 To raise the company's profile
2 To reduce customer complaints by 20 per cent
3 To purchase a two-acre piece of land adjoining the company's headquarters

The **first goal statement** is the most general, and is useful when beginning a decision-making session. It presents a desired end result in general terms and invites people to offer a variety of options. Their options present more specific solutions that can be further discussed.

This discussion helps clarify how each person interprets the idea of raising the company's profile. As a result they can further narrow the focus of their debate. For example, some of the options they generate could include:

- sponsoring a marathon or sports activity
- advertising in a national paper
- getting press coverage for community service projects
- a company executive joining the local school board
- organizing opportunities for executives to speak at conferences or be quoted in the press
- joining professional networking groups.

These six very different options make it obvious that the decision makers have different ideas about what it means to raise the company's profile. So before making a decision about what to do, they have to clarify what they really hope to achieve. For example, do they want to raise their profile nationally or locally? The answer helps them narrow the focus for a second round of suggestions.

The **second goal statement**, to reduce customer complaints by 20 per cent, is more specific. It includes an exact measurement for the decrease. Any option that fails to meet this criterion can be readily eliminated.

When a specific quantity or a precise detail is included in a goal, there should be a good business reason. Details enhance the goal only when they're based on fact and data.

The **third goal statement** is very specific. It limits any options to those that meet all its criteria. This kind of goal is useful when decision makers already know what they need to do. Their task in this case is to generate ideas for how to achieve the goal, rather than to decide what the goal should be.

Stages in the process

The three examples from the previous section show goals that serve decision making at different stages in the process. For example, at the very start it's helpful to have a goal that is phrased in general terms. This invites a variety of options to help the decision makers clarify what needs to be done.

The second style of goal statement is often given to a committee or project team, by bosses, with a mandate to get it done. However, this goal statement usually needs further clarification.

For example, 'customer complaints' might refer to those made to the in-house customer service department, or to blogs, online review sites, social networking sites, or just to the number of items returned after sales. Particularly when this goal statement is non-negotiable and handed ready-formed to decision makers, then it's best to know what it means.

The third style of goal statement usually results after a lot of discussion and hard work about logistical matters of price, timing and legalities. After this goal is identified, however, decision makers may discover that it is impossible to achieve. For example, the landowners may refuse to sell or the price may be too high.

The decision makers must then ask themselves why they wanted that specific piece of land and what else they could do to get the same result without buying that parcel of land. This can open the way to new options they haven't yet considered.

A step-by-step method

There are risks involved in decision making, and the most obvious is making the wrong choice. Decision makers can work to avoid this by using a step-by-step method. Here are the steps:

1 Write a goal statement for the decision.
2 Gather as much information as possible.
3 Generate several options that serve the goal.

4 Ask if the options reveal different interpretations.
5 If so, rephrase the goal statement and repeat step 3.
6 When the goal accurately describes what the decision should achieve, identify at least three options that serve this goal.
7 Test the options using the tally sheets and method described below.
8 Act on the winning option.

Testing the options

Every decision can be met in several ways. That's what creating options is all about. However, when there are several attractive options, it helps if each can be tested against criteria that serve the spirit of the goal. These criteria should be identified just after the goal statement is produced.

There are two levels of criteria: primary requirements and secondary requirements. The **primary requirements** are features that must be satisfied if the goal is to be achieved. **Secondary requirements** support the goal but are not vital.

The crucial difference between primary and secondary requirements is that failure to meet primary requirements will defeat the goal. Primary requirements must be fully met or it is a deal breaker. In contrast, failing to satisfy secondary requirements merely means that the decision is somewhat less suitable, but it still satisfies the goal.

A decision about choosing a holiday illustrates this process. In the following example, a couple has fixed limits for cost, timing and travel method. These are the basis for the holiday's primary requirements. Failure to meet any one of these primary requirements means not having their holiday.

Here are the three primary requirements:

- short travel time – only one work week available
- £2,000 maximum budget for both people
- warm and sunny climate – one person needs the sun to recover from an illness.

In addition, the couple has secondary requirements. These criteria are important to them but not as critical as their primary concerns. Here is a list of their secondary requirements:

● resort on the beach to minimize walking
● travel and hotel package available
● location popular with an age group under 30
● comfortable journey to the hotel
● stable exchange rate
● their native language widely spoken
● sightseeing and night life.

The couple has online information and also brochures for at least 20 resorts. Their goal statement helps them exclude any place featuring adventure sports, educational sightseeing, gourmet dining and a high risk of bad weather. They next list three possible resorts on the tally sheet. Here is a sample of the tally sheet they used:

Goal statement (their desired end result):

Primary requirements	A: Florida World	B: La Plage Splendide	C: Costa Fabula
Short travel time	2 days	1 day	1.5 days
£2,000 maximum budget	£2,500	£1,950	£1,800
Warm and sunny climate	----	yes	yes

They then test their shortlisted resorts against their primary requirements. Both want to go to Florida World, but they have limited holiday time. It would take them a full day of travel to get there – leaving at dawn on a Saturday from a major airport and arriving in Florida late in the evening. Then they would repeat this for their journey home. But they really like the idea and so say, 'Well, maybe,' and write two days in the column.

The next primary requirement refers to cost. Florida World brings them over budget by £500. This is just too much and so reluctantly they decide they have to exclude this option. This means that, even if Florida World meets any further criteria, primary or secondary, it is still off the table.

This illustrates the idea that, if an option fails to meet even one primary requirement, then it is no longer an option.

So the couple looks at La Plage Splendide in France and Costa Fabula in Spain. Both have short journey times. They can reach the French resort from a small airport very near their home, and journey time is about an hour. Total time there and back will be about one day. Costa Fabula is a bit farther from the Spanish airport, but they could still be on the beach by late afternoon of the same day they depart.

Both options are within their budget and also offer sun and dependable weather. Because they meet all their primary requirements, the couple can now test the two options against their list of secondary requirements. They use another tally sheet for this.

After listing their secondary requirements, they score each option, from 1 to 10, against each criterion. This scoring process is subjective and based on how well the couple estimates the option meets the criterion.

The higher the score, the better the option meets the criterion. For example, the French resort has a private beach with cabins, showers and changing rooms on the sand. Costa Fabula's beach is across a road with a narrow strip of sand. So they give Splendide a perfect 10, and Fabula a score of 6.

Secondary requirements	B: La Plage Splendide	C: Costa Fabula
Resort on the beach	10	6
Travel and hotel package	10	7
Location popular with age group	9	8
Comfortable journey to the hotel	10	6
Stable exchange rate	7	7
Native language widely spoken	6	8
Sightseeing and night life	9	6
Total	61	48

Travel to Splendide is easier than to Fabula and so the couple scores them accordingly. Both are good in terms of appealing to their peer group, but once again Splendide wins because the Costa Fabula draws a slightly younger crowd.

The exchange rate for the Eurozone is reasonably stable, so both options score the same. The Spanish resort features ten languages spoken, while the French hotel says its staff speak English, but it's likely they will prefer to speak only French. However, the French resort has better sightseeing, while the Spanish location offers only a night club scene.

The final score for Splendide is higher than the score for Fabula and so is the clear winner. However, at this stage the couple can review these scores to be sure they consider what is really important to them. They could still decide on Fabula if they identify a new secondary requirement.

What they cannot do is return to Florida World. Once an option fails to meet primary requirements, then it is out. Only if decision makers change or eliminate a primary requirement can an option be returned to the tally. But this means that the changed requirement wasn't really critical and should not have been listed as primary.

This decision-making method forces people to make systematic choices based on known information. It helps avoid wavering and returning to options that are unrealistic and unsuitable.

Activity

- Think of a decision you made today.
- Describe this in one or two sentences.
- Did you have any sense of its priority?
- If so, how did you know this?
- How easily could you distinguish between urgency and long-term importance?
- Did you have a goal or know the outcome you wanted the decision to achieve?
- If you could make the same decision a second time, would you do anything differently?

Summary

Making decisions quickly and implementing them are important leadership skills. It requires identifying priorities and setting goals. However, the best way to improve decision making is actually to make a great many decisions and then evaluate them.

Here is a checklist to help you examine decision-making behaviour on a regular basis:

1 Think about the decisions that you made during the last week. Did you set priorities? Score yourself on your **priority-setting skills** from 1 to 10 (1 = low and 10 = high scoring).

2 Did you use the **step-by-step method**? Score yourself on your use of this method from 1 to 10 (1 = low and 10 = high scoring).

3 Score your ability to identify **primary requirements** (1 = low and 10 = high scoring).

4 Score your ability to identify **secondary requirements** (1 = low and 10 = high scoring).

5 What can you do to improve your decision-making skills overall?

Fact-check (answers at the back)

1. In addition to urgency, what does a priority include?
   a) Importance ❏
   b) Limits ❏
   c) Deadlines ❏
   d) Challenge ❏

2. Which of the following describes a goal?
   a) Primary ❏
   b) Target ❏
   c) Timing ❏
   d) Urgent ❏

3. Which of the following belongs to the step-by-step method?
   a) Intuition ❏
   b) Waiting ❏
   c) Patience ❏
   d) Options ❏

4. What are primary requirements ?
   a) Fixed ❏
   b) Standard ❏
   c) Urgent ❏
   d) Long term ❏

5. What are secondary requirements?
   a) Fixed ❏
   b) Absolute ❏
   c) Supportive ❏
   d) Expensive ❏

6. What does a timeline help to manage?
   a) People ❏
   b) Deadlines ❏
   c) Money ❏
   d) Sub-issues ❏

7. Goals help decision makers to do what?
   a) Delay what they need to do ❏
   b) Wonder what they need to do ❏
   c) Hide from what they need to do ❏
   d) Identify what they need to do ❏

8. What do options need to be?
   a) Short term ❏
   b) Fun ❏
   c) Tested ❏
   d) Urgent ❏

9. The scores given to secondary requirements are what?
   a) Subjective ❏
   b) Priorities ❏
   c) Decisions ❏
   d) Basic ❏

10. What gives leaders a way to manage their decisions?
    a) Setting the time ❏
    b) Identifying problems ❏
    c) Setting priorities ❏
    d) Giving orders ❏

CHAPTER 6

Connecting and linking

Connecting and linking are twenty-first-century skills. They are driven by technology and increasingly are starting points for relationships, both business and social. Leaders need to understand technology and also its uses in order to form networks of colleagues, friends and allies.

In the past, isolation at the top put leaders at risk. Because power and status can intimidate people, leaders can gradually be cut off from those who tell them the truth or challenge their point of view. Now social networking applications alongside widely available Internet links allow leaders to contact supporters directly. The three topics that help leaders make connections are:

- living in a small world
- building trust
- leading at a distance.

Living in a small world

Imagine that each of your friends has at least three contacts that you do not know. Then each of these three new contacts also has three more people that you don't know. This means there are at least 12 people that you don't know but who are connected to you through this single friend. This network of potential contacts is invisible, but real, and is essential to help leaders stay connected to their followers.

Microsoft research

A few years ago, computer scientists at Microsoft Research wanted to know how closely connected people are around the world. Because Microsoft owns Microsoft Messenger, they were able to study all of the instant messages their customers sent. An instant message (IM) is a text message sent 'live' over the Internet. The IM service lets people text back and forth at the same time as each other.

These scientists analysed one month's worth of conversations, which included 30 billion messages among 240 million people. Now, obviously those 240 people do not all know one another. However, the scientists wanted to know how many connections might be shared among all these random strangers. They wondered whether someone in Moscow could be linked to someone in India through friends-of-friends, and not even know it.

For example, Juan Perez in Spain uses IM to contact all his family, friends and work colleagues. Each of these people also knows other people. Some of these friends-of-friends are also connected to some of Juan's existing connections. Juan doesn't know that some of these friends-of-friends exist, and certainly doesn't know they are indirectly connected to him. Juan is in the middle of web of contacts, and so is everyone else using the IM service.

The Microsoft scientists decided to study how many friends-of-friends' connections it takes to link every one of its 240 million IM users to everyone else across their whole network. Surprisingly, this turned out to be just 6.6 connections. (The entire research report can be downloaded free of charge from the Internet. Its web address is in the Further reading and information section under 'Microsoft'.)

Leaders are connected to everyone

The idea that everyone is connected is important for leaders because it means they potentially can reach out to anyone, anywhere. As long as there is one person to link a town, village, community or family, then potentially leaders can contact them by going through just six or seven people.

However, making contact is only a first step. Leaders need *something* more to engage people's attention, and that something is trust. Leaders need to be trustworthy if they want friends-of-friends to listen to them because people follow only those they trust.

Building trust

Trust and emotion

Both honest and dishonest people use similar behaviour to win people's trust. For example, many liars make a show of sincerity by using eye contact, a coaxing tone of voice and open-handed gestures. But so do people who are telling the truth. Ironically, because liars put more effort into the lie, they are often more convincing than honest people.

This is also the case with all kinds of tricksters. They work hard, 24/7, to appear trustworthy and often succeed. This is because decisions about trust are often influenced by emotional reactions. Attractive, charming and seemingly wealthy people are made welcome everywhere because people feel relaxed around them.

The more positive an impression they make (see Chapter 3), the safer people feel in their company. In contrast, someone unwashed, sneering and wearing ragged clothes causes alarm, fear and disgust. These emotional reactions bypass rational thought. Sometimes this reaction is correct, but at other times it isn't.

The trust equation

People make hundreds of mini-decisions during the day, about eating or drinking, completing paperwork or taking exercise. Although the majority of these decisions are unrelated to trust, some are and need a more serious evaluation about whether someone is trustworthy. They need awareness that others are also evaluating them.

This is a challenge, but one made easier as a result of the work of David Maister, Charles Green and Robert Galford. They are all experts on trust and invented the idea of the **trust equation.** Their book, *The Trusted Advisor*, is listed in the Further reading and information section.

The trust equation includes four factors that are the essential ingredients of trust and organizes them into an equation. This can be applied to anyone in any situation. The four factors are:

1 credibility (C)
2 reliability (R)
3 interpersonal, or the degree of closeness
   between people (I)
4 self-orientation (S).

Note: Maister, Green and Galford use the term 'intimacy' rather than 'interpersonal'. The change here is to support easy understanding among international readers.

The terms defined

C Credibility refers to experience, skills, qualities and credentials.

R Reliability refers to consistent and regular behaviour.

I Interpersonal is the degree of connection felt with this person.

S Self-orientation is the ego and self-service that the person shows.

T Trust is the belief in the delivery of a promised outcome.

Here is the equation:

$$\frac{C + R + I}{S} = T$$

The equation adds the person's credibility, reliability and interpersonal features (C+R+I) as the numerator or top number of the equation. Then it divides this total by the degree of self-orientation (S), the denominator or bottom number. The result is the person's trustworthiness.

For example, if the person being evaluated has a high degree of credibility, is reliable and is well known to the evaluator, then the sum of these three factors will be high (C+R+I). However, the evaluator also needs to consider whether the person is self-serving. If the score for S is high, then dividing this into the (C+R+I) number produces a low trust score. Here are two problems that show how to apply the trust equation to work situations.

Problem 1

Marie has all the qualifications necessary to lead a project team and has also led similar teams in her previous job. You know that she keeps her promises and stays late to ensure that deadlines are met. You also know her well because she's been open about her family background and interests. This combination means her score for C+R+I is high. As for her self-orientation, Marie is ambitious and makes it clear that she wants a promotion when the right opportunity arises. However, she's a loyal employee. If she leads the team, she serves the company as well as her own career goals. So she gets a low score for self-orientation. Her equation looks like this:

$$\frac{C + R + I}{S} = T \qquad \frac{\text{High}}{\text{Low}} = \text{High trust}$$

Problem 2

Egele is very good at his job. Although he's worked on project teams for five years, he's never been the leader. He is seen to be a risky choice because he disappears for days to work alone when he feels under stress. This leaves his team mates guessing and often unable to finish their work until he reappears. Egele also rarely converses with his colleagues. His response to complaints about his behaviour is just to look away. This combination means his score for C+R+I is very low. As for self-orientation, last year he told a colleague that he was so angry at the company that he thought about sabotaging the project's results. This gives him a high S score. His trust equation looks like this:

$$\frac{C + R + I}{S} = T \qquad \frac{Low}{High} = Low\ trust$$

Adding numbers

The originators of the trust equation, Maister, Green and Galford, also suggested quantifying it – that is, giving a numerical estimate for each of the four factors. These numbers would be based on a subjective assessment of the person. For example, before the boss decides who should assume project leadership, he or she should identify, in advance, the criteria for a top score of 10, and also for a bottom score of 1.

This step helps clarify the standards for project leadership, and should be done for each factor: credibility, reliability, interpersonal and self-orientation. He or she would then score each person wanting the job against these criteria by estimating where they are between scores of 1 and 10. When there are several people wanting the job, a numerical scoring process can improve fairness.

Leading at a distance

Many businesses now depend on smart technology to connect co-workers. This both encourages growth and minimizes costs. However, the increased dependency on technology has an impact on trust. For example, in face-to-face work situations, people see their colleagues' behaviour directly and decide to trust them based on this experience.

When direct contact is removed, people need additional opportunities to experience their colleagues' behaviour in order to support development of mutual trust. Research shows that regular communication, using several methods simultaneously, increases trust among colleagues who work at a distance from each other. Methods can include:

- email
- video telephoning such as Skype
- Twitter – or a clone of this service
- blogging
- an in-house clone of Facebook
- instant messaging or text messages.

In fact, any communication method that helps people learn more about each other will increase their opportunity to connect, bond and form links. Communication supports the I-factor (interpersonal) in the trust equation. Leaders who ask colleagues to work together at a distance also need to offer new ways for them to connect easily.

The table below shows the relationship between eight technology-driven communication methods and the four trust equation factors. Each method supports the equation factors in different ways. For example, people who answer their email immediately can seem reliable. A blog offers opportunities to share candid opinions and therefore helps readers feel as if they know the blogger well. A Facebook clone or social website, organized by the leader, gives co-workers a 'show and tell' opportunity. This can have an effect on credibility.

Technology-driven communication methods

Email means 'electronic mail' and is sent using digital technology.

Skype clone means a software application that allows audio and video calls using digital technology over the Internet.

Blog is an abbreviation of 'web log' and is a website that presents the opinions of the web logger as well as multimedia offerings.

SMS means 'short messaging service' and is text-based using a phone.

MMS means a 'multimedia messaging service' and includes photo, video and audio sent using a phone.

IM means 'instant messaging' and is live, text-based exchanges by two or more people using digital technology over the Internet.

Twitter clone refers to a burst of information sent as a text message over the Internet that uses no more than 140 characters.

Facebook clone means a website that allows people to post information about themselves so that others can access this, learn about them and hear their news.

The relationship between technology-driven communication methods and the four trust equation factors

	Credibility	Reliability	Interpersonal	Self-orientation
Email				
Skype clone				
Blog				
SMS				
MMS				
IM				
Twitter clone				
Facebook clone				

Activity

1 Identify how each communication method supports each of the four equation factors.

2 Choose one networking method from this list that you have never used before. If you've used them all, then choose the one you use least often.

3 Go online and learn more about the method you chose.

4 Identify three benefits to your leadership performance that this method could bring.

5 Experiment with this method; that is, set up an account on a website offering this as a free service, then try the method.

6 Make sure your efforts include a blog or Twitter account.

7 Ask colleagues and friends for their reactions to your efforts.

Summary

This chapter focused on the skills leaders need to bring people together. Of critical importance is their need to be both trustworthy themselves and also to build trust among their colleagues. This becomes more challenging when colleagues work at a distance because people usually depend upon their own senses to decide whom to trust.

Multiple communication methods can act as a substitute for face-to-face contact. Leaders should use these methods frequently and encourage everyone else to participate. The reward for this effort is a well-functioning team.

Here is a checklist to help you assess and improve your colleagues' and your own trustworthiness:

1 Apply the trust equation to each of your co-workers.

2 Whom do you trust and why? Are there any surprises?

3 Is it possible to improve your own trust score:
(a) when making new contacts?
(b) among the people who already know you?

4 How can you support other people to improve their scores?

5 Are you using all the technology available to you to improve communication?

6 If not, how can you increase both the quantity and quality of your communication?

Fact-check (answers at the back)

1. How many links did it take for everyone using Microsoft's instant messaging service to be connected to everyone else?
   a) 10.9 ❏
   b) 108 ❏
   c) 6.6 ❏
   d) 28 ❏

2. Microsoft Research studied how many messages?
   a) 42 million ❏
   b) 2 billion ❏
   c) 30 billion ❏
   d) 260 million ❏

3. Which of the following is a factor in the trust equation?
   a) Reliability ❏
   b) Awareness ❏
   c) Honesty ❏
   d) Friendship ❏

4. A trust equation like this would have what kind of score?

   $$\frac{\text{Low C + R + I}}{\text{High S}}$$

   a) High trust ❏
   b) Low trust ❏
   c) Mid trust ❏
   d) Outer trust ❏

5. A trust equation like this would have which score?

   $$\frac{\text{High C + R + I}}{\text{Low S}}$$

   a) High trust ❏
   b) Low trust ❏
   c) Mid trust ❏
   d) Outer trust ❏

6. When face-to-face contact decreases, what must increase?
   a) Travel ❏
   b) Marketing ❏
   c) Salaries ❏
   d) Communication ❏

7. Credibility refers to experience, qualities credentials and what?
   a) Banking ❏
   b) Skills ❏
   c) References ❏
   d) Honesty ❏

8. What does self-orientation refer to?
   a) Confidence ❏
   b) Knowledge ❏
   c) Mapping ❏
   d) Egotism ❏

9. What does reliability refer to?
   a) Consistency ❏
   b) Promises ❏
   c) Pacing ❏
   d) Timing ❏

10. Interpersonal refers to the degree of what felt with another person?
    a) Psychology ❏
    b) Staffing ❏
    c) Distance ❏
    d) Connection ❏

CHAPTER 7

Vision and inspiration

Vision inspires action and brings people together. Research shows that vision can even be a more effective motivator than cash, bonuses or prized office space.

Vision is like having a light in the distance to guide the way and give direction. When this light is clear and bright, a leader can describe it vividly and well, and so it easily attracts attention, curiosity and interest.

Leaders need to understand and work with vision so that they can inspire others. The topics that support this understanding include:

● meaning and purpose
● seeing the big picture
● the skills of framing and reframing.

Meaning and purpose

Leaders with **vision** remind people that there is more to life than the routine and the ordinary. Vision offers them a common purpose that everyone can achieve together. In general, however, visionaries are not the most comfortable kind of people to be around.

Particularly when their ideas differ from conventional or mainstream points of view, visionaries are often judged by the world to be fanatics, freaks or 'nutters'. Extreme thinking is too unusual for widespread acceptance, and frequently the determined visionary contributes to this negative reaction by behaving in an eccentric way.

However, it's vision, not the behaviour of visionaries, which transforms an ordinary manager or administrator into a leader. Vision suggests that it is possible to make things better and this is inspiring. Here is the definition of leadership that appeared at the beginning of this development programme:

'Leadership is the ability to present a vision so that others want to achieve it. Leaders need the skill to work with other people as well as the belief that they can make a difference.'

Managers and administrators, in contrast to leaders, present ideas, proposals, memos and suggestions. They ask, insist, direct, demand, suggest, convince and encourage their colleagues to co-operate. Depending on their degree of authority and influence, they can also be assured of success. While effective management deserves both praise and reward, it is not leadership.

Leaders have vision, take risks, present dreams, explore possibilities and in general invite their colleagues to join them for a journey to the unknown. Managers write reports, analyse data and ask their colleagues to meet them in the conference room after lunch. Even when leaders blend well into their organizational surroundings, there is something different about them. On close examination, that something is vision.

Whenever individuals lift their attention above routine matters, they open themselves to new possibilities. The ability to imagine something new and better can be acquired with practice. The necessary effort is worthwhile because vision is an essential part of leadership. The next activity is designed to improve your sense of vision.

Activity

1 Ask yourself if there is someone you admire whose point of view surprises you or makes you think. You can choose anyone, including a public figure or someone you actually know.

● What quality or qualities do you imagine inspires their point of view?

2 Remember a time when you've seen this person show this quality in action.

● Can you imagine showing this quality yourself?

3 When you next make plans for your future, take a minute to ask whether you can use this quality while planning.

● Let yourself wonder whether your future plans would improve if you used this quality or whether the person you admire could be there to advise you.

It has already been suggested that people who have vision aren't always comfortable people. They are also often unpopular. The decision to be a leader instead of an effective manager should not be taken lightly. The front line is far more dangerous than the back, and the challenges of leadership are far greater than those of supervision or administration.

Leadership requires a high level of commitment and the loss of much personal choice. The glamour of having vision won't soften the blow if that vision is rejected or is widely misunderstood. This experience is far more painful for a leader than the rejection of a proposal or working paper can be for a manager.

Leaders, by definition, have the kind of relationship with their followers that makes them more vulnerable to their reactions. However tough or macho some leaders may appear, it is hard for them to avoid feeling hurt when their most deeply felt ideas are rejected.

It helps when leaders feel confident that they are the right person for their position. They can also draw on their sense of vision to sustain them when or if they have a difficult time convincing others that their vision is worthwhile. Vision may create vulnerability, but it also supports inner strength when under fire.

Seeing the big picture

'Seeing the big picture' is a phrase often used to describe the act of shifting attention from the details of a situation to see how all the details fit together to make a whole. The big picture integrates all of the details into a coherent image, like seeing that there is a forest rather than a group of single and separate trees. Seeing the big picture is like taking a mental step back to absorb more information. This is an antidote to becoming stuck in petty issues or daily routine.

The purpose of looking at the big picture is to explore the meaning of an existing situation. Leaders who want to see the big picture should first focus very hard on the details of a situation so that each item becomes separate.

Then they should clear their mind and think about the situation again. This time they want to look for a pattern or a picture that ignores specific details. This act of shifting perspective can be shown with an optical illusion:

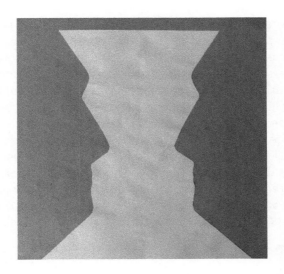

An optical illusion is a trick the eye plays so that a picture can look very different from changing points of view. Looking for the big picture in a situation can be like seeing an optical illusion.

To demonstrate this, focus your gaze on the centre of the picture. Very likely the image of a vase appears. Next, shift your attention to the right side of the picture. Then slowly move your eyes to the middle. A profile of a face is now likely to appear. Then shift your attention to the left side of the picture and move your eye towards the centre. A second profile should emerge.

Just as this picture can be 'read' in two ways, events can change appearance and meaning depending upon point of view. The broader the point of view that leaders take, the more likely they are to include the necessary information to interpret events correctly. They can also gain a fresh perspective and often find solutions to nagging problems. Seeing the big picture allows new patterns to emerge and can create a better understanding about working relationships, circumstances or events.

Artificial divisions can fall away when people and events are seen in a wider context. Sometimes this is called **helicopter viewing** – that is, leaders mentally raise their point of view to look at what is happening as if from above. This can reveal a story that may otherwise be hidden or difficult to see.

On occasion, big-picture thinking reveals hidden threats. In this case, the leader may see a big picture that includes the whole marketplace with allies, enemies and potential business opportunities. This can support action taking before serious difficulties arise.

Courage in the face of adversity is an inspiring leadership quality. Like the hero in an action film, the leader must always believe in the possibility of a happy ending, even if there seems only the remotest chance of this. A leader's core task is to show the way forward in an inspiring way regardless of conflict, problem or challenge. Seeing the big picture helps achieve this.

Activity

1 Watch an exchange between two people that you don't know.

2 Make guesses about this exchange in terms of (a) the purpose of their contact, (b) the underlying emotions they may feel, both positive and negative, and (c) the expressed emotion they both show, both positive and negative.

3 Now focus on just one of the people. Imagine (a) how they got to the meeting, (b) what connection that person has to the other, and (c) where they will go after the meeting.

Shifting perspective like this, on demand, is a core skill for seeing the big picture and is useful to practise.

Framing and reframing

Framing

The dictionary defines framing as 'an established order or system, or the way that a thing may be constructed, organized or formed'. A frame can also be described as the habits of mind that people follow when they interpret what is happening around them. Chapter 3 raised the idea of bias as a mental habit. It is also an example of a frame.

Every single person has a unique **frame of reference.** That's why people can describe the same event seen at the same time in different ways. For example, one person may notice a red jacket because he owns one just like it. Another viewer may see people smiling because she is happy that day herself. Past experience, personal values, attitudes and states of mind influence what viewers choose to look at in a scene.

However, like any other habit, frames can be changed. This takes time, effort and commitment, but is necessary when frames of reference create negative ways of thinking and may stop a leader from doing well.

Reframing

The process of changing a frame of reference or mental habit is called reframing. By definition, this is changing perspective in order to gain new insight and to discover whether any information has been misunderstood. Reframing is consciously choosing to see the world in a new way.

A reframe creates an entirely new story about what is seen, and intentionally interprets information in a different way from usual. The purpose is to break old habits, bias and rigid ideas. By challenging their own points of view, leaders can discover new possibilities.

This is useful when people believe they are stuck. Leaders can feel as if they have no options or are trapped into making only predetermined choices. If those choices are all unattractive, then leaders need to shake themselves up and force themselves to see the world with new eyes.

This skill helps leaders because it creates mental flexibility. It also supports development of vision. Why? Because when people are locked in a single way of seeing the world, they reduce their capacity to invent new things. For them, the distant light on the hill will always be just another all-night petrol station.

Reframing allows new outcomes to emerge. Leaders need the zest that a truly open mind allows them to experience. When they see that light on a distant hill, they think big thoughts and aspire to new things. This is one step beyond the big picture.

Seeing the big picture is a good first step when seeking a new point of view. However, on occasion, when leaders are so caught in routine, this yields nothing. The next step is to reframe what is happening and what is being seen.

Why reframe?

Although the facts of a situation may be indisputable, the frame of reference that each observer uses to interpret those facts differs with each person.

To illustrate this, look at the example of three friends who meet at the end of every week in the coffee room to talk about their weekend plans.

- The boss sees this and thinks: 'Those three are always wasting time.'
- The shy and lonely file clerk looks at them and thinks sadly, 'Those three are such good friends. I wish I could join them, but they would just ignore me.'
- The office busybody sees their meeting as a chance to ask them to help move some furniture.

Based on their different frames of reference, each person interprets the same group of three friends in very different ways. They see what they see through emotional bias. To the extent that each of these three viewers has a rigid bias or mental frame, they limit their opportunity to see things differently.

Reframing gets a leader to choose a different emotional reaction to what is seen or, alternatively, to interpret it differently. Further, reframers do this on purpose and on demand, fully aware that this changes their reactions. For example, the boss in the example above could remember that it is their coffee break and so they can talk about anything they wish. He could also follow his doctor's advice and 'lighten up' and be 'less critical'.

The shy person could recognize that the three people are the most popular people in the office and so decide to study them. Are there any stories they tell or ways of laughing, sitting and being relaxed that make them appear so attractive? If the shy person wishes, this can be a wake-up call. Why not copy them? Why not assume a different attitude towards life?

How to reframe

This activity presents a way to practise reframing:

Activity

1 Choose a magazine or journal. Look through it until you find a picture with people who capture your attention.

● Without reading an explanation of the picture, interpret what you see. This interpretation is your **original frame.**

2 Now look at the picture again and choose to interpret the picture in a completely different way.

● To do this, imagine...

– there is a different emotional atmosphere from the one you first believed you saw

– that the people you see have different motives and intentions from those you first thought

– that the centre of power is changed so that the people who, at first, you thought were less powerful are now the dominant ones.

● This new interpretation is your **reframe.** You can repeat this process whenever you need new insight.

Summary

Presenting a vision is the hardest leadership skill to develop, but it yields a great reward. Vision opens the way to possibility and invites people to feel inspired to create new opportunities.

The following checklist reviews the balance between envisioning new solutions and managing people and resources. The more senior a leader's role, the more time should be spent on using vision to plan for the future and find new solutions.

1 Do you spend all your working time on administration or supervision?

2 Do you give yourself time to imagine new solutions or ideas?

3 How often do you invite your colleagues to think of new solutions or offer new ideas?

4 Do you try to shift your perspective from a narrow field to include a bigger picture?

5 If so, what goes well with this? If not, can you try to frame and reframe for this situation?

6 What do you like and not like about your effort to reframe?

7 How can you improve your reframing skills in future?

Fact-check (answers at the back)

1. Which of the following best relates to 'vision'?
   a) Money ❏
   b) Dreams ❏
   c) Reports ❏
   d) Managers ❏

2. What does 'the big picture' mean?
   a) A map ❏
   b) A movie ❏
   c) An oil painting ❏
   d) The whole ❏

3. What does reframing mean?
   a) Opinions ❏
   b) A survey ❏
   c) Shifting views ❏
   d) Optimism ❏

4. Why do leaders need vision?
   a) To inspire people ❏
   b) To frighten people ❏
   c) To manage people ❏
   d) To control people ❏

5. Which of the following describes an optical illusion?
   a) Myopia ❏
   b) Glasses ❏
   c) Trick ❏
   d) Video ❏

6. What kind of reaction does a reframe change?
   a) An unexpected one ❏
   b) An emotional one ❏
   c) An open one ❏
   d) An interesting one ❏

7. A frame is a mental what?
   a) Problem ❏
   b) Issue ❏
   c) Dream ❏
   d) Habit ❏

8. Vision can make leaders what?
   a) Carefree ❏
   b) Truthful ❏
   c) Unpopular ❏
   d) Lazy ❏

9. What can big-picture thinking reveal?
   a) Hidden threats ❏
   b) Hidden rooms ❏
   c) Hidden ideas ❏
   d) Hidden people ❏

10. What don't managers need?
    a) Power ❏
    b) Direction ❏
    c) Vision ❏
    d) Money ❏

7 × 7

1 Seven key ideas

- **Know yourself.** Self-awareness is a leadership essential. You need to know why you do what you do before you can understand what motivates others.
- **Control your impulses.** Angry, impulsive reactions to people and events waste time and energy. Think things through and manage your behaviour wisely.
- **Look and listen.** Look at people and listen when they speak to you, and pay attention to their whole story, gestures, words and facial expression. This creates understanding.
- **Clear thinking allows clear speaking.** Organize your thoughts before explaining or giving directions. Use simple language, bullet points and short sentences to describe what is needed and by what deadline.
- **Tolerate differences.** Fully accept that other people's choices and priorities are important to them, even if you think they are wrong. Begin a discussion with respect for different points of view and truly listen.
- **Build relationships.** Leaders work through others and so relationships with people above, below and sideways are all equally important.
- **Delegate.** Identify what you need to do yourself and what could and should be done by others. This frees your time to innovate and solve problems.

2 Seven of the best resources

- **Cialdini, Robert**, *Influence: the Psychology of Persuasion* (Harper, 2006). Selling over two million copies and translated into 16 languages, this book offers six principles explaining how influence works.
- **Galford, Robert and Drapeau, Anne Seibold**, *The Trusted Leader* (The Free Press, 2011). Trust supports relationships.

This book explains how to gain trust and assess better when to trust others.

- **Goleman, Daniel**, 'Leadership that gets results' (*Harvard Business Review*, March–April 2000). This article presents six leadership styles and how they influence profits.
- **Leadership testing online.** This website offers free access to personality testing, including a Leadership Test, a Situational Judgement Test and an Interpersonal Skills Test. www.psychometrictest.org.uk/
- **MacGregor Burns, James**, *Leadership* (Harper, 2012). This is a classic and essential for anyone who wants to understand modern leadership. First published in 1978, it explains that leaders and followers depend on each other. His ideas are widely copied all over the world.
- **Mind Tools.** This website is a general resource for ideas about leadership, with blog entries from experts advising how to lead better. www.mindtools.com/pages/article/newLDR_83.htm
- **Weeks, Holly**, *Failure to Communicate: How Conversations Go Wrong and What You Can Do To Right Them* (Harvard Business Press, 2010). Difficult conversations cause stress and jangle nerves. This book serves as a reference for leaders from every profession everywhere.

3 Seven things to avoid

- **Hesitation.** Once you decide, take action. Opportunities are lost when you let doubt take over.
- **Rushing people, ideas, decisions or yourself.** This leads to mistakes and repeated effort. Take time to think things through, decide and then act.
- **Narrow thinking.** Believing that your opinion is the only one that matters is a mistake. This blocks not only your own creativity but other people's as well.
- **Talking too much.** This stops anyone else from sharing ideas and finding solutions. When one person dominates a conversation, this also demotivates everyone else.

- **Stress.** The chemicals surging into your blood with stress damage health and cloud your judgement. Take breaks to recharge. Enjoy a joke. Eat well and be healthy.
- **Confused goals and poor planning.** Leaders are responsible for more than their own success. They need to plan effectively to get the most from shared resources. This means clear goals and getting buy-in to plans.
- **Discourtesy of any kind to anyone.** 'Please', 'Thank you' and 'You're welcome' are key words for leaders. Smiling, waiting your turn and showing respect are key behaviours.

4 Seven inspiring leaders

- **Nelson Mandela**. He faced terrible injustice with resilience, patience and strength. His self-awareness enabled him to rise above hardship and show compassion and tolerance to others.
- **Eleanor Roosevelt**. She led the formation of the United Nations and chaired the commission that drafted and approved the Universal Declaration of Human Rights.
- **Mahatma Gandhi.** He was committed to non-violent and peaceful protest. His inner authority and belief in a just cause drew international attention to India's independence movement.
- **Angela Merkel.** This three-term leader of Germany is widely respected for her judgement and strength of character. She is a decisive and strong world leader.
- **Sir Tim Berners-Lee.** He invented the World Wide Web, not just the idea of global access to information for everyone, but also the computer language that made this happen. Of greater importance, however, is his decision that all access should be free to all.
- **Aung San Suu Kyi.** A Burmese leader who endured 15 years of house arrest, she demonstrated the power of peaceful resistance and brought about social and political change through her writing and example.
- **Steve Jobs.** His name is synonymous with innovation, vision and life-changing products that are both beautiful and functional.

5 Seven great quotes

- 'In any moment of decision, the best thing you can do is the right thing, the next best thing is the wrong thing, and the worst thing you can do is nothing.' Theodore Roosevelt
- 'The single biggest problem with communication is the illusion that it has taken place.' George Bernard Shaw
- 'At one time leadership meant muscle; but today it means getting along with people.' Indira Gandhi
- 'Your time is limited, so don't waste it living someone else's life. Don't be trapped by dogma – which is living with the results of other people's thinking. Don't let the noise of others' opinions drown out your own inner voice. And most important, have the courage to follow your heart and intuition.' Steve Jobs
- 'Trust yourself. Create the kind of self that you will be happy to live with all your life. Make the most of yourself by fanning the tiny, inner sparks of possibility into flames of achievement.' Golda Meir
- 'Excellence is never an accident. It is always the result of high intention, sincere effort, and intelligent execution.' Aristotle
- 'Courage is the most important of all the virtues, because without courage you can't practise any other virtue consistently. You can practise any virtue erratically, but nothing consistently without courage.' Maya Angelou

6 Seven things to do today

- Contact a former colleague that you once knew well – just to say hello.
- Set aside 15 minutes to be alone to think about what you want in your life in five years' time.
- Identify one beneficial project and develop a goal statement for it as well as its primary and secondary requirements.
- At the end of the day, score yourself for self-awareness during the day, giving a 5 for 'excellent' and a 1 for 'didn't try'. Do this every day for the next week.

- Choose someone you believe communicates well. Watch him or her in conversation and identify something to copy.
- At the start of the day, think of your least favourite activity. Decide what you can add or subtract from it to feel more motivated about doing it.
- As you go through the day, think about the kind of power you are using for each activity. Ask if it is the best choice and consider alternatives.

7 Seven trends for tomorrow

- **Social media strategy**: social media will continue to grow and demand your time. Find a balance so that you feel part of things, but are also independent and able to turn off when you like.
- **Personal branding**: the workplace is growing more fluid and you need a single unified message about who you are and what you have to offer. This is the brand you bring with you when changing roles and jobs.
- **The sharing economy**: the move to shared ownership will gather speed with even greater cloud access to images and ideas, along with multi-user cars, bicycles, homes and even garden tools.
- **Diversity**: migration from south to north will increase as more people struggle to gain a foothold in richer European countries. Be prepared to accept and understand differences as the social map continues to change.
- **Social responsibility**: this is an age of social awareness and community responsibility. Leaders need to think beyond their immediate personal interest.
- **The Internet of things**: smart technology connecting ordinary objects means more automation and greater freedom for more fulfilling work and social activity.
- **Big data**: this trend is both a challenge and major social benefit. Through the deluge of information, people everywhere can access data from global sources. This transforms lives.

Further reading and information

Dunbar, Robin, *How Many Friends Does One Person Need?* (Faber, 2011)

Ferrucci, Piero, *What We May Be* (Penguin, 2009)

Galford, Robert and Drapeau, Anne, *The Trusted Leader* (The Free Press, 2002)

Leskovec, Jure and Horvitz, Eric, *Planetary-scale Views on an Instant-messaging Network*, available online at http://arxiv.org/abs/0803.0939 (2008)

Maister, David, Green, Charles and Galford, Robert, *The Trusted Advisor* (The Free Press, 2001)

MacGregor Burns, James, *Leadership* (Harper Perennial Political Classics, 2010)

Maslow, Abraham, *Motivation and Personality*, 3rd edn (Addison-Wesley, 1987)

Maslow, Abraham: official publications website for all of Dr Maslow's books and audio at www.maslow.com

Microsoft Research: Refer to Leskovec, Jure (above), and Sanderson, Katherine (below)

O'Connor, Carol, website: www.visiprac.com or email: carol@visiprac.com

Sanderson, Katherine, *Six Degrees of Messaging*, available at http://www.nature.com/news/2008/080313/full/news.2008.670.html

TED Lectures, available at www.ted.com: an online collection of video-recorded lectures given by leaders in their field

PART 2
Your Motivating People Masterclass

Introduction

This Part of the book will explore motivation from a number of perspectives, including motivation needs, explored in the work of Abraham Maslow and Frederick Herzberg, and motivation drivers, explored in the work of Harry Harlow and Edward Deci.

Traditional thinking around the subject has been that, after satisfying our basic human needs of hunger, thirst and copulation, our primary motivation for behaving in a particular way is based on the rewards or punishment we receive. This can be regarded as **external motivation**.

Over the last century, pioneering work has helped us to recognize the significance of **intrinsic motivation** and the motivation we obtain from the **performance of the task**. Research has shown that we take pleasure (motivational drive) from solving puzzles. Work conducted by Deci in the late 1960s and early 1970s discovered that external rewards (e.g. money) can in some situations create only a short-term gain, and that longer-term motivation and drive come from within. This is now known as **Self-Determination Theory** (SDT) and it deals with people's essential psychological needs and deep-rooted development preferences.

In motivating others, it is a real advantage to have a sound understanding of an individual's level of self-motivation and self-determination. This means gaining an appreciation of the behaviours and motivators behind the choices that people make without any external influence and interference. This insight can help to inform you on how to motivate them.

Even in this short introduction we can begin to see that, while motivating others can be complex, there are some fundamental aspects that, if followed, will help you to do this effectively.

CHAPTER 8

What's in it for me?

Some people are naturally good at motivating others, but for most people it is a leadership skill that they learn. A common mistake is to assume that other people are motivated by the same things you are, so you use that approach with them. Sadly, that rarely works – as a manager you need to view each person as an individual and learn to listen to the language they use, and observe how they behave, in order to work out a personalized strategy for them. That might sound like hard work, particularly if you have a large number of people to manage, but it pays off in the long term, when you develop a highly motivated team.

If you are prepared to embark on the journey of learning how to motivate others, first you have be motivated yourself. Think about what makes you excited and energized at work. Often, when you are motivated and enthusiastic about something, it is easier to bring others along with you. They get caught up in your excitement, which can be contagious.

In this chapter you will be able to reflect on what motivates you, so that you can generate energy and passion for the activities that get you fired up. It will also explain some of the best-known models and theories developed by experts, including Maslow, McClelland and Herzberg, that help us understand more about how people behave and are motivated.

Understanding your motive for action

What's your motive for action?

Any person becomes motivated when they want to do something. This drive, which comes from inside them, causes them to take action. It's their motive. However, this is not the same as being incentivized to take action, which often brings some type of external reward.

Case study: inner motivation

Take the story of George, who had recently been promoted to manager in a large organization. He felt that it was important to get to know his team, so he took time to have coffee with them and learn more about each member. George was motivated to find out what made them tick because he would then be able to manage them better. George's manager also noticed his efforts and later commented that George had fitted into the team really easily and there was a very positive atmosphere. In summary:

Motive for action = To be able to manage team effectively.

Behaviour = He took time to have coffee with each person.

Result = He built rapport and trust with each team member.

Additional benefit = Manager recognized George's efforts.

So it is useful to become more aware of what motivates you to take action. Use the questions below to reflect on this statement. Think of a time at work when you were highly motivated.

- What was going on?
- Who was involved?
- How did you feel?

- What caused it to be motivating for you?
- What did you do?

Then repeat the above exercise for a time when you were really demotivated and lacking energy for work. Analyse both sets of answers, thinking about the specific factors that caused you to behave in different ways.

Now list any insights you have gained that could help you be more motivated and also how you could avoid becoming demotivated.

> **'We cannot change anything until we accept it. Condemnation does not liberate; it oppresses.'**
>
> Carl Jung

Knowing yourself

It is important to be aware of how you are motivated, particularly if you are a manager, because other people will look to you for inspiration – it will be that much harder to encourage other people if you are not motivated yourself.

Think about what motivates you. For some people, it may seem obvious: money is the main motivator at work. While many of us might agree with this view, the research proves otherwise. Surveys and research studies repeatedly show that other factors motivate more than money. For example, a survey published in UK newspaper *The Times* in 2004 showed that the main reasons people leave their jobs were lack of stimulus and no opportunity for advancement.

The notion that long-term motivation really comes from within is important to remember as a manager. Many people fall into the trap of thinking that a salary increase will motivate someone to perform better. It may do in the short term, but over a longer period of time other factors (intrinsic motivators) are also needed.

Motivation must come from within.

To help you learn about motivation, there are some well-known theories and models that are useful to learn about. They will help you understand what's really going inside other people's minds and how this causes them to behave as they do. This then helps you to unlock their potential and work out how to approach each person in ways that will yield positive results.

Herzberg's theory of motivation

Frederick Herzberg's theory of motivation is one of the best-known pieces of research in the field. In 1959 he, together with Bernard Mausner and Barbara Bloch Snyderman, published *The Motivation to Work*, which showed that in general people will be initially motivated to achieve **extrinsic needs** ('hygiene' factors) at work because they are unhappy without them. Examples include good salary, working conditions and interpersonal relationships. Once these needs are satisfied, however, the effect soon wears off – that is, job satisfaction is temporary.

People are only truly motivated when they satisfy the needs that Herzberg identified as **intrinsic needs** ('motivators'), such as achievement, advancement and personal development, which represent a far deeper level of meaning and fulfilment.

Herzberg's theory of motivation

Extrinsic needs (hygiene factors)	Intrinsic needs (notivators)
Company policy	Achievement
Supervision	Recognition
Salary	Work itself
Interpersonal relations	Responsibility
Physical working conditions	Advancement

Think about how Herzberg's theory applies to you.

What gives you the greatest satisfaction at work?

If you were given a choice – you could either take a rewarding job where you had a high degree of personal control over your work, and a salary double what you are earning, or you could have a job on a production line where you performed fairly repetitive tasks with little control over your work, in poor working conditions and limited promotion opportunities and received a salary three times what you are earning – which would you choose for the long term?

Meta Programs – noticing how language motivates you

Another concept that influences our motivation is Meta Programs. These mental processes enable us to filter the mass of information that we take in each day, and to decide on which bits we should pay attention to.

Meta Programs were identified in the 1970s by researchers Richard Bandler and Leslie Cameron-Bandler, and the initial set of Meta Program patterns were then described by Leslie Cameron-Bandler in collaboration with David Gordon, Robert Dilts and Maribeth Meyers-Anderson.

To work out what your filters are, you need to pay attention to the language you use. For example, one person may be motivated by losing weight whereas another may be encouraged by becoming healthier. Both are different ways to describe a similar outcome, and will motivate people according to their Meta Programs. If you use the wrong one to encourage a colleague, you may quickly realize whether it works or not according to their reaction, because they will literally 'filter out' what you are saying. In this example, one is focused on getting away from the problem (being overweight) and avoiding loss and the other is focused on going towards the solution (feeling healthier) and gaining something.

These Meta Programs manage, guide and direct other mental processes and influence how we are motivated. Each one is on a continuum, with the opposite preferences described below being at either end of the spectrum. Both are equally valid, so there is no bad or good preference.

Away from – Towards

People with a 'Towards' preference are motivated by future goals and the enjoyment they get from achieving them. Their language will be future oriented – for example, 'When I achieve this goal I will feel great.'

Those with an 'Away From' preference are focused on avoiding pain or problems, and they talk about what they don't want to happen. Their language will include words and phrases like 'reduce', 'avoid', 'minimize' and 'get away from'.

In business, you might think that most successful people would have a 'Towards' rather than 'away from' focus – after all, in marketing literature we tend to read phrases like 'make a million', 'achieve your ideal future', 'get your dream job'. However, that is not always the case.

The Scottish golfer Colin Montgomerie acknowledges that he was driven as much by the fear of losing as by achieving a win. This also links with the theory of Loss Aversion developed by Daniel Kahneman and Amos Tversky (1984), which highlights people's tendency to strongly prefer avoiding losses to acquiring gains.

Reactive – Proactive

'Proactive' people will put their hand up first to take on a job without having all the parts of the job clearly defined because they just like to get started. People who are 'Reactive' prefer to wait and see what others do first, because they want to reflect and think about what to do before doing it.

Internal – External

People with an 'Internal' preference know inside how they are doing. They don't need to have any recognition from others to feel validated.

Those with an 'External' preference need others to tell them how they are doing. They will want to seek feedback from other people to confirm that they are on the right track.

Options – Procedures

People who have an 'Options' preference will rarely make a quick decision without looking at all the options available. Those with a 'Procedures' focus, by contrast, will expect that there is a 'right way' to achieve a task and like the reassurance of following a tried-and-tested method.

Global – Specific

Those with a 'Global' preference like getting an overview or summary as they like to see the big picture, but may appear vague or provide a lack of detail. Those who prefer 'Specific' enjoy the detail and want others to have all the information that they believe is important.

Summary of the Meta Programs

Key patterns	How they affect people's motivation
Away From – Towards	Towards – will want to know about rewards, future achievements, goals Away From – you will need to explain how the task will avoid pain, problems, outcomes they don't want
Reactive – Proactive	Proactive – like to be told 'go for it' or just do it! Reactive – prefer to be given direction on a task before they get started
External – Internal	Internal – prefer to make their own internal decisions and have no need to get confirmation from others (e.g. a regular review is less important) External – like to refer to the external advice of others (e.g. a regular review will be important as they want to know that they are doing a good job)
Procedures – Options	Options – will enjoy having a variety of options to consider and may feel threatened by lack of choice Procedures – they like processes and knowing the 'right way' of carrying out a task
Specific – Global	Global – like to be presented with the key points or overview and don't mind things being vague Specific – prefer having the precise detail and factual information
Difference – Sameness	Sameness – look for things that match what they already know and want their world to remain the same Difference – notice what's different and prefer change to be constant

Sameness – Difference

People with a 'Sameness' preference enjoy things remaining constant and, if they get a new task, want to know how it's similar to something they are already familiar with.

Those with a 'Difference' preference enjoy change and are motivated by things being new and unfamiliar.

If you think about each pair of preferences and work out which ones you prefer, you will be more aware of how Meta Programs influence your own motivation. Then consider in turn each person that you have to motivate, and notice the language they use so that you can work out which preferences they have, and what words are likely to be more effective when you communicate with them.

Maslow's Hierarchy of Needs

Another model that can help you to work out what drives you is Maslow's Hierarchy of Needs. This is a well-known tool and is likely one that you will refer to time and time again in the future. What it helps you to do is work out what the underlying needs are of those you interact with, including your boss!

For example, when a new employee joins a team their initial behaviour is often driven by the need to feel that they are part of the team. Once they have been accepted, their needs change and they have a greater need to be recognized and have a level of status within the team. However, if the situation at work changed and there was a high degree of uncertainty about even having a job, their need would then be focused on feeling safe and secure.

If you are able to work out what a person's needs are at any given time, you will find it far easier to come up with ways to help address those needs. Abraham Maslow, a professor of psychology, recognized that humans have these differing needs and so he created a hierarchy that explained the sequence in which these needs are satisfied.

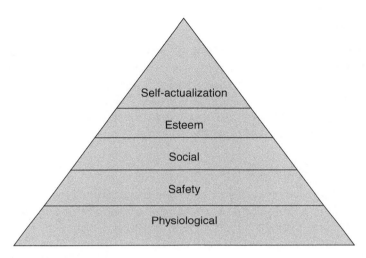

Maslow's Hierarchy of Needs

Physiological needs

Maslow believed that the most basic needs we have are those that are vital to survival – for example water, food, air and sleep. These are the most instinctive needs in the hierarchy and all other needs become secondary until these physiological needs are met.

Safety needs

These include the need for physical safety and security. Security needs are important for survival, but they are not as demanding as physiological needs. Examples of security needs include a desire for steady employment, safe neighbourhoods and shelter from the environment.

Social needs

These include the need to belong and for love and affection. Relationships – whether friendships, romantic attachments or family ties – help fulfil this need for companionship and acceptance, as does involvement in social, community or work groups.

Esteem needs

After the first three needs in the hierarchy have been satisfied, esteem needs become increasingly important. These include the need for things that foster self-esteem, personal worth, social recognition and accomplishment. At work, this can be symbolized by the type of car you drive or the recognition you get from your manager or peers.

Self-actualization

This is the highest level of Maslow's Hierarchy of Needs. Self-actualizing people are self-aware, concerned with personal growth, less concerned with the opinions of others and interested in fulfilling their potential.

The final two levels (esteem needs and self-actualization) are similar to the intrinsic motivators that Herzberg identified in his theory that was outlined earlier, which confirms that humans are ultimately driven to satisfy their need for achievement, recognition and personal fulfilment.

How to apply Maslow's theory to motivate others

The basis of Maslow's theory is that human beings are motivated by unsatisfied needs, and that the lower levels of needs must be satisfied before higher needs. Here are some examples of this:

- You cannot motivate someone to achieve their sales target (Esteem) when they're having problems with their marriage (Social).
- You cannot expect someone to work effectively as a team member (Social) when they believe their job security is threatened (Safety).

Case study: using Maslow's Hierarchy of Needs

Take the experience of Suzie. She had worked in the same accountancy firm for five years and had been promoted twice. As a manager, she now had an office on the first floor, which housed a large desk, two chairs and a meeting table. She felt proud that she had achieved this level of responsibility and that her hard work in studying for additional qualifications had paid off. Suzie also liked the fact that her office was slightly larger than the other offices on this floor, which she felt was a sign of her status.

At the monthly managers' meeting she was told that change was afoot. The firm had decided to move to a flexible working environment because many people were now working in different locations including working from home. As a result, Suzie would no longer have an office. Instead, she could work from a workstation and when meetings were scheduled the quiet rooms could be booked for this purpose. It would mean a bit of chaos while the changes were implemented, but things would be better in the long term. The directors thought that everyone would be pleased, but not so. Suzie was upset: she had worked so hard to be recognized as a manager who had an office, and now it was to be taken away from her. She reacted negatively to this announcement at the meeting and became highly demotivated.

A simple change of environment at work had the potential to demotivate a member of staff. However, it was not the change itself – the real issue was the loss of status (esteem) for Suzie. It might have been quite different for another member of the team who felt more motivated because they could work from home more easily. It would have been far more motivating for Suzie if the director had talked to her separately and reinforced how much she was valued in the organization, and work out with her how her status needs could be met in light of the changes.

> **Motive for action** = To save money and have a flexible workspace
>
> **Behaviour** = Managers told they no longer have offices
>
> **Result** = Loss of esteem and status for Suzie, leading to her becoming demotivated
>
> **Additional need** = Suzie needs to be recognized in other ways

We need to remember that not everyone is motivated by the same things. At various points in their lives and careers, people will be motivated by completely different needs. It is imperative that you identify what the needs of each person are at any particular time. Here are some ways to apply Maslow's theory at work:

- **Physiological needs** Provide ample breaks for lunch and recuperation, and pay salaries that ensure that workers can buy life's essentials.
- **Safety needs** Provide a working environment that is safe, as well as job security and freedom from threats.
- **Social needs** Generate a feeling of acceptance, belonging and community by encouraging team working.
- **Esteem needs** Recognize achievements, assign important projects and provide status to make employees feel valued and appreciated.
- **Self-actualization** Offer challenging and meaningful work assignments that enable innovation, creativity and progress according to long-term goals.

McClelland's Human Motivation Theory

Now that you have learned about Herzberg's and Maslow's theories and worked out your Meta Programs by thinking about what type of language motivates you, you can complete your learning by understanding the theory developed by David McClelland about human motivation.

What his research identified was that there are three motivators that we all have – **achievement**, **affiliation** and **power** – and that each of us will display different characteristics depending on our dominant motivator, which has been shaped by our background, culture and life experiences. The table below summarizes the characteristics of each type of person.

McClelland's dominant motivators

Dominant motivator	Characteristics of the person
Achievement	• Has a need to set and achieve challenging goals • Likes to take risks to achieve their goals • Enjoys getting feedback on progress towards their goals • Often prefers to work alone
Affiliation	• Has a need to be liked and to be part of a group • May tend to go along with what others want in order to maintain harmony and good relations in a group • Does not enjoy risk taking and uncertainty
Power	• Enjoys having power and influence over others • Enjoys competing and winning • Likes recognition and status

You can observe people displaying these different needs in lots of team situations. For example, a group of friends went on a skiing holiday together. Those who had a strong **need for achievement** were focused on discovering the new ski routes they could tackle every day, and were keen to try some of the more difficult runs as soon as they could. They were not bothered if others in the group preferred to ski on easier runs and would arrange to catch up with them at lunchtime or at the end of the day.

Those with a **need for affiliation** would go along with what the majority agreed to do, whether or not they really were keen to do it. So they would often spend quite a bit of time during the day stopping for refreshments and enjoying the conversations with their friends. And those with a **need for power** were the ones that tended to organize the plan each morning and work out what they thought each person should do. They would also encourage competition on the slopes to see who could ski fastest down a particular run.

Think about groups or teams you have been in before and what behaviour you displayed. Which need drives you – power, affiliation or achievement?

Summary

In this chapter you have discovered more about what drives you. This is important because, in order to be able to inspire and motivate others, you need to start by being motivated yourself. This can come from within you (intrinsic motivation) or it can be encouraged by some type of external reward (e.g. money, recognition). Remember that, if you want people to be motivated for a long period of time, the drive must come from within them.

We also looked at concepts related to motivation, including Meta Programs and theories developed by Herzberg, Maslow and McClelland. These help you to make sense of why individuals behave in particular ways at work and what some of the often unconscious intentions behind their actions are.

Fact-check (answers at the back)

1. Long-term motivation should come from:
   a) External sources (e.g. money) ❏
   b) Within yourself ❏
   c) Your manager ❏
   d) Being recognized ❏

2. According to a survey in *The Times*, the main reason people leave their jobs is:
   a) Lack of stimulus and no opportunity for advancement ❏
   b) Lack of a salary increase ❏
   c) They don't like their manager ❏
   d) They don't have a reason ❏

3. Herzberg's theory states that people needs are ultimately satisfied when:
   a) Their extrinsic needs are met ❏
   b) Their intrinsic needs are met ❏
   c) They like the team they are working in ❏
   d) Both their extrinsic and intrinsic needs are met ❏

4. An effective way to discover the Meta Programs that other people use to filter out information is to:
   a) Ask them ❏
   b) Go on a training course ❏
   c) Listen to the language that they use ❏
   d) Use the Meta Programs app ❏

5. The opposite end of the spectrum in the Meta Program 'Towards and _____' is:
   a) Avoiding ❏
   b) Away From ❏
   c) Specific ❏
   d) Difference ❏

6. In Maslow's Hierarchy of Needs, the second highest level of need is:
   a) Self-actualization ❏
   b) Social needs ❏
   c) Esteem needs ❏
   d) Physiological needs ❏

7. According to Maslow, if someone believes their job security is threatened, what is this level of needs?
   a) Self-actualization ❏
   b) Social ❏
   c) Esteem ❏
   d) Safety ❏

8. The three dominant motivators McClelland identified are affiliation, power and:
   a) Achievement ❏
   b) Loyalty ❏
   c) Belonging ❏
   d) Esteem ❏

9. According to McClelland's theory, someone who enjoys competition and winning is driven by a need for:
   a) Affiliation ❏
   b) Power ❏
   c) Belonging ❏
   d) Achievement ❏

10. If you provide ample breaks for lunch and recuperation, and pay decent salaries, you are addressing what level of need, according to Maslow?
    a) Security ❏
    b) Social ❏
    c) Self-actualization ❏
    d) Esteem ❏

CHAPTER 9

Stepping into their world

In the previous chapter you established in your mind what your motivations are. It is now time to take a step into the world of other people and work out what motivates them.

Why? Because it is only when you begin to understand someone by 'stepping into their shoes' that you discover what is likely to motivate and encourage them, and what may be less effective. That might seem like a lot of effort, but it is definitely worth while.

Often, people who are managers make the mistake of assuming that other people are 'just like them' and then try to use the same approach that works for them personally. Or they think that, because it worked with their previous team, it will work again with their new team. This generally does not take into consideration that another person might have different perspectives based on age, gender, culture, background, experience, interests and so on. A 'one size motivates all' approach is unlikely to work.

In this chapter you will be able to develop a framework that will help you to analyse those you need to motivate, by using the theories already learned and a few other important techniques. This will help you to develop personalized strategies for those people you have to motivate to achieve specific goals or tasks, and begin to recognize what is working or what changes in your approach you may need to make.

Taking time to understand other people will help you to build better rapport and trust, and therefore to have a greater likelihood of positively influencing them to achieve the results you want.

> Remember the question that is likely to be in a person's mind is:
> 'What's in it for me?'

Generational differences at work

The labour force is now made up of a number of different generations and it is useful to consider this when working out what is likely to motivate particular individuals. Each of these generations has gone through different experiences in their lifetimes which influence their behaviour and expectations.

● Traditionalists (born 1922–43)
● Baby Boomers (born 1943–60)
● Generation X (born 1960–80)
● Millennials or Generation Y (born 1980–2000)

Today's youngest employees are likely to have quite a different set of perspectives, expectations and outlook compared to those who are older, such as Generation X and Baby Boomers. Some of the characteristics that define each generation are in the table below.

These characteristics can affect behaviour at work and an example of this would be in providing feedback, which is a very useful tool in encouraging motivation. If you were to categorize how the different generations perceive feedback, it might be described as:

● **Traditionalists:** 'No news is good news.'
● **Baby Boomers:** 'Get feedback once a year and lots of documentation.'
● **Generation X:** 'Sorry to interrupt, but how am I doing?'
● **Millennials:** 'Feedback whenever I want it at the push of a button.'

Generational characteristics

Generation	Characteristics
Traditionalists (born 1922–43) *Experienced World War II*	Hard work Dedication and sacrifice Respect for rules Duty before pleasure Honour
Baby Boomers (born 1943–1960) *Era of civil rights, Women's Movement,* *Man on the moon, Cold War,* *Woodstock*	Optimism Team orientation Personal gratification Involvement Personal growth Values
Generation X (born 1960–80) *MTV generation, Thatcher era in UK,* *Reagan era in US*	Diversity Techno-literacy Fun and informality Self-reliance Pragmatism
Millennials (Generation Y) (born 1980–2000) *September 11th Attacks, digital* *technology, pressure to excel*	Optimism Feel civic duty Confidence Achievement orientation Respect for diversity

So the style that might be appealing and helpful to one generation may seem too formal and advisory to another. For example, traditionalists are unlikely to seek out recognition but will appreciate acknowledgement that they have made a difference. The next generation, Baby Boomers, are more used to giving feedback, but less used to receiving it, especially positive feedback, and may appear uncomfortable. The Generation X workers need plenty of positive feedback to encourage them, and the Millennials need much more instant feedback to ensure that they know what they are doing right and what they are doing wrong.

If you are motivating people who are of a different generation to you, it is useful to pay attention to what their expectations may be in terms of feedback and recognition. There is more detail on the subject of recognition and appreciation in Chapter 13.

The impact of values on behaviour

Values are another factor that affect how individuals behave. Values drive our behaviour, and in the workplace it's far easier to motivate staff if you are able to align their personal values with those of the organization.

Values are the rules that we live our lives by and define who we are. For example, if one of your core values is 'family', and you have to work 70 hours per week, it's likely that you will feel internal stress and conflict because you are not being able to spend time with your family.

To think about what your values are, you can ask yourself 'What is important in my work...?' or read the list of values below and identify which ones are important to you. Add in others if your priorities are not listed. If you are not sure, then think about situations where you have felt strongly about something – it's likely that your values were challenged at that time. For example, if you value honesty and are then asked to carry out a task at work that requires you to be dishonest, it is likely that this was challenging one of your values.

- Accomplishment
- Accuracy
- Adventure
- Authenticity
- Being known
- Collaboration
- Community
- Empowerment
- Excellence
- Fairness
- Family
- Freedom
- Friendship
- Fun
- Giving
- Harmony
- Helping others
- Honesty
- Humour
- Independence
- Integrity
- Joy
- Love
- Nurturing
- Order
- Participation
- Peace
- Performance
- Recognition
- Respect
- Reward
- Service
- Sharing
- Status
- Success

Then ask yourself: 'If I had all of these values at work, what would make me leave?' This might generate some other values. To put them in order of priority, look at the first two values on your list and ask yourself, 'If I could satisfy only one of these, which would I choose?' Continue on through the list until you have put them in order. Once you know what your core values are, it's far easier to make decisions about how you live your life and what career you follow.

As a manager, it helps to understand what the values are of those you need to motivate. You can do this by asking them, or by noticing how they behave in particular situations. Then, if you are able to create a connection between the values that an individual has and the organization's values, it is much more powerful in building motivation.

Case study: conflicting values

Bogusia is the manager of a team in a fast-growing technology company. Her experience in this case study is a good example of how individual values can become conflicted in a team. She values hard work and as a result is normally first to arrive and last to leave the office. Bogusia judges other people in a similar way and therefore thinks that Ethan is not committed because he tends to leave work most days around 17.30.

Ethan has 'family' as one of his core values and believes that he can do a good day's work and ensure that he gets home in time to spend time with his family, too. Often, he will deal with emails and last-minute issues after his children have gone to bed, so he works flexibly, which Bogusia is not aware of. It is only when she has a conversation with Ethan that she realizes that this is the case.

What Bogusia needs to learn is to accept that other people may have different values and priorities to her, but that they can still deliver the results that the company requires.

Ethan's motive for action = Fulfil values – to spend time with family

> **Behaviour** = Works in evenings but leaves office at 17.30 every day
>
> **Result** = Manager challenges Ethan's commitment – but he is happier because he is living in accordance with his values
>
> **Additional benefit** = Prompts conversation between manager and Ethan regarding hours worked versus results achieved

By now, you are probably beginning to build up a picture of how complicated it can be to work out what drives the behaviour of any individual. It can be influenced by a myriad of different things, but the more you pay attention to the subtleties of language and actions, the easier it is to work out how to effectively influence and motivate others. Of course, an individual's personality will be another facet of how they behave, and it's worth having a basic understanding of different personality types so that you can readily identify characteristics that affect their behaviour.

Personality types

Historically, there are four temperaments that people display:

- **Sanguine** pleasure-seeking and sociable
- **Choleric** ambitious and leader-like
- **Melancholic** introverted and thoughtful
- **Phlegmatic** relaxed and quiet.

Carl Jung's work built on these temperaments to identify the difference between extravert and introvert personality types, which was then the basis for the creation of the well-known personality inventory, the Myers–Briggs Type Indicator® (MBTI), developed by Katherine Cook Briggs and her daughter Isabel Briggs Myers. This type of personality assessment is a practical way to help people in a team to understand more about themselves and their colleagues, and can be used to generate motivation in a team. This psychometric tool is administered by those who are qualified MBTI assessors.

The MBTI shows that there are four different spectrums highlighting the preferences that someone has in:

- being energized
- receiving information
- making decisions
- living their life.

Just like the Meta Programs described in Chapter 8, people have a preference for either one or the other of a pair (e.g. Sensing or Intuition).

MBTI personality types

Being energized	
E *Extraversion*	I *Introversion*
Likes to talk things through	Likes to think things through
Receiving information	
S *Sensing*	N *Intuition*
Pays attention to the facts and details	Can see the big picture and possibilities
Making decisions	
T *Thinking*	F *Feeling*
Considers situations using logic	Considers others before making decisions
Living your life	
J *Judging*	P *Perceiving*
Enjoys routine and to-do lists	Loves the joy of keeping options open

While everyone has the capability to adapt to all the different styles, we all tend to have four particular preferences – e.g. Extraversion (E), Intuition (N), Feeling (F), Judging (J) – which gives a four-letter descriptor for their type (in this case it is ENFJ). These different types, when described in more detail, can help people in a team, as well as the manager or leader, to understand how their preferences can influence behaviour in a team.

Some ways that these MBTI preferences show up at work are described below.

Working on an individual project

If you ask a person who has an Extraversion preference to work alone for a few days on a project, they are likely to become demotivated fairly quickly because they thrive on being energized by other people. This would not bother those with an Introversion preference quite so much.

Ideas for the future

If you want to quickly engage someone with a Sensing preference, then ensure that you have all the facts and data at your disposal so that they can consider the concrete details on the project. However, if you want ideas for future improvements, then you can motivate someone who has an Intuition preference as they are more likely to be energized by thinking about future possibilities.

Considering the facts in making a decision

An organization that is cutting back its workforce has a meeting to discuss the action plan. The people with the Thinking preference are more likely to have considered all the logical reasons (e.g. cost saving, increased efficiencies, how to create a plan, etc.). Those with a Feeling preference tend to find it easier to think about how the others might feel about the situation, and what should be done to maintain harmony during times of change. Both approaches are required and equally beneficial for the success of the project.

Case study: last-minute preparation

Two team members, Scott and Mary Lou, were preparing to run a course together. Scott, with the Judging preference, had the programme planned a month ahead so that he felt organized and in control. However, he could not get Mary Lou (with a Perceiving preference) to do anything this far ahead. She became focused with three days to go, and then rushed around ensuring that all the final details were correct. When they found that the client had also made some last-minute changes to the programme, this did not bother

> Mary Lou, whereas Scott was frustrated that it was all being left to the last minute and then being changed. However, over time he learned to relax and trust that Mary Lou would cope with the changes and keep him posted.

You can also see below the effect when you add some of the preferences together and how this can impact on behaviour.

- **IS Type** People who are energized by their inner world and have a Sensing preference are motivated by maintaining continuity – *'Let's keep things the same.'*
- **IN Type** People who are energized by their inner world and have an Intuition preference are motivated by thinking through ideas for the future – *'Let's think about possibilities.'*
- **ES Type** People who are energized by the outer world and have a Sensing preference are motivated by action and results which help tasks to be more efficient – *'Let's take action.'*
- **ES Type** People who are energized by the outer world and have an Intuition preference are motivated by change and trying something different or new – *'Let's change it.'*

Recognition and appreciation

The way that someone likes to be recognized or appreciated is quite different for a person with a Thinking preference (T) compared to someone with a Feeling preference (F). Try it out for yourself. Answer the questions below:

- Which word do you prefer – recognition or appreciation?
- What do you like to be recognized or appreciated for?
- How do you like to be recognized or appreciated?
- What happens if you are not recognized or appreciated in this way?

Based on research from Myers–Briggs Type Indicator (in the OPP Myers–Briggs Type Indicator Assessor Training Programme), the way that someone is recognized or appreciated can have a profound effect on their motivation.

As a team leader or manager, it is vital that you don't just 'do unto others as you would like done to you' because it could demotivate those who are different from you. If you heap

Recognition or appreciation?

Question	Thinking types (T)	Feeling types (F)
Which word do you prefer?	• Recognized	• Appreciated
How do you like to be recognized/appreciated?	• By someone I respect • Not too effusively • With money • By being given a larger project	• With personal and genuine thanks • With plenty of appreciation • Must be sincere • Tokens and gestures
What do you like to be recognized/appreciated for?	• For a job well done – achieving an outcome • Not just for an average job • Task-oriented achievement	• A personal contribution • Making a difference because of who I am • Helping others practically
What if you are not recognized/appreciated in this way?	• Get angry or annoyed ('I'll show them') • Reduced input • 'It's their problem not mine' • Feeling down for a short time, but will get over it	• Feel hurt • Become demotivated • Lose confidence • 'What did I do wrong?' • Can have a profound effect and could lead to leaving job

praise for a routine piece of work on a person with a Thinking preference, they are likely to think it is patronizing, particularly if it is not given by someone they respect. And then if you make them stand out in front of all their colleagues to be recognized, that is even worse! You could get the best out of them by focusing on what they have achieved that required real effort, and then give them even more work as a reward.

Building up the picture

By now you should be getting a sense of what to pay attention to when observing other people. This will help you to work out how to motivate them, rather than using the same method that motivates you, and potentially getting it wrong. It might be obvious but you could ask them: 'How do you prefer to be managed and what motivates you?' Their responses will give you clues as to how best to deal with that particular individual. Time taken to do this now will save you problems later on were you to use the wrong approach.

Beliefs drive behaviour

However, there may be some people that you find it difficult to work with, and it can be even more challenging when you have to work with them to achieve an outcome. For example, your perception of an individual is that they are always rude to people who are more junior than them. The important thing to remember is that your beliefs about them will drive your behaviour and you might end up not getting your need met.

Your belief – 'I don't respect this person.'

|

Your feelings – You feel annoyed and irritated.

|

Behaviour – You treat them in an offhand manner.

|

Outcome – They ignore your request and you don't get the task completed on time.

So, if you want to achieve a different outcome, it might mean changing your beliefs about them. Remember, a belief is *not* a fact. It is something that you accept as true or real, and which drives your behaviour.

You might have to accept that in order to get the task completed you need to change your belief about that person. Remember that we are all motivated by two things:

1 the strength of our needs
2 the perception that taking an action will satisfy those needs.

So, if your need is to motivate a person to achieve a task, and your belief or perception is that no matter much you stress the importance of the deadline, they won't achieve it, that is likely to be the outcome you will get. If the need is strong enough, you will probably be motivated to change your belief and adopt a different approach in order to get the outcome you want.

TIP

Accepting, not agreeing...

If you accept that another person has a different set of beliefs from you, that does not mean that you are agreeing with them, only accepting that they are different. This is a key point to pay attention to.

Summary

From this chapter you have gained insights into what drives others and the significance that values and personality preferences can have. When you add these elements to the theories and models on motivation described previously, you should have a better appreciation of what to pay attention to when observing behaviour.

The key to being able to motivate other people is to be able to step into their world and understand what it's like for that individual and what is driving them. Once you take the time to do this, and examine what is really going on for that person, and why they behave as they do, then it is like putting the pieces of a jigsaw together to create a clearer picture of the situation.

The exciting part is then using the information to decide on what strategy you will employ to motivate them.

Fact-check (answers at the back)

1. What is likely to be the key question in the mind of the individual you are seeking to motivate?
   a) 'What's in it for me?' ❏
   b) 'When do we begin?' ❏
   c) 'How much do I get paid?' ❏
   d) 'Who is in the team?'

2. Millennials expect to receive feedback:
   a) Rarely and with lots of documentation ❏
   b) When they have done something wrong ❏
   c) Whenever they want it, at the push of a button ❏
   d) Only if it is positive ❏

3. Generation X...
   a) Are generally optimistic ❏
   b) Feel a sense of duty before pleasure ❏
   c) Are achievement-oriented ❏
   d) Are highly literate with technology ❏

4. One way to identify what your values are is to:
   a) Think about what you feel strongly about ❏
   b) Go on a training course ❏
   c) Speak to your manager and ask them ❏
   d) Keep asking the question 'Why?' ❏

5. Respect, honesty, family and excellence are all examples of:
   a) Values ❏
   b) Motivational theories ❏
   c) 1980s bands ❏
   d) Teams in your organization ❏

6. Which of the following is *not* one of the four temperaments?
   a) Phlegmatic – relaxed and quiet ❏
   b) Careful – thoughtful and detailed ❏
   c) Sanguine – pleasure-seeking and sociable ❏
   d) Choleric – ambitious and leader-like ❏

7. According to the Myers–Briggs Type Indicator, people who are energized by the outer world and have a Sensing preference are more likely to say:
   a) 'Let's keep things the same.' ❏
   b) 'Let's take action.' ❏
   c) 'Let's think differently.' ❏
   d) 'Let's improve things.' ❏

8. People who are Thinking types like to be recognized:
   a) Because of who they are ❏
   b) By being given less work ❏
   c) With genuine appreciation ❏
   d) By money and for a job well done ❏

9. If a Feeling type person is not appreciated over a long period of time, they are likely to:
   a) Have a loss of confidence ❏
   b) Feel down, but get over it ❏
   c) Get angry ❏
   d) Not be bothered ❏

10. A belief is:
    a) A fact ❏
    b) Something that you accept as true or real ❏
    c) A motivational theory ❏
    d) A value ❏

CHAPTER 10

Motivation vs. inspiration

By now you'll have a better idea of what motivates you and some fundamental principles of motivation. Now it's time to clarify your thinking on how you can motivate those you work with.

No matter whether you are a manager, leader or team member or you work on your own, you will have to interact with other people. Therefore it is important to influence others positively. In this chapter we will explore a number of ways in which you can do that:

1 Communication – understanding how, why, when, where, what, and which style to inspire or motivate
2 Decision-making – logic vs. emotion
3 Role models – becoming a catalyst or exemplar for change
4 Self-Determination Theory – helping to encourage autonomy

Being inspirational

So what is the difference between motivation and inspiration? The simple answer is a lot!

The *Merriam-Webster Collegiate Dictionary* provides the following definitions:

> **Motivation** The reason or reasons one has for acting or behaving in a particular way.
>
> **Inspiration** The process of being mentally stimulated to do or feel something.

If you have to motivate others, it's likely that you will have to be inspired and motivated yourself, as well as possibly being a role model for them. Consider the following questions:

- Do you expect that a leader or manager should be a role model?
- What does a role model mean to you?
- Given that anyone can be a role model, how do you motivate or inspire others?
- For whom might you already be a role model or inspiration? (You do not necessarily have to work with them.)

These questions, as well as the key learning points below, will be addressed as we explore how you can motivate and inspire people to achieve organizational and business goals.

> ### 'Motivation is the art of getting people to do what you want them to do because they want to do it.'
> Dwight D. Eisenhower

Think about a leader who has inspired you in the past. It might be someone you have worked for, read about or seen on television. What is it about them that inspired you? This might give you some ideas on what you can do, or are already doing, that might be inspiring to others.

TIP **It's part of the job**
*Providing inspiration as a manager or leader is not just an
extra part of your job. It is an essential element.*

Research carried out by John Zenger, Joseph Folkman and
Scott Edinger over a four-year period to determine what makes
an outstanding leader showed that the ability to 'inspire and
motivate high performance' was the single most powerful
predictor of being perceived as an extraordinary leader.

Here are some examples of things you can do become a
more inspiring leader or manager:

- **Practise effective communication** – you will learn more
  about how to do this over the next few pages.
- **Be the example** – show by your actions that you put into
  practice the behaviours that are valued by the organization. Be
  prepared to set challenging goals yourself and 'walk your talk'.
- **Spend time with those you manage.** View your job as
  enabling your people to succeed, which means you have to
  support and encourage them.
- **Delegate tasks with the development of the other person in
  mind.** Ask yourself: 'Is this task an opportunity for someone
  to develop their skills in — ?'
- **Get around.** Take the time to walk around and speak to
  people; don't just send them an email.
- **Recognize others.** Show genuine appreciation and
  enthusiasm, and remember to pay attention to the different
  preferences that were outlined in Chapter 9.
- **Show humility.** The ability to be humble and not arrogant is
  something that leaders and managers should develop, as it
  helps to build trust and acceptance.
- **Be a positive influence.** Practise being positive; do not fall into
  the trap of only being positive when something good or really
  important has happened. Instead, make being positive your new
  behaviour because, if you do it regularly, it will become a habit.
- **Provide social support.** Help your colleagues and do more
  than just show interest in them and their work.
- **Change your attitude to stress.** Stress is inevitable, so think
  of it as being more positive than negative.

Inspire, then motivate

If you put into practice some of the behaviours above, it's likely that, over time, you will be inspiring other people because they will see that you really want to help them succeed. That inspiration can turn to motivation within them, and as a result they will want to perform the action or task you want them to achieve – and to do so to the best of their ability.

Of course, it's not always easy. You may have to help them to be tenacious and maintain performance and motivation when they find it difficult. This is where being an inspiration can really bring benefits. All too often, the misapprehension is that 'being an inspiration' is the role of iconic leaders who are great orators and have 'presence' or charisma. While it is true that these aspects are important, the ability to be inspirational is not the sole preserve of a few.

Communication

As was mentioned already, how you communicate with people has a direct influence on how you are perceived by others, and the degree to which they are motivated. In Chapter 8 you learned about Meta Programs, which can help you work out the language you should use.

The next step is to consider other people's communication preferences. An effective way to work this out is to draw on knowledge gained through NLP (neuro linguistic programming) – an approach developed by Richard Bandler and John Grinder.

Human beings experience the world through the physical senses. These are described as the **representational system** and they can be split into three groups:

1 **Visual** – the things we see
2 **Auditory** – the things we hear
3 **Kinaesthetic** – the things we feel (touch/emotion), taste and smell.

Your brain uses your senses to build your **internal representation**, or model, of the world around you.

Read the explanation of the preferences below (which are adapted from Tony Nutley, UK College of Personal Development, NLP Programme) and identify which one appeals to you most. This will help you work out your preferred representational system.

Visual

'If I could show you a really brilliant way of communicating that could make you appear more attractive to visionary people, you would at least want to look at it, wouldn't you?'

The benefits of building rapport with people who have a preference for the visual representational system is that it becomes so much clearer to see the way they view the world. It is when you see how things look from other points of view that you catch sight of the bigger picture. From this perspective, it is easier to see the way forward to a really bright future.

Auditory

'If I were to tell you about a way of communicating with people that would really want to make them prick up their ears and listen, you would at least want to hear about it, wouldn't you?'

Striking a harmonious chord with someone with an auditory preference might sound easy, and being in tune with them means that you are talking their language.

Kinaesthetic

'If I were to give you a really concrete way to get in touch with people, so that you can build rapport at a really deep level and get to grips with the way they hold reality, you would at least want to get a feel for it, wouldn't you?'

When you find common ground with people, you may feel that things move along more smoothly, that new connections are being made and that the path ahead becomes a stroll in the park.

TIP **Building rapport**
By understanding your own preferred representational system, it can help you to work out why it might seem easier to communicate with some people than others. And for those that you find it more difficult to talk to, if

you begin to notice which system they tend to use, you can notice how they react to you. If you then adapt how you communicate, it is likely that you'll have a better chance of building rapport with them.

Another element of communication that is helpful to be aware of is to pick up some of the non-verbal changes that happen in the person you are speaking to.

Case study: using sensory acuity

Sergey was asking a member of his team for an update on a task he had been given to complete. While the individual explained that progress was being made, and that it should be finished by the agreed deadline, the person's non-verbal communication told a different story.

Sergey couldn't help noticing that he was fidgeting and would not look directly at him. He spoke more quickly than usual and his face was reddening. So Sergey calmly enquired: 'Although you tell me everything is OK, my sense is that something's not right, because you are a bit agitated. Is there a problem?' At that point the person confessed that he was a bit unsure about one element of the task and had not done anything about it yet. Sergey had used his **sensory acuity** to identify that there was an issue, which meant he could deal with it.

The table below shows the key physical signs to be alert to:

Sensory acuity

Senses	Signs	Senses	Signs
Voice	Tone/pitch/pace	Facial movements	Eyebrows, muscle twitching
Skin tone	Colour and/or shininess	Lip size	Thinning
Eye movements	Up/down, left/right combinations	Head	Angle
Pupil of eye	Dilation or widening	Physical gestures	Hand/arm/foot/leg movements, fidgeting

Remember that few, if any, of the above signals 'mean' anything on their own. Reading body language is not about learning to attach some arbitrary meaning to each of the above, but to consider them along with all the other information you are getting from another person.

Communication methods in business

As a manager who wants to inspire or motivate others, you are likely to be under time pressure to get tasks completed. There can be a temptation to use the quickest method, which might not always be the most effective.

So make sure you have thought through which method(s) are best for the particular person you are motivating. Some people prefer to communicate by email, which can allow time for thinking and reflection, whereas others thrive on the stimulus of regular face-to-face contact.

In today's world a simple representation of communication methods is:

- **One-dimensional (1D) communication = written (e.g. SMS text, email, Internet)**
  The vocabulary used and construction of the words within the communication are what will convey meaning. However, this can be misinterpreted as the initiator is not present so cannot use the other senses to gauge the person's situation or mood, and cannot make adjustments to the communication 'in the moment'.
- **Two-dimensional (2D) communication = verbal (e.g. telephone, Skype call)**
  Through the tone, pace and volume of voice, those present in the call can better evaluate the communication, ask questions to clarify understanding and make adjustments. Both parties will gain more meaning than in a written (1D) communication.

- **Three-dimensional (3D) communication = in person (i.e. meeting someone face to face)**
  Visual conference calls could be regarded as 2D rather than as 3D, although advances in technology and greater familiarity with it may change this view. In this mode, there is the full range of conscious communications taking place, plus other subtler subconscious non-verbal signals (e.g. body language).

The most effective form of communication is 3D and the most convenient is 1D. Emails, SMS texts and social media are the most popular forms of communication now, and with them often comes the expectation of a rapid response, which can cause people problems as they send messages without fully thinking them through.

Gauging what and when to communicate is a critical success factor in influencing others. So, when you want to motivate or inspire someone else, think about which communication mode you should use and remember to pay close attention to the state the recipient is in and the representational system that works best for them.

Logic vs. emotion

Think of a situation where you had a bulletproof case or justification for an action and where the facts, the reasons and logic behind it were clear. Yet the other person dug their heels in and refused to budge. Your logic did not succeed.

Decision-making is invariably emotional rather than just purely logical – through neuroscience the reasons for this are becoming better understood. Decisions are made by not just working out the pros and cons, but also relying on feelings, which some may describe as using their instincts.

If you want to successfully influence others, then using the organization's goals and values as the sole reason for action may not be enough. It is better to help others discover for themselves what feels right, too. This may involve spending some time with them building up their trust in you. By understanding their situation (e.g. their problems, concerns and objectives), you can indicate that what *you* want to achieve, can also help *them* with the issues they have. In other words, you achieve a win–win outcome.

One way to try to access people's emotions is to ask open-ended questions, as these will help to get someone talking and expressing themselves. It encourages the person to begin a dialogue and so set the course of the conversation, which can help them to start feeling safer and achieving greater self-expression.

Examples of open-ended questions

'What is bothering you?' ('Is something bothering you?' is an example of a closed question and one that is likely to result in a one-word answer!)

'What would you like to talk about?'

'What's been happening since we last met?'

'How do you think this could be improved?'

'What makes you think it may be time for this to be changed?'

'Tell me about a time when this worked well for you?'

'What else?'

'Such as?'

'What else would you like to discuss?'

Practising asking open questions could prove helpful. However, be aware that, if you use this approach too often or in the wrong circumstances, you could be viewed as indecisive or as a procrastinator. In this situation, you should switch to using closed questions that encourage a 'yes' or 'no' answer, and help someone to commit to an action.

Examples of closed questions

'Are you going to complete the report by tomorrow?'

'Have you managed to work out a solution to this?'

'Is Mary attending the meeting, too?'

So now you are likely to have a greater awareness of the nuances of communication that can make a difference in how you motivate people. Take time to observe, and to practise behaviours that are different from your normal preferences.

Role models

If you have a leadership or management role in an organization, then you will be aware that your staff tends to take their cues as to how to behave based on what they observe you doing. So are you behaving as a role model?

What does a role model mean to you?
Who are your role models?
Why are they role models?

As well as being a role model, you may find it very helpful to have role models whom you can learn from and aspire to be. A lot can be gained by studying others and, if possible, by discussing their careers and decisions with them. People are often flattered when others ask them for help, so don't be afraid to do so.

Positive energy

Both motivation and inspiration require positive energy, and by developing positive habits of nurturing, supporting and recognizing the efforts of others you will discover new levels of pleasure in how you work, which are likely to be mirrored by those who work with you.

Keep your integrity
Be mindful of not becoming so agile and adaptable that what you say or do becomes an 'act'. If you adapt yourself too much, you are likely to dilute your values to a point you do not really believe in what you are saying or doing. This runs the risk of being considered disingenuous.

Self-Determination Theory

Traditional thinking has been that motivation in the workplace is driven by external reward; more recently, recognition has also been added to the mix. This has led to quantity becoming the focus – that is, 'more is better'. Over the last 40 years important work done by psychologists and neuroscientists has given us a better understanding of motivation that challenges this thinking.

Two research psychologists, Edward Deci and Richard Ryan, have developed their Self–Determination Theory, in which they propose the importance of the *quality* of motivation over the *quantity* of motivation. A central theme to their view is that there are two types of motivation – **controlled** and **autonomous**.

Controlled and autonomous motivation

	Approach	Method	Effect
Controlled motivation ('carrot and stick')			
	Seduce	Reward	Pressure
	Coerce	Threat	Pressure
Autonomous motivation ('self-determination')			
	Choice	Inclusion	Willingness
	Endorsement	Support	Enjoyment
	Interest	Belief	Feeling valued

The benefits of autonomous motivation are that it leads to better creativity, problem solving, task performance and a positive emotional state. These benefits are achieved because the person has:

● had their own perspective / internal frame of reference considered
● been engaged in the decision-making process
● been shown a willingness to explore new ways

- discovered a higher level of 'self-starter' energy within themselves
- found the rationale behind what is meaningful (i.e., related to their values and beliefs)
- gained a sense of enjoyment through the approach.

Deci and Ryan's Self-Determination Theory is a theory of motivation that aims to explain individuals' goal-directed behaviour. They believe that motivation resides along a continuum, with intrinsic motivation on the far right, extrinsic motivation in the middle and amotivation on the far left – which is a state of lacking any motivation to engage in an activity (being apathetic):

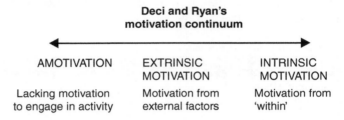

Deci and Ryan's motivation continuum

AMOTIVATION	EXTRINSIC MOTIVATION	INTRINSIC MOTIVATION
Lacking motivation to engage in activity	Motivation from external factors	Motivation from 'within'

The critical component of the theory concerns the degree to which individuals fulfil their basic psychological needs. So the more someone attains these needs, the more their behaviour is self-determined. The three main psychological needs they identified are:

1 **autonomy**
2 **competence**
3 **relatedness**.

'Motivation is the energy for action.'

Edward Deci

How to encourage autonomy

So how do you encourage autonomy while ensuring that the goals of the organization are met? Here are some guidelines adapted from Ryan and Deci:

- **Share decision-making.** This is not practical in all circumstances, but it is in more cases than we often assume. If goals are non-negotiable, allow people to determine how they will get there. The more people participate in the decisions that affect them, the more engaged they will be.
- **Explain the reasons for goals and rules.** Take time to explain why a rule exists, or how a task is important to a larger objective, as it helps to encourage engagement.
- **Adopt the other's perspective.** Once you understand another person's perspective, it's easier to work out – together – how you might help achieve the organizational goals.
- **Foster an alliance.** Hierarchical relationships have their place, but work-related or behaviour-related goals are often shared. The manager is not responsible for an employee's mistakes, but they are responsible for the final product. Make your mutual interest clear – as well as your offer of support.

Summary

Motivation, as Edward Deci writes, is 'energy for action' and it comes from within, and if you want to influence another person's motivation you have to appeal to them at a logical and an emotional level.

Inspiration is built upon positive energy, an appealing vision and compelling behaviour. Through your behaviour you can inspire other people. You may not think that it is your job to inspire others, but do not underestimate the positive effect it can have on other people. They may never tell you, but you will know it by the way they behave towards you.

In order to motivate or inspire, you will need to positively influence others and be able to assess and react to a situation well. You also need to be agile in how you adapt your thinking, behaviour and communications to different people and situations.

To influence effectively is a skill that can be learned. The level to which one can influence is also a factor of your character. While you might argue that your character cannot be changed, it can be – if you want it to be. So you have to find the motivation – the reason from within that makes it worth while to change.

Fact-check (answers at the back)

1. Inspiration is:
   a) the process of being mentally stimulated to do or feel something ❏
   b) the reason or reasons one has for acting or behaving in a particular way ❏
   c) difficult to do if you are demotivated ❏
   d) something that only those with charisma can give ❏

2. What is an essential element of your job as a manager or leader?
   a) Using your mobile phone at the weekend ❏
   b) Keeping your salary confidential ❏
   c) Getting everyone a cup of coffee ❏
   d) Inspiring others ❏

3. Which answer below is *not* something you should do to become more inspiring?
   a) Spend time with those you manage ❏
   b) Show humility ❏
   c) Take all the credit for tasks your team achieve ❏
   d) Delegate tasks with the development of the other person in mind ❏

4. According to NLP, which of the following is *not* a representational system?
   a) Auditory ❏
   b) Kinaesthetic ❏
   c) Telepathic ❏
   d) Visual ❏

5. Meeting someone face to face would be an example of:
   a) 1D communication ❏
   b) 2D communication ❏
   c) 3D communication ❏
   d) 4D communication ❏

6. An example of an open-ended question is:
   a) 'What's been happening since we last met?' ❏
   b) 'Have you completed the report yet?' ❏
   c) 'Is George attending the meeting?' ❏
   d) 'Could you collect the manager from the station?' ❏

7. An example of a closed question is:
   a) 'How is the report progressing?' ❏
   b) 'Which option do you think is best for our office reorganization?' ❏
   c) 'What training requirements do you have for the next 12 months?' ❏
   d) 'Are you going to complete the report by tomorrow?' ❏

8. Becoming too agile and adaptable in your communication style could result in:
   a) You being clear about who 'you' really are ❏
   b) Being seen as weak ❏
   c) Spending a lot of time of this activity ❏
   d) Others seeing you as disingenuous and putting on an act ❏

9. Deci and Ryan's Self-Determination Theory states:

a) That the carrot-and-stick approach is a key facet ❏

b) That the more someone attains their basic psychological needs, the more their behaviour is self-determined ❏

c) That the three main psychological needs are power, affiliation and achievement ❏

d) That seducing and coercing are two approaches to use ❏

10. One effective way to encourage autonomy is:

a) Set ambitious goals ❏

b) Share decision-making ❏

c) Take responsibility for the employee's mistakes ❏

d) Use the carrot-and-stick approach ❏

CHAPTER 11

Taking the wider perspective

In order to develop your ability to influence and inspire others it is hugely important to look outside your 'local environment'. When looking further afield you can discover fresh ideas, new examples of best practice and gain a broader appreciation of the context in which you work. Invariably, the nuances that can improve things can be sensed only when you branch out further than the world in which you work. By doing this, you can put work pressures into a more meaningful perspective, which in turn can fuel your motivation and that of others with whom you work.

In this chapter you will learn how to benefit from working in a matrix environment where you can find yourself working with people from other departments who have different skills and experiences from you. There may also be people who are more senior or junior to you in the organization, plus people from other organizations (e.g. suppliers, technical partners or clients) or from other countries, which introduces you to a range of different cultures.

Following on from this, we will also discuss the challenges of influencing, and being influenced by, other functions and disciplines in an organization. This will then take you into a brief exploration of the importance of organizational awareness and finding people who can support and work with you to achieve the results you need to deliver.

Maintaining motivation in a matrix world

When you are faced with the ever–increasing demands of organizational life, where matrix management, multiple projects, stretch goals and various other organizational initiatives and programmes can make working life quite challenging, it can be hard to maintain your own motivation, let alone think about being an inspiration to others.

Juggling priorities is hard enough, so when it is compounded by having to contend with changes that can come from outside your local world (e.g. from a person in a sister company or partnership business where you have no visibility in their world), it can be quite a surprise and a potential demotivator.

> *'People expect their leaders to help them to achieve the common task: To build the synergy of teamwork and to respond to individuals and meet their needs.'*
>
> John Adair

The work of John Adair offers two useful leadership concepts that can help you to understand and use techniques that will enhance your motivational skills in this type of environment.

1 Action-Centred Leadership

John Adair created an 'organizational needs' model that considers the effectiveness of a leader through three areas of need:

Type of function	Type of need
Task functions	Sense of direction
Team functions	Sense of belonging
Individual functions	Sense of identity

The model is known as Action-Centred Leadership. Below is a simple diagram of the model showing how the three needs and functions are related.

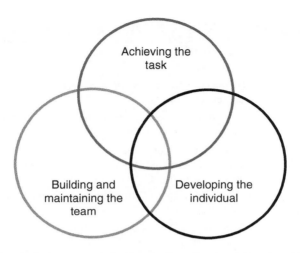

In order to help you relate the Action-Centred Leadership model to how you help motivate and inspire others, look at the sets of questions below, based on further work from John Adair. These will help you to analyse the way you can help to motivate the team you are part of, and then identify areas for improvement.

As you answer the questions, you might like to draw your own version of the model and consider:

- to what degree the circles overlap
- what are the causes of the overlaps
- actions you might wish to take to balance the model.

Action-Centred Leadership: checklists

Achieving the task		
Purpose	Am I clear about what the task is?	
Responsibilities	Am I clear what my responsibilities are?	
Objectives	Have I agreed the objectives with my manager, or the person accountable for the group?	
Targets	Has each team member clearly defined and agreed to the targets?	
Priorities	Have I planned how to prioritize the time?	
Progress	Do I check progress regularly, evaluate and encourage?	
Role model	Do I set standards by my behaviour?	

Building and maintaining the team		
Objectives	Does the team clearly understand and accept the objectives?	
Standards	Do they know what standards of performance are expected?	
Team members	Are the right people working together? Is there a need to create subgroups?	
Team spirit	Do I look for opportunities for building teamwork into jobs? Do methods of pay and bonus help to develop team spirit?	
Consultation	Is this genuine? Do I encourage and welcome ideas and suggestions?	
Briefing	Is this regular? Does it cover current plans, progress and future developments?	
Support	Do I see people at their work when the team is apart? Do I fairly represent the whole team in my manner and encouragement?	

Developing the individual		
Targets	Have the targets been agreed and quantified with each individual?	
Achievement	Does each person know how their work contributes to the overall result?	
Responsibilities	Has each person got a clear and accurate job description? Can I delegate more to him/her?	
Authority	Does she or he have sufficient authority for his/her task?	
Training	Has adequate provision been made for training people in skills they require and about being a team member?	
Recognition	Do I spend enough time with individuals listening and developing them? Do I recognize people's successes?	
Appraisal	Is the overall performance of each individual regularly reviewed in a face-to-face discussion?	

Now that you have answered the questions, you might like to review whether:

- the Task/Team/Individual circles overlap sufficiently to provide and maintain morale in the face of difficult challenges
- there are adequate systems or procedures in place to resolve tensions and conflicts effectively.

2 Influencing across borders – the '50/50 Rule'

The second concept of John Adair's that is useful to remember is the 50/50 Rule – 50 per cent of motivation comes from within a person and 50 per cent from his or her environment, especially from the leadership encountered there. The rule, like the popular management tool known as the Pareto Principle (commonly known as the '80/20 Rule'), provides a very useful guideline.

When trying to motivate others, it is also helpful to consider your view and their view on the situation and to make sure that you are not being manipulative rather than legitimately exerting your influence. What is the difference between the two? Manipulation occurs when your motives are grounded in your own purposes rather than in a common purpose (which in the work context is shared by you, the individual and the organization).

If you are motivating other people who report to other departments or organizations or who work remotely, then it is paramount that your relationship with them is one where all parties want to keep in touch. One way of developing relationships is to show a greater awareness and sensitivity to their wellbeing and work situation rather than simply being work/task-focused.

Another approach is to be useful to them – for example, as a source of knowledge or as a useful sounding board for working out problems or exploring ideas.

One common characteristic found in most people is the desire for recognition, which will be addressed in detail in Chapter 13. While praise is assumed to be the most popular method of recognition, the ability to be genuinely interested in, and concerned about, other people is something that will inform your thinking as well as help your relationships to develop.

An additional benefit is that, through others trusting and respecting you more, they are likely to want to keep you informed and take you into their confidence. All of these methods will help you to gain a wider appreciation of situations and be able to influence decisions.

Let's look at an extended case study on influencing.

Case study: influencing

Two contemporaries, Megan and Deirdre, had begun working at Rusty Clothes Peg, the global retro female clothing brand, at the same time. After completing the graduate training scheme, Megan moved back to the United States to be based at the clothing design centre in San Francisco, while Deirdre started in the European 'satellite' office in Dublin where she worked on the European clothing range, specializing in sourcing accessories for Europe.

In Dublin, Deirdre soon became involved in liaising with a number of accessory suppliers in Asia. Her natural curiosity, patience and attention to detail meant that the suppliers liked working with her, and it made her popular. This popularity did not seem to reduce even when the pressures of seasonal launches were at their peak. While Deirdre knew she was detail-focused and placed a lot of importance on her performance, she was naturally competitive. From a young age she had learned the importance of teamwork and team spirit while competing at hockey at county level. She had progressed to the position of captain in the hockey team and was proud of this achievement.

Megan, her friend in the States, loved fashion and liked to be seen as a trendsetter rather than fashion follower. Like Deirdre, she had learned about competition from a young age when she rode in various pony trials and show-jumping competitions. Now at work in San Francisco, she had to liaise with the manufacturers in Asia and South America. Her approach was sometimes brusque and direct, and she was seen by them as an intense and highly focused individual.

Although both Megan and Deirdre were valued by the organization, the Chief Operating Officer, Glen, was fascinated to discover during a tour of the main suppliers in Asia that there was a distinct preference for dealing with the European office over the US office. Upon exploring this in more detail, Glen soon learned that the major factor was that Deirdre in Dublin had established a level of rapport with suppliers, whereas Megan in San Francisco had not. Specifically, Deirdre talked *with* people and made them feel involved, whereas Megan tended to talk *at* them.

Inside the organization, the Chief Operating Officer had recently been in a talent review meeting where Megan had been considered to be a decisive person and proactive. Indeed, she had a reputation with the senior team inside the business as a solid person you could rely on for quick action. By contrast, others thought that Deirdre was somewhat tentative at times. This seemed odd because a couple of major clients had made positive comments about Deirdre.

Below are summaries of the Chief Operating Officer's observations about the two employees, after he had gained some feedback on both individuals from their manager, peers and team members, together with his conclusions.

How Megan is seen by others

By having a positive outlook and not restricting her presence to her own department, Megan puts herself in the position where she makes sure that others learn of her success. Megan seems to have fallen into the trap of thinking that, by saying 'Fantastic', 'Well done' or 'Great job', she is recognizing other people's efforts in a positive way. However, this can be viewed as insincere at times. She has demonstrated a focus on delivering results, so that more challenging and prestigious projects are being considered for her.

How Deirdre is seen by others

Deirdre's ability to listen actively and interpret the non-verbal skills is superior to Megan's. She demonstrates that the empathy, interest and knowledge she has gleaned about other people's situations means that she is able to put into context why she thinks they have done a great job when giving positive feedback. However, she has not actively worked towards building a positive reputation inside the company but has focused on doing a good job.

Organizational awareness

1 Do you know what each function does in your organization?
2 Do you know how the work of each function affects the financial performance of your organization?

If the answer to either of those questions is 'no' then ask yourself: 'How can I find out?'

Below is a case study that is a good example of how organizational awareness can have an impact on your work.

Case study: organizational awareness

Marcus was a very confident character who was always very positive and a quick thinker. Some people described him as a 'good talker' as someone 'who could persuade anyone'. As a 'shooting star' in the organization's talent programme, he was asked to lead a small international project. Wanting to impress and complete the project early, he approached the Finance Manager, Alex, during his lunch break and explained what he needed for the project. He also wanted to tell Alex about the benefits that the project could bring to the organization in the second half of the year.

A few days later Marcus attended the weekly project update meeting. His manager, Paulette, told him that his project had been postponed. Marcus was dismayed: 'That can't be right. When I talked with Alex he said that what I was doing was interesting.'

At the end of the meeting Paulette asked Marcus to stay behind. When everyone else had left the meeting she asked him:

- Why did you approach Alex?
- How essential was it that you involved Alex?
- What other options did you have?
- What do you think the wider implications were?

When Marcus started to give Paulette vague long answers; she stopped him and explained that he urgently needed to pay more attention to how he was thinking and behaving. Although he was talented, his interpersonal skills were not as good as he thought. His team were becoming quite demotivated because he was not really listening to them or involving them.

She also told him that the pace at which he was driving the project meant he was placing unnecessary pressure on his team. Because it was an international project he should have used video and telephone conference calls more, and emails less. Because of his bullish approach, he had missed some obvious non-verbal signals (e.g. tone of voice and body language).

Lastly, his growing confidence had turned into arrogance in the eyes of his project team and a number of his peer group. Instead of using the incredible network he had at his disposal through the 'shooting star' talent programme, he had ignored this route, which could have helped him to understand what the real impact of his project could be and to work out who his allies were.

Paulette suggested that Alex should have spoken with some of the other departments and introduced himself, outlined the project, and explained how he valued their input. The simple gesture of reaching across borders would have had a tremendously positive effect on the people he interacted with.

In closing the conversation, Paulette offered Marcus the following comments about being more organizationally aware.

Before approaching people outside of his normal day-to-day work, he should:

- take the time to understand his work in the wider context of the whole organization
- know who the real influencers are and importantly how well aligned they are to the organizational core values
- consider whether his timing is right – so, with very senior people, he should check with someone in his network who either knows them or can find out whether your approach will be well received.

Paulette also explained that, after Marcus spoke to Alex and outlined his concerns, Alex passed this information on to the Financial Director. She then mentioned the project to the Chief Financial Officer, who had already had concerns about Marcus's readiness for the talent programme. It was therefore decided that, as the organization needed the project to succeed, and as it did not absolutely have to be done this financial year, the CFO had postponed it for now.

It was a salutary lesson for Marcus that he needed to develop more organizational awareness.

Inform your thinking

In what ways do you keep yourself up to date on what's going on in your organization? Some people are naturally conservative or work in highly prescriptive roles or organizations, so they may not seek a wider perspective in order to stimulate their thinking.

In a similar vein, how does your thinking inform your ideas? A manager or leader is often expected to come up with ideas to help solve problems or move solutions forward, so it is worth considering how you can stimulate your thinking and problem-solving skills.

A common phrase used for innovative thinking is 'thinking outside the box'. Peter Drucker, in his book *Innovation and Entrepreneurship,* wrote about seven 'sources of innovation'. The first three sources occur within an organization and the remaining four sources involve changes outside the organization:

- **Inside the organization**
  - Unexpected successes and unexpected failures
  - Process needs
  - Incongruities
- **Outside the organization**
  - Changes in industry and market structure
  - Changes in demographics
  - Changes in meaning and perception
  - New knowledge

Expanding upon his model, Drucker proposed that systematic innovation means monitoring the seven sources regularly as they can provide opportunities for innovation. Often, the lines between these seven sources can be fuzzy and overlap. You should try, however, to treat each area separately as this will produce a better result.

The unexpected

No matter whether the unexpected is a success, a failure or an external event (within the organization or team you are in), consider whether any part of your work or the organization can benefit. If there is something, then ask (as appropriate):

1 How did the unexpected success/failure happen?
2 What would it mean to the organization if it were able to exploit the unexpected success?
3 What would have to be done to convert the unexpected failure into an opportunity?

Set aside time to discuss unexpected success or failures – they can lead to an improvement and a source of fresh motivation.

Process needs

These relate to process improvement through innovation. An example of this is where technology has been used to streamline a process, as in airlines that have developed the concept of using only online check-in for flights. As a result, they have saved time and money, as the check-in activity is carried out by the customer, not a member of staff.

Incongruities

Be vigilant for incongruity – this is the discrepancy that lies between reality as it 'actually is' and reality as it 'is assumed to be' or as it 'ought to be'. A good way to discover incongruities is to listen out for complaints or extreme views that don't seem quite right to you. Your sense of incongruity will help you to be curious about and explore what lies beneath what you have heard. For example, you might hear one department member complaining about a member of another department: 'We all work for one organization, yet despite our requests they keep not giving us the information we need.' This type of comment may indicate that the values or priorities in each department are different and can provide an opportunity to explore what could be done differently so that the information required is transferred correctly and on time. This will help future communication to be more effective and can lead to greater success.

Changes in industry and market structure

This relates to a change in a market such as the introduction of low-cost airlines into the travel industry. This changed the travelling habits of the general public. Similarly, when an industry grows very fast and demand outstrips supply, the changes and opportunities that arise can lead to innovation.

Demographics

Typically, this refers to population changes such as changes in size, age profile, educational status and income. For example, when a new shopping mall, distribution centre or major employer moves in, or out, of an area, things will change. (Note: although classed as external, this opportunity can occur when organizations are merged.)

Changes in meaning and perception

An example of this source of innovation is how business opportunities continue to develop as we continue to live longer and remain healthy and active for longer. This has created a range of opportunities – in everything from travel, hobbies and fashion to financial planning – as well as a mood of greater opportunity and enjoyment in retirement.

New knowledge

It is said in some quarters that we have moved from the Information Age to the Hybrid Age, though others have called it the Connected Age. What is certain is that, if we don't keep pace with all the new knowledge, then individuals and organizations fall behind very quickly. Therefore having areas of specialism and working collaboratively is for many organizations the only way to keep up with the rapidly changing opportunities that technology and innovation are providing. That, of course, is impossible for all but bionic brains, but we can stay informed in our respective areas of endeavours, and get together with associates and friends from differing backgrounds in order to exchange ideas.

 Keep yourself informed
As a manager or leader, you would not want to be thought of as myopic or negative, so having a broad range of knowledge and social awareness as well as a positive outlook will make you more interesting and informed. This can help you to anticipate issues, be an 'out-of-the-box' thinker and, ultimately, be a source of inspirational thinking that others will want to access.

Solution support

- How often do you seek support from others – regularly, occasionally or only when you need to?
- What causes you to seek support? A problem you cannot solve or the desire to improve?
- Whom do you go to for support? The same 'comfortable' group of people, or do you challenge yourself and ask people who you know have the knowledge but might be more difficult to deal with?

If you don't seek support when trying to solve problems or at least check that who you ask for advice is worthy of providing it, how do you know you have found a good solution?

When you are managing or leading others, it is important to involve them when generating new ideas or options that could bring about changes or improvements. Sometimes we make excuses that there is not enough time and we prefer to solve our problems on our own, but if you are able to work with, and learn from, others who think and behave quite differently from you, then it can generate new ideas and approaches.

Teamwork can be frenetic, competitive and complex, and can be highly results-focused. However, given good team spirit and a willingness to engage in debate and even face disagreement, the personal benefits can outweigh working in isolation.

Obviously, working in a team is not the only way to gain support from others; specialists can offer valuable knowledge and experience, as can confidants. As you develop in an organization, the ability to get inspiration and ideas from other people is vital. This can help to improve your performance and, ultimately, also the performance of those whom you manage and lead.

Summary

In this chapter you will have learned more about taking in the wider perspective and how it can help you motivate others. Being able to step out from within ourselves to consider the wider environment will add richness to the way that we and our teams operate.

If you want to help motivate or inspire others, then being a positive influence needs to be fundamental to your approach and requires you to be positive in your thoughts as well as actions. When working in multi-departmental teams or groups, try to be inclusive and open-minded, as these are attributes that will help to endear you to others and encourage them to be influenced by you.

When your behaviour is observed by other departments or organizations, they make judgements about your ability, and being able to take note of their different perspectives can be helpful when navigating your way in an organization.

Finally, bear in mind that the impressions you transmit as well as those you receive are vital motivational influencers.

Fact-check (answers at the back)

1. Which of the following is *not* part of Adair's Action-Centred Leadership model?
   a) Sense of identity ❏
   b) Sense of purpose ❏
   c) Sense of direction ❏
   d) Sense of belonging ❏

2. Activities that can help you in 'achieving the task' can include:
   a) Standards ❏
   b) Briefing ❏
   c) Team spirit ❏
   d) Clarifying the purpose ❏

3. Activities that can help you to build and maintain a team are:
   a) Supporting others ❏
   b) Recognition ❏
   c) Targets ❏
   d) Progress ❏

4. 'Developing the individual' can involve:
   a) Targets ❏
   b) Briefing ❏
   c) Training ❏
   d) Team spirit ❏

5. John Adair's 50/50 Rule refers to the fact that:
   a) 50 per cent of your problems come from 50 per cent of your team ❏
   b) There's a 50:50 chance that you will work with motivated people in your team ❏
   c) Praise and recognition will increase motivation by 50 per cent ❏
   d) 50 per cent of motivation comes from within a person and 50 per cent from his or her environment, especially from the leadership encountered there ❏

6. Developing organizational awareness is:
   a) Managing your boss more effectively ❏
   b) About getting a better job ❏
   c) Finding out about companies that are similar to the one you work in ❏
   d) Understanding how other departments in the organization operate ❏

7. When leaders have a sound understanding of how the business and organization around them works:
a) They know how to find the expertise they require, where to find it and how to access it ❏
b) They know which boss is difficult to work with ❏
c) They have been distracted from the job of getting on with the real work ❏
d) They know how to work the system ❏

8. Which one of the following does not feature among Drucker's seven sources of innovation?
a) New knowledge ❏
b) The 50/50 Rule ❏
c) Changes in demographics ❏
d) Unexpected successes or failures ❏

9. When you are looking to generate new ideas or innovative ways of solving a problem, it is useful to:
a) Ask people who have the knowledge but might be more difficult to deal with ❏
b) Just save time and try to fix the problem yourself ❏
c) Speak to the same people you always speak to ❏
d) Ask your manager ❏

10. Which activity below has potentially a long-lasting negative impact?
a) Trying to fix all your problems on your own without asking for help ❏
b) Speaking to your boss's boss without checking that it is OK first ❏
c) Scowling at or showing no interest in someone the first time you meet them ❏
d) Working collaboratively with your peers at work ❏

CHAPTER 12

Dealing with difficult situations

You should now have gained a greater understanding of the key elements that influence motivation, as well as of some of the actions you can take, as a manager, to inspire and motivate other people.

You will also now realize how important it is to create the right environment so that people can perform at their best, while enabling them to have a degree of autonomy in their work. If these things, along with your encouragement and direction, are in place, you are likely to have happier and more engaged people in your team.

However, it is also likely that there will be times when the motivation level of individuals in your team can dip. This can be because of external factors such as the economy, or changes in their personal circumstances such as marriage breakdown or family tensions. It can also be due to issues within your organization such as unsettling internal politics, difficult colleagues or unrealistic time pressures.

Now we will focus on some of the common problems that cause people to become demotivated, and how to address them as a manager.

Managing internal politics

Case study: the dangers of ignoring internal politics

Jorgen had been working on a report for a week. Along with his team, he had done a great job in analysing and collating all the data required to prove the need for an additional member of staff to work in the accounting function. He was confident that when he presented the arguments to Katarina, the company director, she would agree to what was proposed. After all, everyone had seemed enthusiastic about the idea at the monthly meeting.

When Jorgen presented the proposal to Katarina, she thanked him, and said she would let him know what the decision was. After a few days, she told him that the proposal had been rejected because another manager had made a stronger case, and so they would get the additional resourcing. Jorgen was furious. It had all seemed so straightforward – so something must have changed.

What Jorgen was not aware of was that the other manager had been subtly influencing Katarina for some time, so that by the time Jorgen submitted his proposal the other manager had succeeded in winning over Katarina. Jorgen had been beaten by internal politics.

It is important, particularly within large organizations, to understand how the internal politics operate, because those who have power and influence are likely to have an impact on your ability to get things done. You don't have to like everyone you work with, but you have to be able to get on with them. Make sure that you develop good peer relationships so that you know what's going on.

There can be a dark side to organizational politics – people behave in a selfish manner, have personal conflicts, compete for power and leadership, and use influence to build personal status by controlling access to information or not revealing the true intent behind their behaviour. Some people avoid 'playing the game' because they don't like this type of behaviour and therefore miss out on the positive benefits that can be gained by having informal networks and being able to assert their presence in an authentic and positive way.

Think back to the key points about what motivates people to take action:

- the strength of their needs
- their perception that taking an action will satisfy those needs.

If you perceive that investing time in building relationships and getting to know key people will not bring you any benefit, then it is unlikely that you will be motivated to spend time on this activity. However, if you consider this in a different way, and ask yourself the question 'How will building relationships with key people help my team to get their work done more effectively?', you might come up with a different response. It is likely that the quality of relationships and breadth of the network you create will have a degree of influence over how peers respond to requests from you or your team members.

Case study: learning how to influence

Henri was an up-and-coming manager in a biotechnology company. He wanted to be able to influence the Chief Scientific Officer (CSO) more effectively, but found it difficult to speak to him in team meetings, and, as a result, his ideas and concerns were getting ignored. The CSO had a very direct style and did not suffer fools gladly. Every time Henri asked a challenging question, the CSO seemed to respond abruptly and glare at him.

Frustrated at his lack of progress, Henri confided in his colleague Arianna, who was also a manager. He explained his issue and asked for her thoughts. 'Have you ever paid attention to how other people influence the CSO?' she replied. 'They make sure they catch him at the water cooler, and strike up a conversation with him about his passion, which is golf. Then they move the discussion on to whatever is concerning them and see what he thinks. In this way, if there is a disagreement, it is done informally and never in the team meeting. I think that your challenging questions in the meeting put him on the spot and so he gets defensive.' Henri had never considered this before. He thanked Arianne and reflected on how he could influence the CSO in a different manner.

By taking time to stop and observe what was happening, and asking a colleague for advice, he was able to understand the subtle politics that were at play and how others got things done. This enabled him to adopt an approach that still felt authentic, but helped him to avoid confronting the CSO in public, which was not delivering the result he wanted.

Motive for action = To get the CSO to buy in to Henri's ideas

Behaviour = Asking peers what their observations were

Result = Understanding the politics helped to create more options for different approaches Henri could take

Additional benefit = Less frustration for Henri and a stronger relationship with his colleague Arianna

External influences

As a manager, it is essential that you also pay attention to anything going on in the wider world that could have an impact on the behaviour and motivation levels of people in the workplace. For example, the global financial crisis made its mark on many people financially through job losses or reduced work hours, organizational cost cutting, the suspension or cancelling of projects, and so on. There was a change from a period of high confidence to one of uncertainty, anxiety and concern. Coping with uncertain times meant that employees tended to focus on their own financial security, family obligations and future employment prospects (remember the first and second level of Maslow's Hierarchy of Needs).

This uncertainty can escalate into rumour and gossip and before long people feel disinclined to perform at their best.

There are a number of ways in which you can support your team in managing their distress and anxiety. Communication is a key element here:

- Don't ignore reality. If there are external issues that are causing concern, recognize this and talk about them openly with your team.
- Use a variety of methods to communicate with your team so as to ensure that they are aware.
- Check that they have understood what you have communicated.
- Find out what the rumours and gossip are so that you are 'in the loop'.
- Take time to listen to the concerns of your staff but don't get bogged down in the uncertainty yourself.
- Encourage people to focus on the aspects of the situation that they can control, and to stop worrying about what is beyond their control.
- Every challenge can also be an opportunity, so think about what the opportunity could be.
- Turn the focus back on to what still has to be achieved despite any uncertainty. Satisfaction can still be gained from achieving results.

Get great results in times of uncertainty
Great results can still be achieved in times of disruption and uncertainty if a team focuses on what they can change, rather than on what they cannot change. As a manager, you can empathize but do not join the team in feeling disempowered or ineffective. Make sure that you are aware of your own emotions, because they can have an impact on your behaviour and your team will notice your own feelings of uncertainty or negativity.

Unrealistic timescales

Another external influence that can either inspire or demotivate people is being given a task that has an unrealistic timescale in which to achieve it. Most people have experienced this at some stage in their working lives, when they find that they are asked to complete a job in a time that they believe is impossible.

Case study: giving people a choice

Dean was a graphic designer in a design and print company. Their client suddenly changed the design of the invitations for an event the evening before they were due to be printed and sent out. Normally, Dean finished work at 17:30, and when his manager asked him to revise the design at 17:00 he knew that the timescale was unrealistic.

Dean's manager explained the reason for the change and how important this client was to their overall business. He added: 'I know I don't normally ask you to work late, but on this occasion, if you are able to, you would be helping out not just me and the client, but the entire company. I would really appreciate it if you are able to help.'

This gave Dean an element of control and choice in his decision, and although he knew there was not really any choice in reality, he appreciated that his manager had spoken to him in this way, rather than just telling him to stay late and get on with it. By giving Dean a choice, his manager was using the Self-Determination Theory we looked at in Chapter 10, and as a result Dean was willing to stay late.

The other approach that Dean's manager could have taken was one of coercion and command. An American social psychologist, Douglas McGregor, describes this type of strategy as typical of a Theory X manager. McGregor's ideas suggested that there are two fundamental approaches to managing people. Many managers tend towards Theory X and generally get poor results.

Enlightened managers use Theory Y, which is similar to how Dean's manager behaved, which can produce better performance and results, and allows people to grow and develop.

Contrasting beliefs of Theory X and Theory Y managers

Beliefs of Theory X manager (authoritarian management style)	Beliefs of Theory Y manager (participative management style)
The average person dislikes work and will avoid it if they can. Most people must be forced with the threat of punishment to work towards organizational objectives. The average person prefers to be directed, to avoid responsibility, is relatively unambitious, and wants security above all else.	The effort people put in at work is as natural as work and play. People will apply self-control and self-direction in the pursuit of organizational objectives, without external control or the threat of punishment. People usually accept and often seek responsibility. Commitment to objectives is a function of the rewards associated with their achievement. The capacity to use a high degree of imagination, ingenuity and creativity in solving organizational problems is widely, not narrowly, distributed in the population. In industry, the intellectual potential of the average person is only partly utilized.

If Dean's manager had been a Theory X manager, it is likely that his approach with Dean would have been quite different – he would have just told him that they needed the revised invitation by 19:00 that night and to get it done. This is because Theory X managers tend to be results-oriented and focused on the facts and figures, and don't understand, or have any interest, in the 'people' issues.

If you have to work with a Theory X manager, it is useful to have some knowledge of how to work with them effectively – and thereby influence them.

Things to know about Theory X managers

- **They are results-oriented** – so focus your own discussions and dealings with them around results, on what you can deliver and when. Focus and get agreement on the results and deadlines – if you deliver consistently, you'll increasingly be given more leeway on how you go about the tasks, which amounts to more freedom.
- **They are focused on facts and figures** – so cut out the incidental information and be able to measure and

substantiate anything you say and do for them, especially when reporting on results and activities.

- **They do not understand or have an interest in people issues** – so don't try to appeal to their sense of humanity. Set your own objectives to meet their organizational aims and agree these with them. Show them that you are self-motivating, self-disciplined and well organized.

Ways to deal with Theory X managers

- **Always deliver on your commitments and promises.** If you are given an unrealistic task and/or deadline, state the reason why it is not realistic but be very sure of your ground. Try to be constructive as to how the overall aim can be achieved in a way that you know you can deliver.
- **Stand up for yourself but avoid confrontation.** Never threaten to go over their heads if you are dissatisfied. If you do, you'll be in big trouble afterwards and life will be a lot more difficult.
- **Don't add to their problems.** Be aware that many managers are forced to adopt a Theory X approach by the short-term demands of the organization and their own superiors. A Theory X manager is usually someone with their own problems, so try not to give them any more.

Dealing with underperformers

Another challenge that you may face as a manager is finding a way to deal with underperformers. Failure to do so can lead to an entire team becoming discontent. If a manager continually avoids addressing the issue, it can ultimately be the manager who is managed out of the organization! Use the following strategy:

1 Find out the reason

Make sure that you do not make assumptions about what is causing the poor performance. Reasons can vary from lack of skill and clear goals, to lack of interest and focus due to personal issues outside work. Is it just this one person in one situation?

Has it developed over a period of time? How do you know they are not performing – what is the measure you are using?

Sometimes underperformance can be due to poor management, because no overall goals or objectives have been jointly set, so be prepared to look at your own practices as a manager before jumping to conclusions.

2 Take action

The longer that a person is left to underperform, the greater effect their underperformance is likely to have on the overall team – morale and productivity will slip as others see that the issue is not being addressed. So take action by having a discussion with the person and allowing them time to improve their performance. Make sure that you both have clarity about what level of performance is expected, and what changes in behaviour you wish to observe, and by when. Explain the consequences if the behaviour does not improve within the agreed timescales.

3 Consider the wider consequences

The way that a manager handles underperformance will be noticed by others in the organization. If people see that managers give underperformers a chance to improve, and support to do so, and that there are consequences if they do not do so, they will understand better what the likely implications for them could be if they did not deliver results. However, if a team notices that the manager fails to tackle poor performance, or that there is an overall absence of clear goals and expectations of what should be achieved, they are more likely to be apathetic and less keen to perform well.

4 Choose the appropriate leadership style

Picking up on point 2, if the style that you normally adopt as a manager to motivate members of your team is not working, it may be worth while considering a different approach. A *Harvard Business Review* article by Robert Tannenbaum and Warren H.

Schmidt entitled 'How to Choose a Leadership Pattern' offers a continuum of leadership behaviour that relates the degree of authority used by a manager to the degree of freedom available to their subordinates.

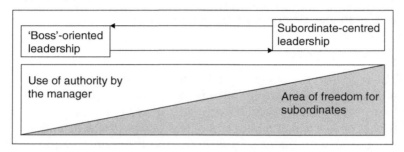

Tannenbaum and Schmidt's continuum of leadership behaviour

This continuum provides a useful reference for the different approaches you may select for making a decision, and assessing the potential consequences. At the right-hand end of the continuum subordinates enjoy a high degree of freedom. (This is similar to the degree of autonomy described in Deci's Self-Determination Theory, where the more autonomy that individuals have, the more their motivation will come from within.)

There are four main styles: tell, sell, consult and involve:

- The **Tell manager** will identify a problem, choose a decision or action plan and instruct the subordinates/team.
- The **Sell manager**, unlike the Tell manager, recognizes that subordinates may be resistant or have issues. So, although the Sell manager will have already come to a decision, they will attempt to persuade the subordinates to adopt the decision and action plan.
- The **Consult manager** will have views on what a decision and action plan should be but will not state those until the subordinates/team have had an opportunity to discuss the problem/task. Only after that will the Consult manager decide on the action plan, which enables individuals to feel they have had a say in the decision.

- The **Involve manager** will define the problem/task and the limits of responsibility, and will then involve the subordinates/team totally in the decision process – there will be a discussion and then the team, along with the manager, will make the decision/action plan.

This range of styles can give you a wider range of options for managing people, and it can be helpful to review which style seems to help/hinder performance with particular individuals.

Personal issues that impact on work

You already know how to create a work environment that gives employees a sense of identity, belonging and direction. However, there may be situations when you notice that those you have to manage seem to be 'off their game' and it's your job to understand what is going on so that you can help them get back to being at their best.

Sometimes personal issues outside work can have an impact on their performance. For example, if a family member is ill or they have financial worries, when the person is at work they will find it difficult to concentrate. While providing support and empathy as a manager is helpful, it is also useful to make it clear to the person that you still need them to deliver results at work. At times, it may also be difficult to interpret an individual's behaviour because they may not always be willing to talk about the underlying cause.

It can be beneficial to liaise with the human resources department, which can support the employee and direct the individual to any additional resources that might be available such as employee assistance, occupational health or a stress management programme.

In addition to these unexpected personal issues, there may be other influences that a person may not be consciously aware of that causes them to behave in a manner that is out of the norm. In this case, their behaviour can be driven by underlying personality traits that may not be normally observable. Consider the following:

- **Their level of desire for independence** If you put a person who normally works independently into a team situation, they may find it difficult to operate.
- **Willingness to tolerate ambiguity** Some people can operate with a high degree of uncertainty whereas others prefer to minimize risks and be more in control of an outcome.
- **Knowledge and experience to deal with tasks** Some people find it hard to admit that they don't know how to do something, so, if you give them a task and assume that they know what to do, they might find it hard to tell you otherwise.
- **Willingness to share knowledge in the decision-making process** This point can be linked to the independence issue above, particularly if the organization has a culture where 'information is power'. It is likely to be difficult for a person to accept that others may have to be involved in the process of making a decision, because it could mean having to disclose information.

Continuum of leadership behaviour: making a decision

Manager-led	Subordinate-led
Manager makes decision and announces it	Manager presents problem, receives suggestions and makes decision
Manager 'sells' decision	Manager defines the boundaries and asks individuals to make decision
Manager presents ideas and invites questions	Manager permits subordinates to function within limits defined by business or their 'boss'
Manager presents tentative decision, subject to change	

Summary

Now you should now have a better idea of ways to deal with problems that you may encounter as a manager when having to motivate other people. Whether it is being able to understand the politics that operate within an organization, or becoming aware of how external factors can influence how people react at work, it can be good to have a greater knowledge of what is going on, and how to navigate these situations.

As a manager, sometimes your own motivation can be tested if you are given unrealistic timescales in which to achieve particular results. The section on Theory X and Y managers will resonate with what you read earlier in the book about Self-Determination Theory and the importance of meeting underlying needs such as autonomy, competence and relatedness.

Getting to grips with underperformers may call for tough talk and straight dealing as well as empathy and understanding. Being a manager for all types of people demands the ability to adapt your style, so practise flexing your style to see how both you and other people react to different behaviours!

Fact-check (answers at the back)

1. Understanding organizational politics is about:
   a) Being nice to the boss ❑
   b) Knowing how informal influence is used within the organization ❑
   c) Taking a short cut on the career ladder ❑
   d) Getting ahead with your job by getting to know the CEO ❑

2. In order to gauge your manager's views on a subject that is to be discussed at a meeting, you could:
   a) Find out who your manager goes to lunch with, and ask them ❑
   b) Send your manager an email giving your views ❑
   c) Casually ask for their thoughts on the subject prior to the meeting ❑
   d) Grab them in the coffee lounge and spend ten minutes giving your point of view ❑

3. Which of the following is *not* something that will help you cope when external issues impact on your team?
   a) Recognizing when issues are causing concern, and talking about them openly with your team ❑
   b) Turning the focus back on to what still has to be achieved despite any uncertainty ❑
   c) Panicking and starting to get worried ❑
   d) Finding out what the rumours and gossip are so you are informed ❑

4. Theory X managers:
   a) Do not understand or have an interest in people issues ❑
   b) Are interested in lots of extra detail and extraneous information ❑
   c) Are focused on the big picture ❑
   d) Take time to really get to know their staff to build good relationships ❑

5. Theory Y managers:
   a) Think that the average person prefers to be directed ❑
   b) Believe that people must be forced to work towards goals by the threat of punishment ❑
   c) Believe that people are inherently lazy and not interested in work ❑
   d) Have a participative management style ❑

6. If you have a Theory X manager, you should:
   a) Threaten them, and go over their head if you are upset ❑
   b) Appeal to their sense of humanity ❑
   c) Deliver on your commitments and promises ❑
   d) Have a vague and rambling discussion with them ❑

7. Which of the following is *not* an action to take when dealing with underperformers?
   a) Find out the reason ❑
   b) Take action ❑
   c) Consider the wider consequences ❑
   d) Accept that it is just how they are ❑

8. The four different management styles discussed by Tannenbaum and Schmidt are:
   a) Tell, Sell, Consult, Involve ❏
   b) See, Hear, Do, Predict ❏
   c) Task, Team, Individual, Purpose ❏
   d) Participative, Coercive, Team-focused, Autonomous ❏

9. When individuals' personal issues impact on their work, as a manager you should:
   a) Be empathetic and understanding, but clear about expectations ❏
   b) Tell them to get a grip and focus on their work ❏
   c) Send them to HR and avoid dealing with the issue ❏
   d) Ignore them and hope that things change ❏

10. Which of the following theories of motivation highlight the issue of 'intrinsic motivation'? (There are more than one.)
   a) Maslow's Hierarchy of Needs ❏
   b) Herzberg's Theory of Motivation ❏
   c) Deci and Ryan's Self-determination Theory ❏
   d) McGregor's Theory X and Theory Y ❏

CHAPTER 13

Rewards and recognition

Sometimes, no matter how hard you work, you just don't get recognized. In this chapter we focus on this subject because it is so important to motivation. We will use an extended case study to illustrate the key learning points.

We will take a look at different aspects of reward and recognition to which it is critical for you, as a manager, to pay attention. These aspects are:

- monetary rewards
- non-financial rewards
- appreciation and recognition
- incentives.

Sometimes hard work goes unnoticed...

Let's begin by introducing our case study.

Case study: Llewellyn feels his extra work goes unappreciated

For three weeks Llewellyn had been working late on a Friday evening and been expected to come in over the weekend to maintain the company IT system. Everyone else had gone home, and while he was waiting for an upgrade to finish he allowed his mind to drift and reflect back over the last six months. His partner, Alfredo, had recently asked him: 'Lew, why do you spend so much time at work when the company won't invest in improving the IT system? If it wasn't for your knowledge and goodwill, they would be stuck, yet they don't even pay you anything for the extra hours you work. It must be 20 hours every week and that's before you include the time you are checking things remotely from home!'

It was the word 'goodwill' that Llewellyn was reflecting on. On a mental blank page he was jotting down where and when he had received any positive communication from anyone senior in the organization. It stayed blank. By contrast, he had already filled up another mental page with all the IT-related issues and problems the organization had brought to him. Eight-seven per cent of them were as a result of a policy of minimal investment in the proper upgrading of firmware, software and hardware, or providing any training for users.

Monetary rewards

'How much do you earn?' is a question you will be asked at some time in your career and it is no doubt a question you would like to ask others. As a manager or leader, it is so important to do your utmost to ensure fairness in terms of monetary rewards. This means checking that those you are responsible for are fairly paid for their job role, their level of responsibility and the performance they deliver at work.

Fairness is important, not just in your area of direct responsibility, but across other comparable roles in your organization, because it is inevitable that employees will discover what others earn. For example, if sales administration staff have higher salaries than purchasing administration, even though their jobs are similar, you can anticipate significant demotivation in the purchasing team.

Rewards aren't just a question of money
As a manager, it is also useful to be aware of the different elements that constitute rewards because money is only one element. To help you gain this wider perspective, this chapter addresses other elements of reward and recognition that play a part in having motivated employees.

Case study: Llewellyn's salary

What would have happened if the company had paid Llewellyn more in recognition of the value he delivers to the business and the unsociable extra hours he works? Were he to be paid more, do you think he would be fully satisfied?

The likelihood is that the frustration Llewellyn experienced would continue unless he developed greater job satisfaction internally, and also won appreciation or recognition from his managers. It is important not to assume that monetary rewards should be the first and only way of rewarding people, as was highlighted in Chapter 9 in the section on recognition and appreciation.

Sometimes managers operate by giving positive feedback by 'exception' and commenting only when something has gone wrong, rather than noticing what has been done well. For someone like Llewellyn, it is likely to be demotivating, as his personality preference appears to show that he is more externally referenced – he likes to know that he is doing a good job.

Non-financial rewards

In many companies, managers have no ability to give additional financial rewards, so they have to think about how they can reward someone without increasing their earnings. Below are listed six categories of non-financial reward. This is not an exhaustive list but should provide a good basis for you to work from.

1 **Achievement or contribution** – for example publicly mentioning an individual's successes, efforts (even in failure), solutions or ideas and how they have helped
2 **Growth opportunities** – giving the individual the chance to develop their professional status or knowledge (e.g. investment in time off to take a course or academic qualification)
3 **Networking** – giving the individual the opportunity to meet and work with other people of significance from around the organization or further afield (e.g. key clients or suppliers can provide employees with great opportunities to learn skills and interpersonal relations plus extend their network)
4 **Advancement** – enabling the individual to become part of a project team, and thereby stretching their skills and developing their opportunities for advancement
5 **Leadership** – projects or initiatives can provide a great 'incubator' for people to demonstrate their leadership and management potential offline from the organization structure
6 **Environment** – upgrading an individual's tools (e.g. computer) or improving their physical working conditions

These non-monetary rewards are incorporated into the 'Total Reward' approach, as proposed by Patricia K. Zingheim and Jay R. Schuster in *Pay People Right!* This breaks down rewards into the following four elements:

The components of Zingheim and Schuster's 'Total Reward'

Individual growth	Compelling future
Investment in employees	Compelling vision
Development and training	Company growth and success
Opportunity to be multi-skilled and take on different roles	Company image and reputation
	Win–win over time
Total pay	**Positive work environment**
Base pay	Inspiring leadership
Variable pay (e.g. bonus)	Operating infrastructure
Share options for key people	Colleagues
Benefits (e.g. coffee, holidays)	Work itself
Recognition	Effective relationships

These components enable an individual to understand the broader perspective when it comes to thinking about how they are rewarded. Often, employees compare their current situation to others, only by using salary as the benchmark, but the truth is that rewards are made up of far more than money. If an employee is helped to look at the other elements of reward, they can begin to judge their situation in a different way. For example, the fact that an organization has a strong brand reputation and a clear vision for where the business is heading will influence how employees feel about working there.

So encourage those you have to motivate to consider the wider view of rewards rather than just their salary.

Case study: improving Llewellyn's non-financial rewards

From the various categories above there are a number of positive actions the organization could take as part of an improved reward strategy for Llewellyn. What would you suggest?

Appreciation and recognition

All too often, appreciation or recognition is assumed but not expressed. Many organizations are managed on a problem-solving basis, which means that a lot of energy is expended on anticipating, identifying, monitoring and solving problems. Proportionally, a lot less energy is used in appreciating the efforts and performance of its people. In Chapter 9, we explained the difference between appreciation and recognition and the suitability of each for motivating different members of your team.

We have also highlighted that the amount of power and influence you can wield through exhibiting positive energy is quite remarkable, especially when it is delivered face to face and on a one-to-one basis. What can make a demonstration of appreciation even more powerful is when you put that appreciation into context.

Acknowledging someone's effort in working late by saying 'Thank you' is good if you can show that:

● you understand what was required from them in order to do it
● you understand what their effort and/or result means to the organization
● you are genuinely thinking about them and their needs.

For example, according to the Myers-Briggs Type Indicator, someone with a Thinking preference is likely to be prefer recognition from someone significant in the organization whom they respect, and they also might want to be given more work as a reward. By contrast, those with a Feeling preference are more likely to appreciate receiving a handwritten thank-you card or box of chocolates that has been selected specially for them. It is not the monetary value that is the issue, but the personal consideration that has been shown to them.

Get to know your team
By getting to know more about the people you have to manage, you can learn about their interests outside work and which gifts would mean the most to them. The choice of gift will be a good indicator to the recipient of your true appreciation.

'If then' or 'now that' rewards

It is important not to express your intention of giving a gift until the work is complete. To mention a gift beforehand could have the effect of being an incentive rather than the genuine sign of appreciation that you intend. Daniel Pink, in *Drive: The Surprising Truth about What Motivates Us*, describes this difference as that between 'if then' and 'now that' rewards.

'Now that' is used after the event as a method of recognition – for example, 'Now that you have worked extra hours over the weekend to help sort out the IT system, I'd like to give you a day off in lieu of the hours worked.' This reward is unexpected and does not set up the employee to expect this to happen all the time.

'If then' is used as an incentive or form of extrinsic motivation before the action is taken – for example, 'If you come in over the weekend and help out, then you can have an extra day off.' The downside of this approach is that it can reduce an individual's intrinsic motivation (see Herzberg's theory of motivation). This sets up an expectation in the person's mind that, the next time they are asked to help out, they can expect a similar reward. So it can actually achieve the opposite effect for the organization in the longer term, as it encourages employees to do extra work only when there is some sort of reward for doing so.

Case study: showing Llewellyn appreciation

From the case study it would seem that Llewellyn was not given even the most basic appreciation. His manager could have said 'thank you' or made an occasional phone call when he was working late to find out how he was getting on. Expressing appreciation for his efforts could have changed the level of motivation that Llewellyn had for doing the work.

What else would you suggest could be done in terms of recognizing Llewellyn's efforts?

Incentives

Commonly, the reason for introducing an incentive is to encourage your team members to put in a greater effort. Being clear about what incentivizing means to you is extremely beneficial because, if you aren't, incentive programmes can end up not having the desired effect. It is also worth while understanding how those you have to manage like to be incentivized, too.

When considering the use of an incentive, it is important to ask yourself whether the incentive you are thinking of using is one that appeals to the values and needs of all concerned (i.e. you, the organization and the individuals to be incentivized). Do not fall into the trap of making assumptions about this because what works for you is not necessarily likely to work for everyone else.

Also, you should decide on the level of performance you are seeking through the incentive. If the change you are expecting to get is a permanent or major one, then will the incentive remain valid and sustainable throughout? It may be that the extra motivation you think will be gained by offering a 'carrot' at the end is not continued over time because intrinsic motivation is reduced (see Daniel Pink's 'if then' approach).

For example, If Llewellyn's manager had offered him a bonus for working over the weekend, it might do the trick on the first occasion. However, if he is required to continue working at weekends, Llewellyn is likely to expect a bonus every time, and if this is not forthcoming, then he is likely to become even more demotivated than he was before being offered the incentive.

Incentives encourage people to be forward thinking – but at what cost? If the incentive period is short, then will any sacrifices of behaviour, practices and values be made in order to achieve the incentive?

There is also the risk with incentives that they are too materially oriented and become the norm. If an incentive becomes the assumed expectation (i.e. the reason for doing something), then the likelihood is that the motivational driver is no longer about core values and the organizational mission – it is about personal gain. A likely consequence is that incentives devalue appreciation and a 'thank you' becomes ineffective.

Finally, when considering using incentives, make sure they are part of an integrated approach that supports the organization and complements any reward programme. The context of the incentive is something worth spending time explaining when launching and reinforcing its purpose during the period that it is in place.

> ## Case study: benefits for Llewellyn and the organization
>
> Given the way in which Llewellyn applied himself, it would seem that his work ethic is very strong, so would more appreciation and recognition of his efforts and performance be more effective for him and the organization?

In future, make sure your recognition is:

- **timely** – try to catch people doing something right
- **authentic** – make sure that you really mean what you say (don't just thoughtlessly say 'Great job!')
- **in context** – relevant to the scale of the achievement
- **linked to the person's own values, and not your own** – step into their shoes and make the reward meaningful to them.

Summary

In this chapter you have assembled a number of strategies and techniques for demonstrating your appreciation and recognition of others for their effort and performance. Equally, you will now have spent time thinking about how, why and when you might use incentives and rewards to help motivate and focus people on issues important to you and the organization.

While commonly people associate the term 'reward' with money, you will now have ideas for alternative, non-monetary rewards. How a person's role is structured, their autonomy and the support they receive, along with the degree to which they are interested and stimulated by the role and work content, will all influence the degree to which they are motivated. It does not take much for people to become demotivated when managers are not fully attentive to the non-verbal signals people display.

In the next chapter you can re-evaluate your strategy for strengthening how you motivate yourself and how you can help to motivate and inspire others.

Fact-check (answers at the back)

1. Which of the following forms of reward and recognition tend to reduce intrinsic motivation?
   a) Monetary rewards ❏
   b) Non-monetary rewards ❏
   c) Appreciation and recognition ❏
   d) Incentives ❏

2. Financial rewards in a team should be based on:
   a) Fairness and parity ❏
   b) Giving the most to those who do the most work ❏
   c) Years of service ❏
   d) Ability to do the job ❏

3. You can reward someone while not directly increasing their earnings by:
   a) Encouraging them to work longer hours ❏
   b) Providing opportunities for training and development ❏
   c) Moving them to a new location ❏
   d) Highlighting their individual successes ❏

4. Which of the elements below is *not* part of Zingheim and Schuster's 'Total Reward' approach?
   a) Individual growth ❏
   b) Compelling future ❏
   c) Positive work environment ❏
   d) Bonus and incentives ❏

5. Methods of appreciation do *not* include:
   a) Giving a bonus ❏
   b) Saying 'Thank you' ❏
   c) Giving a personalized gift or token ❏
   d) Thanking an individual in front of others ❏

6. Acknowledging someone's effort can be good if you can show that you understood:
   a) What was required from them in order to do it ❏
   b) How it benefits you ❏
   c) How much they will be paid ❏
   d) Why other team members did not step up and help out ❏

7. Daniel Pink's 'now that' approach is used:
   a) As a way of showing off and bragging to your colleagues ❏
   b) Like a carrot to incentivize activity ❏
   c) After the event as a method of recognition ❏
   d) To tap into extrinsic motivation ❏

8. Daniel Pink's 'if then' approach is used:
   a) To reward success after an individual has done over and above what was expected ❏
   b) To get people to do things they don't want to do ❏
   c) After the event as a form of recognition ❏
   d) As an incentive and form of extrinsic motivation ❏

9. One of the main risks of using incentives is that:

a) They encourage long-term behaviour change ☐

b) They are too materially focused and become the norm ☐

c) They don't deliver the desired outcome ☐

d) People are so enthusiastic that it costs the company a lot of money ☐

10. Which of the following should recognition *not* necessarily be?

a) Timely ☐

b) Authentic ☐

c) Linked to the person's values ☐

d) A rare occurrence ☐

CHAPTER 14

Reviewing progress

It is time to draw together what you have read, learned and remembered from your previous experiences, and then think about how you will review the progress you have made in motivating others. In this chapter we will consider three areas:

1 What you have learned
2 How you can review the progress of those you are trying to motivate and inspire
3 How you can encourage those you have to motivate to review their own progress.

You will also be able to explore ways in which you can prepare, conduct and learn from the reviews you do to help others develop their motivation.

In particular, we will explore how reviewing can influence motivation, as well as how language influences what is reviewed and how reviewing is carried out. In addition, there are some monitoring tools that can be used to assess progress.

Measurement is a key part of the process of motivation because the mere activity of measuring progress can act as a motive for continuing action. For example, if you are trying to lose weight, by stepping on the scales once a week you get a measure of progress. The information you get will potentially motivate you to continue because the measure shows you are losing weight, will serve to motivate you to do better if you are not losing weight, or will cause you to give up if the goal is perceived as being too difficult to achieve. Whatever the result, without the existence of a monitoring process you do not know whether you are moving towards or away from your goal.

Context: your progress/ performance

If you are responsible for motivating others to achieve certain results, part of your strategy should be putting in place a monitoring process. This could be a daily, weekly or monthly meeting, or an update via text message or an emailed report.

Before conducting a progress review on a face-to-face basis, especially one regarding personal issues such as motivation and performance, it is important for the reviewer to be clear about how their own performance may have had some influence on the outcome so far.

So, before discussing the preparation, structure and methods of the review process, it is useful to revisit the principles behind motivation and influencing, as these will provide valuable reminders of how to put yourself 'into the shoes' of another person so that you communicate with them effectively.

Remember: people are generally motivated by their desire to satisfy a hierarchy of needs (Maslow):

- **Physiological** – hunger, thirst, sleep
- **Safety** – security, protection from danger
- **Social** – belonging, acceptance, social life, friendship and love
- **Esteem** – self-respect, achievement, status, recognition
- **Self-actualization** – growth, accomplishment, personal development

Each person you have to motivate is not necessarily focused on fulfilling the same needs, and so may need to be motivated in a different way. If a person is seeking to have their esteem needs met, it is likely that they are more interested in measuring success and receiving positive feedback, and may find it hard to be challenged or receive critical feedback that could detract from their own positive self-perception.

Reviewing intrinsic motivation

In Chapter 10 you read about Ryan and Deci's Self-determination Theory, where a critical distinction is made between intrinsic and extrinsic motivation.

- **Intrinsically motivated behaviours** are performed out of personal interest and personal desire – they satisfy our innate psychological needs for competence and autonomy (i.e. they form the basis for self-determined behaviour).
- **Extrinsically motivated behaviours** derive from the 'carrot and stick' approach, which is underpinned by the belief that someone would not want to do something unless there was a reward at the end (e.g. a bonus or avoiding being berated by the manager). Such behaviours are based on threat, enticement or coercion.

A tool that can help people to review their intrinsic motivation is to encourage them to ask 'active questions'. According to Marshall Goldsmith, people who ask themselves active questions on a regular basis have reported more happiness, more meaning in their lives, and better relationships. Here are some active questions you should be asking yourself regularly:

- 'What did I do to make sure I knew what was expected of me at work?'
- 'Did I do my best to progress towards my goals today?'
- 'Did I do my best to be engaged?'

The principle of active questions gets away from the passive approach in which employees can get into 'victim' mode and avoid action because they think that the organization is responsible for doing something – not them. The use of active questions enables employees to take more initiative and become more autonomous. With that greater sense of control comes greater satisfaction at work.

It is worth while remembering that there may be some generational differences related to this. For example, the high degree of self-reliance characterized by Generation X means that they are more likely to be proactive and take action themselves to solve problems and get the job done. Millennials, by contrast, are more likely to sit back and expect the 'organization' to provide. The use of active questions as a form of review can help people to avoid passive behaviour.

You can also use active questions to assess your own level of leadership. The table below draws on the five characteristics of exemplary leadership as identified by Jim Kouzes and Barry Posner, in *The Leadership Challenge: How to Make Extraordinary Things Happen in Organizations*. As you work through the questions, note down any reflections as these can become your personal development plan and source of self-motivation.

Reviewing your level of influence

Influencing has been a common theme throughout this Part and so, in discussing the topic of reviewing progress, it is worth mentioning the Influence Model, as proposed by Allen R. Cohen and David L. Bradford. The model is based on the Law of Reciprocity, which states that all transmissions of energy result in a return of energy in a similar way. This belief is sometimes summarized as 'What you put out you get back', which is a point well worth remembering – and not just when conducting a review!

The Influence Model has six fundamental steps:

1 Assume that the person you are attempting to influence is your ally.
2 Clarify your goals and priorities.
3 Think about the other person and their world view, vision and values.

4 Identify relevant 'currencies' – what matters to you and the other person.
5 Understand and deal with your relationship with that person.
6 Influence the person through give and take.

You can use these steps as a checklist for your behaviour when trying to motivate other people, by asking yourself: 'Did I do my best to 1) assume that the other person was my ally... 2) clarify my goals and priorities...?' and so on.

Kouzes and Posner's five practices of exemplary leadership

Did you do your best to...		
... model the way?	• Set the example • Plan small wins	Leaders, through their own leadership behaviour and actions, get the process moving.
... inspire a shared vision?	• Envision the future • Enlist others	Leaders enable people to join in the direction or vision.
... challenge the process?	• Search for opportunities • Experiment and take risks	Leaders are constantly challenging other people to exceed their own limitations.
... enable others to act?	• Strengthen others • Foster collaboration	Leaders understand that success requires a team effort
... encourage the heart?	• Recognize individual contributions • Celebrate accomplishments	Leaders show regard for the efforts of others and they celebrate team successes.

Meta Programs – are you being filtered out?

In Chapter 8, we looked at Meta Programs – the mental processes that enable us to filter the mass of information that we take in every day, and decide on which bits to pay attention to. There are two in particular that are particularly relevant to the reviewing progress:

1 Towards – Away From
2 Internal – External.

Remember that those with the Towards preference are going to be focused on the future and what progress has been made towards the agreed goals. Those with the Away From preference will be focused on progress that has enabled the problem to be minimized or reduced. The language and focus used by each preference type is likely to be quite different.

With regard to the internal and external filters, those who are internally referenced will know whether they are doing a good job or not, without having to be told by anyone else. They are therefore likely to work on their tasks independently and you, as their manager, may not get any feedback from them unless you specifically ask for it. This can be unnerving, particularly if you have a need to know how things are progressing or you don't entirely trust your team members.

Those who have an external filter are probably going to be seeking your approval at more regular intervals, and this can have its disadvantages, particularly if they lack confidence. It can often mean that a manager ends up doing most of the work themselves, rather than investing their time in supporting and building the confidence of the team member to trust their own capabilities.

So, rather than taking a job back to do it yourself, it can be more beneficial in the long term if you ask the person to come prepared with possible solutions rather than bringing problems for you to solve. You can then ask questions to encourage them to think, rather than telling them what to do, which reduces their autonomy and therefore their sense of personal satisfaction in completing the work. It's also important to provide recognition (e.g. 'I believe you have the capability to do this') so that they know you are supporting them.

Here are some questions to use:

- 'What is it that you want to achieve?'
- 'What alternatives do you suggest?'
- 'What are the pros and cons of each idea?'
- 'If you were in charge, which option would you select, and why?'
- 'What might happen if we don't...?'
- 'What else do you think is possible?'

Monitoring tools

As a manager or leader, knowing how things are progressing is important. However, sometimes the process of monitoring can be demotivating to a greater or lesser extent for those who are doing the task being monitored. Therefore, how you have agreed

● what is being measured
● for what purpose *it is being measured*
● what the information is used for

will have a significant bearing on people's motivation to do the task.

It is important that the tool you select is right for the individual and not biased by your own preferences. An effective method for trying to find the appropriate balance between retaining control and delegating is to ask the person who is carrying out the task to write down all the decisions that they regularly have to handle in performing their function. This can be done just by asking them to make a list or by being more creative and brainstorming the question to see whether you can flush out some of the other, more unusual functions and decisions they have to handle. In some cases, it may be preferable for the manager to generate and maintain the list themselves.

The RADAR system below offers a useful way to ensure that everyone is clear about what activities are being monitored, and how.

The RADAR system

Job/task	Recommend	Act	Delegate	Alerts	Reviews
A	✓			Face to face	Daily
B		✓		Email/phone	Weekly – Thursday
C			✓	Email report	Weekly – Monday 1hr (phone) Monthly – 2 hrs (face-to-face meeting)

Together with your team member, use this table to outline the list of jobs or tasks, and agree in which one of the three columns (Recommend, Act, Delegate) the task should be placed.

- **Recommend** This means that when the decision occurs the person comes directly to you with a recommended course of action, and will take no further action without your agreement.
- **Act** This indicates that the person can make the decision themselves.
- **Delegate** This indicates that the person will be delegating the decision to someone who reports to them (i.e. the decision need no longer appear on their list).

Depending on the nature of the job and the relationship you have with the team member, you may also want to discuss and agree the way in which you wish to be informed of alerts or issues. These two final columns, 'Alerts' and 'Reviews', are where you state how often you will review the task and also the communication style of that review (e.g. face-to-face meeting, telephone/Skype call, email report).

- **Alert** This confirms the way in which you would like to be informed of issues or alerts.
- **Review** This describes the type of review (e.g., frequency, type, location) and, perhaps, those attending.

Once you have generated this list, it can be advantageous to consolidate it into a series of subject headings and/or themes.

Review using Action-Centred Leadership

Case study: the high cost of completing a task

These days, the activity of reviewing is probably carried out less often than it ought to be because, often, once a task has been completed, people move straight on to the next activity without reflecting on what has happened during the previous one.

Milo's team had worked really hard to deliver the software upgrade on time, but it had been achieved at the cost of team cohesion. If Milo had asked the team members whether they wanted to work together on another project in future, the answer would have been a resounding 'no'. This was because Milo has encouraged the team to focus solely on the completion of the task, and ignored the team and individual functions.

If, however, Milo had invested some time in maintaining morale, attending to personal problems and giving praise and feedback, he could have helped to create a high-performing team with a strong sense of identity and belonging.

If you are a manager, you need to make sure that you use mechanisms to review progress regarding not just the task but also team and individual functions. That can be as simple as asking the team to score themselves on their team effectiveness on a scale of 1 to 10, and then, if this is low, asking them what needs to change in order to make the score increase. You can use the checklist below as a way of ensuring that you have paid attention to all three areas – task, team and individual. This is based on the Action-Centred Leadership model described in Chapter 11.

Task, Team and Individual functions checklist

Task functions – sense of direction	Tick (✓)	Team functions – sense of belonging	Tick (✓)	Individual functions – sense of identity	Tick (✓)
Achieving objectives		Maintaining morale – building team spirit		Meeting the needs of individuals (within the group)	
Defining group tasks		Cohesiveness of the group		Attending to personal problems	
Planning the work		Setting standards and maintaining discipline		Giving praise and feedback (performance and progress)	
Allocation of resource		Systems for communication		Resolving conflicts	
Organization of duties and responsibilities		Training – the team		Training	
Controlling quality		Selection of sub-leaders		One-to-one meetings	

Summary

In this chapter you have discovered how reviewing progress is a motivational tool in itself, though its effectiveness depends, of course, on how it is used. Reviewing can provide the 'motive for action' and helps individuals to pay attention to what they can proactively do, rather than being passive and waiting for others to take action.

Now that you have spent time reading about motivating others, you should consider how you are going to put this all into practice. Remember that in order to motivate others you must begin by motivating yourself. When you find that energy and enthusiasm it will rub off on others, and you will be able to start off your actions on a positive note. If the going gets tough, there are many tools in this book that can help you to overcome challenges and deliver results by motivating your team.

So get started now, and see what amazing things you can influence others to achieve.

Fact-check [answers at the back]

1. Measurement is a key part of the process of motivation because:
   a) It also begins with the letter 'M' ❏
   b) The activity of measuring progress can provide the ongoing 'motive for action' ❏
   c) It is like an incentive ❏
   d) It gives you extrinsic motivation ❏

2. Before you begin the process of reviewing someone else's performance, you should:
   a) Be clear about how your own performance may have influenced it ❏
   b) Prepare a plan ❏
   c) Observe them to get your own perspective ❏
   d) Be prepared to shout at them if they have not delivered results ❏

3. What type of questions help people to assess their intrinsic motivation?
   a) Open questions ❏
   b) Hypothetical questions ❏
   c) Leading questions ❏
   d) Active questions ❏

4. If a person is given a task to deliver and another department does not provide the information, what generation of employee is likely to be proactive and seek alternative ways to find the solution?
   a) Millennials ❏
   b) Generation X ❏
   c) Traditionalists ❏
   d) Baby boomers ❏

5. According to Kouzes and Posner, which of the following is *not* a characteristic of exemplary leadership?
   a) Challenging the process ❏
   b) Inspiring a shared vision ❏
   c) Enabling others to act ❏
   d) Rearranging priorities ❏

6. Those who are 'internally referenced' are likely to update you on progress:
   a) Rarely, unless you have agreed it with them ❏
   b) Daily ❏
   c) Weekly ❏
   d) At team meetings ❏

7. The D in the RADAR monitoring tool stands for:
   a) Drive ❏
   b) Delegate ❏
   c) Defer until later ❏
   d) Daily monitoring ❏

8. Which of the following is *not* one of the senses to be measured in the Action-Centred Leadership model?
a) Sense of direction ❏
b) Sense of belonging ❏
c) Sense of identify ❏
d) Sense of motivation ❏

9. The Law of Reciprocity is based on the idea that:
a) Feedback drives the motive for action ❏
b) People who are extrinsically motivated will be satisfied only in the short term ❏
c) What you put out you get back ❏
d) 80 per cent of motivational issues are caused by 20 per cent of your people ❏

10. Measuring progress should be carried out:
a) Rarely, because it takes too much time ❏
b) As a part of the process of setting and achieving goals ❏
c) Only by the person doing the job ❏
d) Only if it provide quantitative results ❏

7 × 7

1 Seven key ideas

- In order to motivate others, you must first be motivated yourself.
- Create the right environment by focusing on physical working conditions, rewards and interpersonal relations.
- Others' behaviour will always be driven by the need to satisfy their underlying needs.
- Remember to consider factors that could be influencing others that are outside of your immediate focus.
- The greater flexibility you have in your communication style, the easier it will be to influence other people.
- Provide a level of autonomy by enabling people to have a level of control, comfort and choice over what they do.
- Give others recognition for their efforts and regular feedback.

2 Seven best resources

- How to motivate your employees: http://www.wikihow.com/Motivate-Your-Employees
- Daniel Pink, 'The Puzzle of Motivation': http://www.ted.com/talks/dan_pink_on_motivation?language=en
- 'The Power of Small Wins' by Teresa Amabile and Steven J. Kramer: https://hbr.org/2011/05/the-power-of-small-wins
- Dan Ariely 'What makes us feel good about our work?': www.ted.com/talks/dan_ariely_what_makes_us_feel_good_about_our_work?language=en
- Infographic showing how major companies motivate their employees: www.business2community.com/infographics/major-companies-motivate-employees-infographic-01033558

- Seven unusual ways to motivate your employees: https://www.inc.com/ss/7-unusual-ways-motivate-employees
- Six ways to inspire and motivate top performance: www.forbes.com/sites/joefolkman/2013/05/20/everything-counts-the-6-ways-to-inspire-and-motivate-top-performance/

3 Seven great companies

- **South West Airlines** By putting its people first and enabling them to find purpose in their work.
- **Google** Employees cite many reasons why they like working at Google including that they believe their work has a positive impact on the lives of others.
- **Popeyes® Louisiana Kitchen Inc.** Cheryl Bachelder transformed an ailing restaurant chain into the darling of the industry by using servant leadership to inspire her employees.
- **SumAll** This data analytics company took a bold approach to motivating its employees, revealing everyone's salaries, how much everyone has invested, and involving all levels in decision-making.
- **Atlassian** Atlassian was named as number 1 in the Best Places to Work in Australia, 2015. It began a tradition whereby software developers can spend one day a quarter tackling any problem they like.
- **Marriott** One of the largest hotel chains in the world, Marriott has been listed as one of the 'Best Companies to Work For' consistently for the last 18 years.
- **Godrej Consumer Products Ltd** Indian Managing Director Vivek Gambhir writes a blog for his employees every Monday morning about leadership or personal effectiveness, and includes practical tips that employees can apply immediately.

4 Seven inspiring people

- **Oprah Winfrey**, talk show host, actress and media owner has had a profound influence over the way people around the world read, eat, exercise, feel and think about themselves and the world around them.
- **Eddie Jones**, when head coach of the Japan national rugby union team, he inspired the team to win against South Africa, with a last-minute try in their first pool match in the Rugby World Cup 2015.
- **Anne Mulcahy**, Chairman and CEO of Xerox Corporation led the company from the brink of collapse in the late 1990s. She said her biggest leadership lesson from that time was that good leaders listen.
- **Adam Garone** is co-founder of the Movember movement designed to raise awareness of men's health and prostate cancer. It began with 30 people involved in 2003 and has had over 5 million people involved to date.
- **Nelson Mandela**, worked with National Party President F.W. de Klerk to abolish apartheid in South Africa and became the country's first black president from 1994 to 1999.
- **Ernest Shackleton** was a polar explorer who led his men to eventual safety after their ship, *Endurance*, became trapped in pack ice in Antarctica. Many business leaders use his inspirational leadership lessons today.
- **Aung San Suu Kyi** became an international symbol of peaceful resistance in the face of oppression, as a result of her 15 years under house arrest while attempting to bring democracy to military-ruled Myanmar.

5 Seven great quotes

- 'Desire is the key to motivation, but it's determination and commitment to an unrelenting pursuit of your goal – a commitment to excellence – that will enable you to attain the success you seek.' *Mario Andretti*

- 'You have to walk in the other guy's moccasins. You have to think what they think. If you want to bring somebody on to your side, you have to figure out what motivates them. What do they need?' *Chuck Schumer*
- 'If your actions create a legacy that inspires others to dream more, learn more, do more and become more, then you are an excellent leader.' *Dolly Parton*
- 'You manage things; you lead people.' *Grace Murray Hopper, US Navy Rear Admiral*
- 'Motivation is the art of getting people to do what you want them to do because they want to do it.' *Dwight Eisenhower*
- 'A leader takes people where they want to go. A great leader takes people where they don't necessarily want to go, but ought to be.' *Rosalynn Carter, former First Lady*
- 'You have to look at leadership through the eyes of the followers and you have to live the message. What I have learned is that people become motivated when you guide them to the source of their own power and when you make heroes out of employees who personify what you want to see in the organization.' *Anita Roddick*

6 Seven things to do today

- Treat each person as an individual – there is no 'one size fits all' approach when motivating people.
- Try saying 'Thank you' or 'Well done' to those you lead – and mean it! It can make a positive difference to them.
- Take time to speak to your team regularly and really listen to what they say and how they say it. It will enable you to have a better relationship with them.
- Smile and say good morning to others when you arrive at work, even if you don't feel like doing so.
- If someone is not doing what he or she should be doing, think about whether it's lack of SKILL or WILL (motivation) that is stopping them.
- Motivating a team is like doing a jigsaw puzzle. It takes time and resilience and you need to keep the big picture in mind, but every small action will take you forwards.

- Every day think about the internal PR or 'good news' that you can convey to those you motivate. Everyone likes good news!

7 Seven trends for tomorrow

- Leadership drives culture, and culture drives performance, so leaders need to pay attention to the culture they create.
- '87 per cent of organizations around the world cite culture and engagement as one of their top challenges.' (Employee engagement and culture, Deloitte University Press, Global Human Capital Trends 2015)
- The needs of Millennials in the workplace are quite different from those of previous generations, and companies must consider how to address this.
- The new world of work is changing the way that employers engage people, as employees are now more mobile, work longer hours, and often in a virtual environment and a matrix structure.
- As work has to become more meaningful for individuals, it highlights the importance of performance management, coaching and empowering individuals.
- Employers will need to think of their employees more as customers and treat them in a similar manner.
- The motivated employees of the future are likely to be the ones most able to deal with ambiguity and uncertainty.

References and further reading

Adair, J.E., *Action-Centered Leadership* (New York: McGraw-Hill, 1973).

——, *The John Adair Handbook of Management and Leadership* (London: Thorogood, 2004).

Cohen, A.R., and D.L. Bradford, *Influence without Authority*, 2nd edn (Hoboken, NJ: John Wiley, 2005).

Drucker, P., *Innovation and Entrepreneurship* (New York: Harper & Row, 1985).

Goldsmith, M., *Mojo: How to Get it, How to Keep It and How to Get It Back If You Lose It*, 2nd edn (New York: Hyperion, 2010).

Herzberg, F., B. Mausner and B.B. Snyderman, *The Motivation to Work* (New York: John Wiley, 1959).

Kahneman, D., and A. Tversky, 'Choices, Values, and Frames', *American Psychologist* 39:4 (1984): 341–50.

Kouzes, J. and B. Posner, *The Leadership Challenge: How to Make Extraordinary Things Happen in Organizations*, 4th edn (Hoboken, NJ: Jossey-Bass, 2012).

McGregor, D., *The Human Side of Enterprise* (New York: McGraw-Hill, 1960).

Pink, D.H., *Drive: The Surprising Truth about What Motivates Us* (Edinburgh: Canongate Books, 2009).

Ryan, R.M., and E.L. Deci, 'Self-determination Theory and the Facilitation of Intrinsic Motivation, Social Development, and Well-being', *American Psychologist* 55 (2000), 68–78.

——, 'The "What" and "Why" of Goal Pursuits: Human Needs and the Self-determination of Behaviour', *Psychological Inquiry* 11 (2000), 227–68.

Tannenbaum, R., and W.H. Schmidt, 'How to Choose a Leadership Pattern', *Harvard Business Review* 36 (March–April), 95–101.

Zenger, J., J. Folkman and S. Edinger, *The Inspiring Leader* (New York: McGraw-Hill, 2009).

Zingheim, P.K., and J.R. Schuster, *Pay People Right!* (New York: Jossey-Bass, 2000).

PART 3

**Your Business
Communication
Masterclass**

Introduction

We live in an age when the number of ways in which we communicate in business is constantly increasing. Years ago, we simply had face-to-face communication, phone and letter. Now we also have more, including email, websites, blogs... and yet, if we are honest, alongside this increase in the ways in which we communicate has come a decrease in the level of effective communication.

How familiar are you with the following?

Working relationships that show low levels of trust
'There's too much information and I can't "see the wood for the trees"'
Colleagues who talk only in jargon that no one understands
The minutes of a meeting are unclear
PowerPoint presentations that have too many points but are vague in their core message

Unfortunately, the list could easily go on. We are all too aware of poor communication at all levels in business. What can we do? This Part of the book will offer some positive guidelines to help *you* communicate more effectively. You may not be able to change the way your company or organization works, but you can change the way in which *you* work.

CHAPTER 15

Know your aims

In this chapter we are going to look at:

- basic aims in communicating: if we know where we are going, we are more likely to arrive at our destination than if we wander aimlessly
- different ways in which people learn: one of the key themes of this Part is to make sure that our communication is focused not on ourselves but on the person we want to communicate with. If that is so, we need to make sure that our message is expressed in the way that is most appropriate for them
- various ways in which you can communicate: another of the key themes of this Part is that there is more to business communication than just typing an email and then pressing 'send'. We will therefore explore some of these different ways of communicating here
- some barriers in communication... and how we can overcome them.

The basics of communication

I often begin my workshops on communication with the memory prompt **AIR**:

- **A**udience
- **I**ntention
- **R**esponse.

TIP *There is more to business communication than just typing an email and then pressing 'send'.*

Audience

'Audience' means: know who you want to communicate with. Here the focus is not on you, but on the person/people you are trying to communicate with. This means the question you should ask yourself is *not* so much 'What should I say/write?' but 'What does my audience need to hear?' To answer that question well, you need to think about who your audience is and what their response to your communication is likely to be.

For example, if you are writing a document, the person who you are writing to should affect the way in which you write. Are you writing to your boss or to someone who has written to your company or organization with a complaint? In each case, how you express what you are trying to say will be different.

If you are emailing your boss, you may simply give him or her the information that he or she has asked for:

Hi Robert,

Sales for 2012 were 10% up on 'Introduction to Project Management'. We have sold just over 3,000 copies and we reprinted a further 1,000 copies of that title last month.

Harry

Your boss wants the information quickly, with no extras. If you are responding to a complaint, however, your tone will be different:

Dear Mrs Brown,

Thank you for taking the trouble to write to us to express your dissatisfaction with the service you recently received at one of our restaurants. I am very sorry that you found our service unsatisfactory.

I have checked the details from your letter and it appears that the member of staff you dealt with on 3 October in Grantchester was a temporary worker. He was unfamiliar with our company policy on the high levels of service we require from all our staff.

I have now taken the necessary steps to ensure that such a situation will not occur again.

Thank you again for writing. Please be assured that we aim to offer our customers the highest possible level of service at all times.

Yours sincerely,

John Duckworth

Do you see the difference? The email to your boss is short and to the point. The letter responding to the complaint is expanded and also, crucially, the *tone* is much softer.

So you need to know who your audience is. When I am preparing a talk, I will often think of one or two people I know who will be in the audience, and I gauge how they are likely to receive what I am saying, their present level of understanding and the point I want them to reach by the end of my talk.

Intention

By 'intention' I mean the message: the key point(s) you want to put over. In the above examples, the key points to your boss are stated very briefly, and the intention in replying to the person who complained was to defuse their anger and say that you had looked into the matter.

You may face some difficulties in identifying what the intention/message of your communication is.

You may not know it yourself. If this is the case, *think*. To take an example, my website was recently down and I was without one, so it made me think, 'What is the purpose of my website? Do I want people simply to find out about me and my services or to buy books from me or to contact me with questions?' Think hard until you can identify your key messages definitely and precisely. We will explore more on this crucial area of thinking and the role of mind maps or pattern notes in Chapter 17.

Is your message clear? If it isn't clear to you, then it will hardly be clear to those you are trying to communicate with. On one of my courses I discovered that the key message of one document was in a 67-word sentence in brackets near the end of the document!

Even if you do know what your key message is, you may need to explain some background to that key message before you can get to it.

TIP *If your message isn't clear to you, then it will not be clear to those you are trying to communicate with.*

Introducing change

John was hired by Denton Manufacturing Company to introduce change. There was a culture of 'we've always done it this way – why do we need to change?' in the company, but its traditional outlook meant that it was being quickly overtaken by smaller, newer firms. He gathered his fellow directors and senior staff on an awayday. His first task was to enable his colleagues to see the weaknesses in their present way of working and to create a sense of dissatisfaction that would lead them to want to change. Because John identified his primary message clearly, he could focus on that as a successful first step in introducing change.

Response

What do you want the person you are communicating with to do with your communication? Sometimes we can be so preoccupied with working out all the details of what we are trying to say that we forget what we want our readers, for example, to do with the information we give them. You may be writing to them simply to inform the people you are writing to – but it is more likely that you want them to make some decision.

Is it crystal clear how they are to respond? What are the next steps you want them to take? For example, suppose you are writing a fundraising email. You need to include in clear terms which website your readers can donate money on, giving bank account codes as necessary, and how donors can gift-aid their contributions.

Different ways of learning

Every individual is different and, if we want to communicate effectively with a range of individuals, we would be wise to try to discover their preferred learning style. There are three main learning styles:

- **visual** – those who like to see information in the written word, pictures or diagrams to take it in well
- **auditory** – those who learn by listening to information
- **kinaesthetic** – those who learn by actively doing things, for example by role play.

It can be very useful for you to discern where your own personal preference lies. I am more visual and auditory rather than kinaesthetic. The aim here is to challenge your assumption that the way in which other people learn is the same as how you learn. You need this reminder that other people's learning styles will be different from yours. To be an effective communicator, you therefore need to be alert to the styles of those you want to communicate with.

You can discern others' styles from how they respond and you can then at least use words that are appropriate to their style, for example:

- **visual** – *see, look, picture, focus*
- **auditory** – *hear* ('I hear what you're saying'), *buzz, rings a bell*
- **kinaesthetic** – *feel, concrete, get to grips with, contact.*

Different methods of communication

You can use your knowledge of the different styles in which people learn to find the best way to communicate with them. To communicate most effectively, you should send your communication in the form that is most suited to your audience. We can therefore immediately see that email will not be useful for everyone in all circumstances. For auditory learners, a phone call may well be more effective; for kinaesthetic learners, a meeting that puts suggestions into action will help.

We can also distinguish some groups further. For example, among visual learners, some will respond more to words, others to pictures or diagrams. This has significance. To give two examples: (1) If I am preparing a PowerPoint presentation, I will not simply list headings in words but I will also work hard to find a picture that encapsulates the key idea visually. This can be very time-consuming, but I am sure it is worth it. (An example: a picture of buttresses supporting a cathedral may help to communicate the concepts of strengthening and confirming.) (2) When preparing a map, don't only give directions ('After five miles on the A21, at the roundabout, turn left...') but also draw a map with lines in a diagram.

The two approaches (words and picture/diagram) in examples 1 and 2 reflect the fact that one approach (words or picture/diagram) will appeal to some but not to others. By combining two approaches I hope to reach many more people than I would have done if I had followed only one approach.

Making an informal contract

Peter had to commission several university lecturers to write a series of books for the publishing company he worked for.

As he began to email prospective authors, Peter quickly realized that some responded to emails but many did not. Later, as he met up with those he was going to commission and began to work more closely with them, he deliberately made an informal contract with them. He asked them which communication method (e.g. email or phone) they preferred and, especially if by phone, what days/times were best for them to be contacted. Having this knowledge meant that his frustration at their lack of response was significantly less than if he did not have such information and so his communication with his writers was more effective.

Email is very useful for communicating information, quick checks and seeking quick agreement. It is weak, however, in building good business relationships.

Phone calls are useful for discussions, because you can discern immediately whether or not someone has understood what you are trying to say. Unless you have a way of screening phone calls, however, they can interrupt your work. So it can be useful (1) to arrange in advance a convenient time to call or (2) to ask at the beginning of a call 'Is now a convenient time to talk?'

Be aware that your mood will often be detected by the person you are speaking to on the phone. Without being able to see the person you are speaking to, we tend to build up a mental picture of them. As far as you can, convey enthusiasm as you talk. One way that is often recommended is to smile as you speak.

Before making an important call, jot down the points you want to discuss. How often do we finish a call and then realize that we have not discussed something important?

It can also be useful to signal the scope of the call at the beginning ('Ray, I think there are three areas we need to discuss today'). Unless the matters are sensitive, aim to discuss the most important matter first, in case either party cannot continue talking and has to finish the call quickly. If one of the matters is sensitive, then you can ease yourself into tackling it by discussing less significant matters first and then proceeding to the more delicate one.

If you are trying to persuade a colleague to do something, before you begin the call list to yourself the possible objections they might raise and deal with each one. In this way, you will be prepared for what they will say.

Don't be afraid of summarizing where you have got to at a certain point in a phone call ('OK, so we've agreed quantities and delivery dates, now let's move on to prices').

Face-to-face meetings are more expensive but are indispensable in business. As we email and phone colleagues around the world we probably build up a mental picture of their appearance and manner – and when, perhaps much later, we meet them our perceptions may well be proved wrong. When two people meet face to face in such circumstances, one may well say to the other, 'It is good to put a face to a name.'

Face-to-face meetings also often provide opportunities for more informal relationship building; during a mid-morning break or lunch we can discuss our colleague's family or holiday plans, for example.

Barriers in communication

We conclude this chapter by looking at barriers to effective communication.

What is effective communication? I often present it like this:

This means that A wants to communicate content A (whatever it is), represented by a triangle. What we want B to receive and understand is a triangle, not a square, circle or a partially formed triangle.

So what prevents effective communication from taking place? What are some of the barriers to good communication and how can they be resolved?

- Your presentation is poorly focused, unclear and vague. Resolve by preparing well and being clear and precise.
- You give too little information. Resolve by getting to know your audience better and knowing the amount of information they need to make a decision.
- You give too much unnecessary detail and too much information. Resolve by getting to know your audience better and knowing the amount of information they need to make a decision.
- You use incomprehensible words and phrases. Every business has its own jargon and set of abbreviations. Resolve by using only those terms that you know your audience can understand.
- The person you are trying to communicate with is significantly less able to communicate in your language. Resolve by being far simpler in what you are trying to communicate.
- Inaccurate information undermines the credibility of the rest of what you want to communicate. Resolve by checking your facts first.
- You have negative feelings towards certain individuals; for example, someone may be perceived as too abrupt and insensitive. We devote two chapters (16 and 20) to dealing with this.
- You lack trust in a person: their words may sound right but you don't believe them. Credibility is gained and kept not only by someone's knowledge and expertise but also by the relationship you have with that person.
- The politics and/or processes of your company or organization may hinder good communication. For example, I recently heard of an organization running a conference whose management released details of the speaker and other essential details *to their own staff* only three weeks before the conference was due to take place!

- Formal channels of communication in a business setting are unclear and colleagues rely on unofficial means of communication ('the grapevine') for information, which will include rumours rather than facts. Resolve by being more decisive and, probably, more open about communicating.
- The approach is badly timed. For example, asking for an immediate decision on an important matter that requires much thought should be done at a time that is appropriate. Resolve by finding out and planning what that appropriate time is.
- Your body language is in conflict with your message. For example, you may try to sound friendly but your awkward posture and lack of eye contact with the person you are speaking to express your attitude more fully.
- In meetings, you allow the discussion to wander. On this and other deficiencies in meetings, see Chapter 18.

Summary

In this chapter we have looked at knowing the basics of communication. In particular, it is essential that you are aware of AIR: (A) your audience, who you are trying to communicate with; (I) your intention/message, what you are trying to communicate; (R) the response you are trying to gain from the person you are communicating with.

In considering who our audience is, we considered the style in which they best learn. We distinguished *visual, auditory* and *kinaesthetic* styles and can use that as a basis to determine the most appropriate way in which we can communicate with them.

Follow-up

1 Think of a *good* piece of communication that you have been involved in.

   A Audience: who were you communicating with?

   I Intention: what was your message? What were you trying to say?

   R Response: what response did you receive?

Why was it successful? How do you know?

2 Think of a *bad* piece of communication that you have been involved in.

   A Audience: who were you communicating with?

   I Intention: what was your message?

What were you trying to say?

   R Response: what response did you receive?

Why was it not successful? How do you know?

Fact-check (answers at the back)

1. To stop and think about what exactly you are trying to communicate is:
   a) A luxury ❑
   b) A nice to have ❑
   c) Essential ❑
   d) A waste of time ❑

2. Effective communication needs:
   a) Spontaneity ❑
   b) No planning ❑
   c) Improvisation ❑
   d) Thought and planning ❑

3. Thinking about the basics of communication, the letters AIR stand for:
   a) Abbreviations, Image, Reputation ❑
   b) Activity, Information, Reflection ❑
   c) Audience, Intention, Response ❑
   d) Attachments, Internet, Receptivity ❑

4. Clarifying who you are communicating to is:
   a) Vital ❑
   b) A waste of time ❑
   c) Unnecessary ❑
   d) Quite important ❑

5. What you are trying to communicate should be:
   a) Vague ❑
   b) Clear ❑
   c) Confusing ❑
   d) Ambiguous ❑

6. You have forgotten to think about what response you want from the information in an email you are about to send. Should you:
   a) Press 'send', knowing they can email back if they want to pursue it? ❑
   b) Rewrite the email before you press 'send'? ❑
   c) Hope that the recipient will not notice? ❑
   d) Tell your boss about it tomorrow? ❑

7. The statement 'Everyone learns in the same way as I do' is:
   a) Always false ❑
   b) Always true ❑
   c) True sometimes ❑
   d) False sometimes ❑

8. Email is the best way to communicate in business. Is this:
   a) Always true? ❑
   b) Sometimes true? ❑
   c) False? ❑
   d) True? ❑

9. Telephoning business contacts is good:
   a) For socializing ❑
   b) For finding out about your competitors ❑
   c) For developing better working relationships ❑
   d) Only when your email is down ❑

255

10. How would you respond to someone who says: 'There are so many barriers to effective communication that I feel like giving up now'?

a) 'Yes – leave work early and don't come back.' ❏

b) 'Sorry, what did you say?' ❏

c) 'I'll think about it and come back to you later on it.' ❏

d) 'No – that's all the more reason to listen well, develop good business relationships and work hard.' ❏

CHAPTER 16

Listen carefully

When thinking about communication, we tend immediately to think of speaking or writing. However, before we can consider those, we need to remember that our communication is not isolated from its context. We speak or write in certain situations, and listening carefully has to come before speaking or writing to enable what we say or write to be effective.

So now we consider:

- the importance of listening
- how to listen more attentively, focusing on what the other person is saying
- steps to help us listen more effectively.

In contrast to speaking and writing, which are productive skills, listening is a receptive skill. We will also look at the other receptive skill, reading, and suggest ways in which we can improve our techniques for reading texts and statistics.

Listen more attentively

In this chapter we're going to focus on listening in face-to-face relationships. As a manager, you will be expected to do a lot of listening: to your boss as he/she directs your work; to colleagues as you talk about your work; in meetings as you discuss a range of subjects and make decisions, and as you interview staff, solve problems and use the phone.

Listening is hard work

There are many reasons why listening is difficult:

- We tend to focus on what we want to say; by contrast, listening demands that our concentration is on someone else as we follow the sequence of their thoughts.
- The person we are listening to may speak unclearly, too fast or repeat himself/herself.
- The person we are listening to may be a non-native speaker and so does not speak in standard English.
- We were probably not taught to listen. I vaguely remember school lessons in which we were taught to read, write and speak but I don't think I was ever taught to listen (or maybe I wasn't listening during those lessons!).

But listening is a really valuable skill. Have you ever felt really burdened by something and opened your heart to someone else? At the end you feel relieved and can say, 'Thank you for listening.'

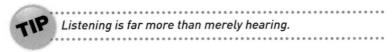

TIP *Listening is far more than merely hearing.*

The importance of listening

Listening:

- focuses on the other person. Often when someone else is talking, we are focusing on thinking about what we are going to say as a reply.

- values the person you are listening to as an individual in their own right, so that you understand 'where they are coming from', why they are working or speaking as they are.
- helps you understand the point at which a person is. For example, if you are trying to sell something to customers, you want to build a good relationship with them. By listening, you will discern who is interested and who is not, so you can use your time more valuably and concentrate on the likelier potential clients.
- encourages you to ask the right questions. As you focus on the other person (not yourself), you will want to know more. We can distinguish:
  - *closed* questions: ones that can be answered by a straight 'yes' or 'no': 'Was the project late?' 'Yes.' 'Will you be able to give me the figures by 5.00 p.m.?' 'No.'
  - *open* questions: ones that get people talking. Open questions begin with why, how, who, when, where, what. 'Why do you think the project is running late?' 'Because we did not plan enough time for the extra work the customer now wants.' Most of the questions you should ask as a manager should be open questions.
- means that you do not listen only to the words a colleague is speaking: you can perceive their response to what you are saying by being sensitive to their body language and tone of voice.
- allows you to 'listen between the lines', to become aware of any underlying messages – your response could be, for example, 'So I guess what you're saying is that you need someone else to help you complete this task on time.'
- allows you to distinguish between facts and opinions. You will hear both, and you can discern what is objective information and what are the subjective thoughts on such information. You are then in a position to evaluate what has been said.
- enables you to gather information so that you can solve problems and make decisions more efficiently.
- builds trust between people: you show that you are genuinely interested in them. This forms the basis to help you work well with them. Listening often improves relationships. Rather than someone keeping angry feelings to himself/herself

and becoming increasingly tense, listening – and allowing someone to speak openly about his/her difficulties – provides a release for them.

- offers an opportunity to develop more all-round relationships. For example, if a colleague says, 'I'm off on holiday tomorrow,' you can either ignore that signal (but ignoring it is possibly slightly rude) or you can use that as a hint that they want to tell you more about themselves: 'Great, where are you going to?' 'Hong Kong.' You can then remember to ask them 'How was Hong Kong?' when you next see them.
- can resolve disagreements. If colleagues are in conflict with one another, listening to, and understanding, the opinions of the other side – not necessarily agreeing with them – is an important first step in settling a disagreement.
- helps you understand people better. As you listen carefully to someone, you will discover more about that person: what is important to them, how they think and what they are feeling.

Recently a stressed-out colleague told me, 'I want to go back to Australia.' That seemed to tell me a lot about her: a desire to be released from present tensions and return to a former, more relaxed environment. Having such knowledge helps you work better with them, even if you don't like them or agree with their opinions.

Susie was angry

Susie was angry. She worked late every evening to complete her tasks in the project but she felt her work was not appreciated or valued. It was only when a new colleague, Jan, started to work alongside her that something happened. Jan was concerned less about herself and her own work (which she did well) and more about her colleague; she cared enough to stop and listen to Susie. Susie was in tears as she poured out her heart to Jan, telling her about the real pressures she was working under. At the end of their conversation Susie told Jan, 'Thanks for listening. You're the first person I've been able to talk to about these things.'

Tips on better listening

Here are some ways to help you improve your listening skills:

- Be responsible. Realize that listening is an active skill and as such is hard work. Concentrate. For example, when I meet someone for the first time, I listen particularly attentively to catch their name. If I think I have heard it accurately, I will say it back to them, for instance 'Great to meet you, Nick!' If I didn't hear their name properly, I will say, 'I'm sorry, I didn't quite catch your name' or ask (if it is unusual to me and seems difficult to spell) 'Could you spell that for me, please?' (The first time I met the girl who became my wife I spelt her name correctly and was the first person she had met to do so!)
- Focus on the other person, not yourself. Don't be tempted to interrupt the other person while he/she is talking. Stop and really listen to what the other person is saying. Make eye contact with him/her. Be interested in him/her. Rephrase what he/she has said in your own way to help you clarify the meaning in your own mind; for example, 'So what you're really saying is that we should have put in place more effective monitoring controls.' Such a rephrasing process is called 'reflective listening'.
- Be willing to accept the reasoning and opinions of others as valid. Be willing to acknowledge that you may make false assumptions and may have prejudices.
- Don't be so critical that you make an immediate decision about someone based on their appearance, their style of presentation or your first impression of their personality.
- Discern the main points of what is being said. Speakers may or may not structure their argument well. Often, in informal talks or meetings it can be difficult to distinguish between facts, opinions, examples and ideas, but try to work out the speaker's main point(s).
- Do your best to remain attentive, even if the other person is not; don't become distracted.
- Write down in note form what a speaker is saying if you need to remember what he/she is saying and you might otherwise forget it. Making notes can help you concentrate

and avoid the sense that 'things go in one ear and out of the other'.

● Don't be afraid of silence. Silence is part of a conversation. It can be:
  – a junction: which way will a conversation turn?
  – a time to catch up and digest what has been said
  – an opportunity for the other person to express their thoughts further
  – an opportunity to reflect on what has been said.

Read more effectively

So far we have thought about listening. The other receptive skill in communication is reading. As a manager you will have a lot of material to read, for example emails, reports, websites, professional literature, contracts, technical manuals.

How do you read?

It can be helpful to stop and reflect on the way in which you read. Do you:

● pronounce the words in your head as you read?
● go over every word in every sentence?
● read through a piece of writing quickly to see which parts are important and then go back to those parts again?
● stop at words you don't understand and so make very slow progress through a long piece of writing?

Here are some guidelines to help you read more effectively:

● Decide on your aims in reading a particular text. Do you want to simply check a fact, gain an overall sense of a text, grasp a detailed knowledge of a subject (for example for a report or presentation you have to prepare) or evaluate the writer's arguments and views?
● Vary the speed at which you read a text, depending on the kind of text you are reading. Spend more time on important and/or difficult parts of the text and less time on less important and/or easier parts.

- Try not to mouth words as you read them. Mouthing words in this way not only slows you down but also means that you focus on the words rather than their meaning.
- Read more widely. (At school, we were constantly encouraged to do this, but I can't remember being told why. For the reason why reading is good, see the rest of this paragraph.) Don't just read material for work. Read a newspaper or magazine (hard copy or digital). It can help if you read material on a subject that interests you, as your motivation will be higher. Choose an article. Read it once for sense, and a second time to look at the language used. Recently, I did this with some students whose use of prepositions was weak, so in the article we were reading I pointed out: *the results* **of** *the survey*; **at** *fault*; *responsible* **for**. Almost unconsciously, you will pick up new words and phrases. Consult a dictionary (again, either as hard copy or online) for certain words that you do not know.
- For some important work, take notes of what you have read (see earlier for comments on taking notes in listening). Summarizing the author's argument in your own words can be a particularly useful tool.
- If you want to undertake a more detailed read of part of a text:
  - Find out which sections of the text you want to read. Consult the table of contents/list of chapters or index. Survey or scan the text to get a wider view of it. As you do that, you will begin to see the writer's key words and phrases.
  - Look out for the signposts: the introduction and conclusions; the words *firstly*, *secondly*; the beginning of paragraphs; such expressions as *on the one hand* and *on the other hand*. These guide you to see the structure of the text and can be helpful to your understanding.
  - Focus on the key words and, even more important, key phrases. There is less need to concentrate on such functional grammatical words as *the, of, has, be* and a greater need to concentrate on significant words.

- Reword the main points in your mind, on computer or on paper. Express the author's key points in your own way. This will help increase your understanding.
- Think about the author's argument: do you agree with him/her? Does the text make assumptions that you disagree with? Ask questions of the text and see whether they are answered. Engage your mind.
- At the end of reading, check whether you can recall the main points or, even better, if you can explain the main points to someone else. You could even review what you have read later to check that you still recall it.

The following text concerns the evaluation stage at the end of a project. The key words and phrases to concentrate on in reading are in bold:

Identify what you have achieved. Specifically, **list** what you have delivered:

- The project was built on a **solid foundation.**
- You received **strong support** from your **Project Sponsor.**
- You delivered the **desired output** in terms of the **products, services**, etc.
- **Outputs achieved** the agreed **quality standards.**
- The **actual expenditure** was **on track** compared with the **original budget.**
- **Return on investment** was **good**. The **benefits** that your company received from the project are **greater** than the **costs** incurred.
- The **actual time** taken compared well with the **original schedule:** you delivered the outcomes **on time.**
- **Robust control procedures** were in place to **track** and **monitor costs** and **schedules effectively.**
- **Customers/users** and other stakeholders were **satisfied** with the project's **outcomes.**

Effective reading... and good time management

As a manager, Sarah was methodical about her reading. She checked her emails only a few times a day, dealing with essential matters as they arose. She didn't bother to check the many junk emails she received but simply deleted them.

She allocated Friday mornings, when she knew she generally received fewer emails, to important, but not urgent, reading material that enabled her to do her job more effectively.

As she was preparing to relax for the weekend on Friday afternoons, she read non-urgent but useful material that kept her up to date with other trends in the industry which were not directly related to her job but developed her wider professional knowledge.

Of course, sometimes very urgent matters arose, which meant that she could not always keep to this methodical time allocation, so in such cases she was flexible. Generally, however, Sarah was able to allot sufficient resources of time to reading what was useful and essential and to manage her time well.

Reading statistics

Here are some guidelines on reading and understanding numbers presented in tables:

- Check the basics: the dates covered, the sources used, the scale used, the context of the figures – for example, if the figures represent a sample, how large is that sample? Are the assumptions reasonable? Are certain figures omitted? Why? Check the definitions of terms used. Are they sound? If percentages are shown, percentages of what?
- Take one row or column and think through its content and implications to understand the data.

- Compare figures in columns and see whether you can discern any patterns in the data. Consider any trends: do the numbers show a consistent pattern that increases or decreases? For instance, is actual expenditure consistently higher than budgeted?
- Consider averages. Calculate the average for a particular row or column and see what variations and exceptions there are. Try to work out reasons for such differences, for example variations because of higher or lower income or differing levels of employment.
- Read the text that accompanies the data and check you agree with it; be particularly wary of such expressions as 'significant' or 'these figures of course show'.
- Be careful about putting too much confidence in extrapolations of data that assume a trend will continue.

Summary

In this chapter we have considered listening and reading, the receptive skills in communication. Improving your listening skills will mean that, when you come to speak, you will know more about who you are talking to and so you can choose your words more accurately and therefore be more effective.

Improving your reading skills will mean that you will know why you are reading a certain passage and so you can focus your energies more appropriately.

Follow-up

1 Ask colleagues whether they think you are a good listener or not. Listen (!) to their response.

2 Think about a recent business conversation. Were you too busy thinking about what to say that you did not really listen to the person you were talking to?

3 What steps can you take to improve your listening skills? Be ruthlessly practical with yourself.

4 As you have read this chapter, what struck you as new? What action will you take as a result of your reading?

Fact-check (answers at the back)

1. The key skill in listening is:
a) Looking at a person's face ❏
b) Thinking about what you
want to say ❏
c) Focusing on what the other
person is saying ❏
d) Looking at the floor ❏

2. Good listening:
a) Develops worse relationships ❏
b) Provokes arguments ❏
c) Relaxes people ❏
d) Develops better working
relationships ❏

3. Listening is:
a) Easy – that's why I'm the
manager ❏
b) Hard work, but rewarding ❏
c) Not worth bothering about ❏
d) Useful if you have the time ❏

4. When I listen well, I:
a) Can discern the main
points someone is trying to
communicate ❏
b) Am confused ❏
c) Get easily distracted ❏
d) Interrupt the other person ❏

5. Listening provides a basis
for me to:
a) Express my own opinion to
anyone who will listen ❏
b) Direct what I want to say
more accurately ❏
c) Decide what to eat for
lunch ❏
d) Work out who I like and
who I don't ❏

6. When I read:
a) I read everything fast ❏
b) I read everything slowly ❏
c) I decide why I am reading
something and use that as
a basis to work out my
approach ❏
d) I question why I have
to read it ❏

7. To make sure I understand
a difficult passage:
a) I read it through quickly
and hope for the best ❏
b) I read it through slowly
and hope for the best ❏
c) I learn it off by heart,
although I'm not sure
I grasp its meaning ❏
d) I take notes, summarizing
the author's message in
my own words ❏

8. In reading I focus on:
a) Why I disagree with
the author ❏
b) The middle of paragraphs ❏
c) The key phrases, especially
at the beginning of
paragraphs ❏
d) The page numbers ❏

9. I read other material outside
my subject field:
a) Never ❏
b) Not at all – I'm too busy to
do that ❏
c) Often ❏
d) Very rarely. ❏

10. When I read numbers in a table:

a) I focus on what regular patterns I can see between the columns ❏

b) I get hopelessly lost ❏

c) I never read numbers ❏

d) I always extrapolate the figures to see where they lead ❏

CHAPTER 17

Write clearly

Expressing yourself clearly is essential to communicating effectively and now we are going to look at the steps you need to take to express yourself clearly in writing.

First of all, we will consider general principles of writing, which apply especially to longer documents, and then we will consider specific media of writing: emails, letters and reports.

We can break down the writing process into different steps:

- thinking
- organizing
- writing your first draft
- editing your draft.

It is important to note that there are different steps; it isn't simply a matter of typing an email with the first thing that comes into your mind and then pressing 'send'!

The writing process

Thinking

Think about what you want to write. One good way of helping you start thinking what to write is to draw a pattern diagram (also known as a mind map). Take a blank piece of A4 paper. Arrange it in landscape position and write the subject matter of the report in the middle. (Write a word or few words, but not a whole sentence.) You may find it helpful to work in pencil, so that you can rub out what you write if necessary.

Now write around your central word(s) the different key aspects that come to your mind, maybe as a result of your reading. You don't need to list ideas in order of importance; simply write them down. To begin with, you don't need to join the ideas up with lines linking connected items.

If you get stuck at any point, ask yourself the question words *why, how, what, who, when, where* and *how much*. These may well set you thinking.

When I do this, I am often amazed at: (1) How easy the task is; it doesn't feel like work! The ideas and concepts seem to flow naturally and spontaneously. (2) How valuable that piece of paper is. I have captured all (or at least some or many) of the key points. I don't want to lose that piece of paper!

An example of a pattern diagram for a report on buying new computer systems can be seen in Figure 1.

Organizing

After you have completed the thinking stages with a pattern diagram, there are two further stages before you can begin writing. It is probably better to do them in the order shown here, but if that is difficult then do **2** then **1**.

1 **Refine the key message(s) of what you are trying to communicate.** This can take some time – if you find it difficult, you can at least eliminate parts that are less important. For example, if you are analysing the disadvantages of an old computer system, then the exact technical details of the software are probably less significant

Users

Which company departments will use the system?

Accounts department

· Will they move over to new system?
· They introduced new system only 6 months ago

Cost

· Budget
· Check figures with Finance Director

Time available

Should be ready for 1 January

Locations

· On company's two sites

IT department

· Who will build the new system?
· Who will install the new system?

New computer system

Old system

· Keeps crashing
· Secure?
· Software: out of date
· Slow, constant problems

Kinds of computers

· Laptops
· iPads
· Latest technology
· How long intended to last?

Link with Intranet

Website maintenance

Security

· Privacy policy

Figure 1 Example of a pattern diagram

than the fact that it has serious drawbacks, is out of date and no longer fulfils its original purpose.

To work out what your key message is, you also need to consider your document's audience and response. If you are writing a report for your Finance Director, for example, you will want to present the financial facts (e.g. cost, return on investment) as your key message. However, if your Finance Director has already given the go-ahead to installing the new system and you are writing a report for colleagues in Research and Development who will be using the system, then your approach will be different. Your key message may then be on the usability of the new system and its advantages compared with the old one.

2 **Organize the information.** In other words, you need to arrange the information you are giving in a certain order. The aim here is to find the most appropriate logical way to present what you want to say. Ways include:

- arranging in terms of importance, probably listing the most important first
- comparing the advantages and disadvantages
- analysing different aspects of a scheme, for example under the headings *Political, Legal, Social, Economic, Financial*
- arranging in a chronological approach – considering a time sequence.

Writing the first draft

So you have prepared a pattern diagram and organized your thoughts in an appropriate order, and you now have come to the actual writing stage.

Now is the time to begin to write the following:

- an **introduction** to explain why you are writing your document
- the **main part** of your document, containing facts, explanations and other relevant information, together with your interpretation

● the **conclusion:** a summary of the key points, drawing together the issues you have raised.

Don't be tempted to ignore the preparation you have already done; build on that.

Let's now look at an example in the main part of your document. For example, you have on your pattern diagram the section:

Old system
- keeps crashing
- secure?
- software: out of date
- slow, constant problems

This is fine as a basis, but you need to expand these notes into sentences.

Let's say that this is a paragraph in your report. 'Old system' isn't adequate as a heading, so you write: 'Disadvantages of the existing system'. As you consider this subject, you realize that the key thought is 'The existing system, which was installed ten years ago, has been overtaken by many new technological features', so you put that as the opening sentence in your paragraph. (This is called 'the topic sentence' – one that represents the whole paragraph in a single sentence, showing what the paragraph is about.)

You can then fill out the rest of the paragraph, expanding on the note form of your original structure to express your meaning in sentences. If you are unsure what to write, keep asking yourself, 'What am I trying to say?' It can be very helpful to discuss this with another individual in person (not by email!) to sharpen up precisely what you want to communicate.

A first draft of the paragraph might read as follows. The raised numbers discuss certain aspects of the writing process. See the notes for further explanation.

Disadvantages of the existing system

The existing system, which was installed ten years ago, has been overtaken by many new technological features. The present[1] system experiences too many failures[2], which cause colleagues a great deal of inconvenience.[3] Even when[4] the present system is functioning well[5], it is slow and often becomes locked[6]. Moreover[7], when handling large amounts of data, the existing system has been known to develop faults and some data has been lost. There are also doubts about how secure certain aspects of the system are.

Notes

1 To avoid repeating 'existing', I chose the synonym 'present'. Consult a thesaurus to help you with synonyms (words with similar meaning).
2 I thought that 'crash' was too informal for this report. I consulted a dictionary to help me find an alternative word.
3 I expanded on the effect of the computer failure.
4 'Even when' adds emphasis and a note of surprise considering the previous statement.
5 In my mind, I had 'running smoothly' but I felt that was too informal so I changed that to 'functioning well'.
6 In my mind, I thought of a computer 'freezing'; I thought that was too informal so consulted a dictionary and changed that to 'becomes locked'.
7 'Moreover' introduces a further similar line of reasoning; this additional thought occurred to me as I was writing, so I included it.

Editing

After completing a draft, go back over it and refine it. The aim here is to ensure that what you have written is clear and as you want it. When I am editing a document, I check first what is there and second what is not there. Has the first draft missed out a vital step in the argument? Alternatively, you may find that you have written too much about something that on further reflection was not very important and you have not written enough about something more important. Now is the time to redress that balance. Don't leave it as it is, thinking that it will go away or that the readers will not notice weaknesses in your argument.

Here are some tips for editing. Check that what you write:

- is accurate.
  - Check the content. We have all received emails inviting us to a meeting on Tuesday 14 September, only to discover that 14 September is a Wednesday. The result is that many colleagues spend precious time emailing requests for clarification and then having to respond to them with the exact date. It would have been better if the person who originally sent the message had checked the details before sending it.
  - Check totals of numbers, for example that percentages in a list all add up to 100.
  - Check punctuation. For example, are apostrophes and commas used correctly?
  - Check spellings. Be aware of words you often misspell. If your report contains basic errors, for example confusing *its* and *it's*, *effect* and *affect*, *of* and *off*, *principal* and *principle*, then they will undermine the overall credibility of your message.
- is brief. You may have heard of the saying, 'I wrote you a long letter because I didn't have time to write you a short one.' Sentences should be 15–20 words in length. Any longer and your readers may have difficulty following the meaning. Edit down – that is, cut out – some parts of your text that do not add anything significant to your argument.
- is clear. Is your overall message clear? If it isn't to you, it will not be to your readers.
- contains appropriate language for the medium you are using.
  - Watch the tone of your writing. There is a tendency to be too informal in more formal contexts. For example, if you are describing the role of a project manager, you could say he/she needs to be able to 'keep many balls in the air', but such language would be inappropriate in a formal report, which might instead say 'tackle a wide range of activities at the same time'. There is also a tendency to be

too formal, for example to use *necessitate* instead of *need*, or *terminate* instead of *stop* or *end*. The crucial point is to know who your audience is and write with them in mind.

- There is a tendency these days to write using a sequence of nouns but a more effective way of communicating would be to use more verbs. For example, 'an examination of the maintenance records took place' would be better expressed as 'the maintenance records were examined' (passive) or, even better, 'the manager examined the maintenance records' (active, naming who examined the records).
- Sometimes the language can be simplified: 'the repercussions regarding the effects subsequent to the explosion will be perused by the staff' can be simplified to 'the managers will consider the effects of the explosion'.
- Avoid abbreviations that are not generally known as well as jargon and slang.

● follows a logical sequence of thought.

- Often when you write a first draft, you tend to put down unrelated thoughts. At the editing stage, focus on each sentence to make sure that it fits into a logical sequence of your thoughts. In the example above, I constantly used the phrases 'existing system' or 'present system' in the paragraphs to make sure that the content of each sentence was clearly focused.
- Similarly, the progression of your paragraphs should follow a logical thought: each paragraph or series of paragraphs should deal fully with one particular idea before you move on to the next idea or thought. You can sometimes use linking words and phrases to show the connection or contrast (for example: to reinforce a point already made, *moreover, furthermore*; to introduce a contrast, *however, conversely, on the other hand*).

● expresses the meaning you want to communicate.

- Look back at the final sentence in my example: 'There are also doubts as to how secure certain aspects of the system are.' An alternative that rounds off the text better would be: 'Furthermore, faults in the present system have occasionally jeopardized (or *compromised*) the security of the overall network.'

Lists in bullet points

Consider whether the use of a list in bullet-point form is appropriate, especially for short phrases. People sometimes ask me about punctuation in bullet points: the trend these days is only to put a full stop at the end of the final point and not to have anything at the end of each point.

A more frequent mistake is that individual lines do not run on grammatically from the opening text, for example:

The successful candidate will be:

✔ skilled in numeracy and literacy

✔ able to speak at least two European languages

✘ have experience in using project-management software.

The error here is in the third bullet point, which does not follow on grammatically from the opening line, and should be changed to:

✔ experienced in using project-management software.

I have deliberately gone into some depth at this editing stage to be very practical in what to write and how to express it.

All the above applies to extended documents; we can now turn to some specific kinds of document.

Writing emails

Emails are great. We can communicate with colleagues all round the world instantly. However, emails also have their disadvantages. We can receive too many unwanted ones that stop us dealing with the tasks we are supposed to be dealing with.

Here are a few tips:

● Put a clear subject in the subject line (more than 'Hi Jane'). Being specific about your subject will help your reader know what the email is about.
● Use 'cc' ('carbon copy', from the days of paper) and 'bcc' ('blind carbon copy') sparingly. Send copies only to those

who really need to see the email. To explain 'cc' and 'bcc': if I am emailing Colin and cc Derek and bcc Ed, then Colin will see I have copied the email to Derek but Colin will not see I have copied the email to Ed. Using 'bcc' can also be useful for bulk emails when you don't want individuals to know the identity of the people on your emailing list.

- Unless you are writing to a close colleague, include some form of opening and closing greetings. The policy of your company and organization and your own personality will guide you to what is acceptable (e.g. I find 'Hi Martin' difficult to accept from someone I don't know at all).
- In a long email, put the key information at the beginning, so that it will be clear on the opening screen as your reader opens the email. Spend some time laying out your email. Group sentences that concern one subject in paragraphs. Remember that, if your message isn't clear to you, then it certainly won't be clear to your readers!
- Watch the tone of your email to make sure that it is not too abrupt. Consider adding softer opening and closing statements. Even 'Thank you' can help in this respect.
- Use only those abbreviations that are known to your readers.
- Don't type whole words in capital letters, which strongly suggest shouting.
- As part of your email 'signature', also include other contact information at the end of your email, including your job title, phone numbers (landline, mobile) and postal address. Your reader might want to phone you to clarify a point.

Writing letters

Although use of email is widespread, letters are useful for more formal statements. Business letters follow certain conventions:

- **Opening greeting.** If this is the first time you are writing to someone, use their title: Mr, Mrs, Ms and so on. If you know their first name, use that: 'Dear Freda'. You can also use the style of the person's first name and surname, especially if you are uncertain from the name (e.g. Sam, Jo, Chris) whether the recipient is male or female: 'Dear Sam Smith'. The style 'Dear Sir' or 'Dear Sir or Madam' is very formal and more impersonal.

- **Closing greeting.** If the opening greeting is 'Dear Freda', 'Dear Mrs Jones' or 'Dear Sam Smith', then the close is 'Yours sincerely' (capital 'Y' on 'Yours' and lower-case 's' on 'sincerely'). You can also add 'With best wishes' or 'Best wishes' before 'Yours sincerely'. If you have used 'Dear Sir' or 'Dear Sir or Madam', then the close is 'Yours faithfully' (capital 'Y' on 'Yours' and lower-case 'f' on 'faithfully').

Writing reports

The basics of writing reports

All the advice above on writing is important here, especially knowing why you are writing the report, who will be reading it and how you will structure it.

Kinds of report include:

- a progress report
- a health and safety report
- an investigation into the causes of an accident
- a company report
- a feasibility report
- a legal report used as evidence.

Your audience may be colleagues, shareholders, a board of directors, a project board, a team of advisers or consultants, a committee or users of a new product.

The purpose of your report may be to:

- examine whether a particular project, product or whatever is financially viable
- present a case for a decision on buying a product or service
- persuade someone to act in a certain way
- explain how a new product works
- describe the achievements, financial condition and so forth of a company
- inform colleagues of the progress of a project
- outline the cause of an accident or the nature of an incident.

Be clear about your audience, intention and response. Knowing these will determine, for example, how much information you should include in your reports. If in doubt, discuss with colleagues. In other words, do not agonize over writing ten pages when senior management want only one page. Moreover, your company or organization may already have a report template to give a structure to your report.

The content of reports

Reports normally have the following as a minimum:

- **Introduction**: this provides the report's purpose, including its scope or terms of reference.
- **Body of the report**: its main sections, outlining the procedure you have followed and findings, supported by facts and other information. Such objective evidence should be distinguished from your interpretation of those facts in your argument.
- **Conclusions**: a clear summary that draws all your arguments together, and recommends the necessary actions arising from your conclusions that must be taken to implement the report's findings.

Reports are often structured with clear numbers and headings (e.g. 1, 1.1, 1.1.1, 1.1.2, 1.2) to help readers refer to different parts easily.

Depending on the length of the report, you may also include:

- **An executive summary of the whole report.** Such a summary should be able to stand by itself and be a concise statement of all the report's significant information.
- **Appendices:** a section at the end of the report that contains technical information that is too long or too detailed to be included in the body of the text.
- **Bibliography:** a list of references and other sources of information used and/or quoted in the report.

Summary

In this chapter we have looked at writing – first of all at the general principles that apply especially to longer documents:

- thinking
- organizing
- writing your first draft
- editing.

We then looked specifically at writing different kinds of documents: emails, letters and reports.

Follow-up

1 Think which stage of writing you have most difficulty with (e.g. thinking, organizing, drafting, editing) and read again the relevant parts of this chapter.

2 Look at an email that you have just received from a colleague. Is its message clear? Is its tone appropriate? Is the action your colleague wanted you to take clear?

3 Look at an email that you have just written. Is its message clear? Is its tone appropriate? Is the action that you want the reader to take clear?

4 What practical steps will you take to improve your emails?

Fact-check (answers at the back)

1. 'I just start writing without any thinking or planning.' Do you think this way of approaching a piece of writing is:
   a) Good? ❑
   b) Bad? ❑
   c) Neither good nor bad? ❑
   d) A waste of time? ❑

2. When writing in business, what should you keep in mind?
   a) Yourself ❑
   b) The weather ❑
   c) Your readers ❑
   d) Your boss ❑

3. When I write a long document, I organize my material before I write:
   a) Never ❑
   b) Sometimes ❑
   c) Why bother? ❑
   d) Always ❑

4. Getting the tone of an email right is:
   a) Important ❑
   b) A luxury if you have the time ❑
   c) A waste of time ❑
   d) Unnecessary ❑

5. To help me write, I use a thesaurus or dictionary:
   a) Never ❑
   b) What's a thesaurus? ❑
   c) Very rarely ❑
   d) Often ❑

6. After you have drafted an email you should:
   a) Press 'send' ❑
   b) Go home ❑
   c) Keep on rewriting it ❑
   d) Check it. ❑

7. When rechecking an email before I send it:
   a) I never find anything I want to change ❑
   b) I'm a perfectionist, so I change so much that I forget to send it ❑
   c) I often change things ❑
   d) I don't bother to check them ❑

8. When I send an email, I send a copy to:
   a) Everyone in my address book ❑
   b) Only those who need to see it ❑
   c) No one: I don't know how to do that ❑
   d) My boss always, to protect myself ❑

9. When writing a report:
   a) I structure my material carefully ❑
   b) I don't bother structuring my material ❑
   c) I ask someone else to structure it ❑
   d) My structure is so elaborate even I don't understand it ❑

10. When writing a report:
    a) I put all the material down, hoping that readers will be able to make sense of it ❑
    b) I carefully distinguish facts and interpretations ❑
    c) I put everything in lists of bullet points ❑
    d) I get so lost in writing that I don't really think about what I am writing ❑

CHAPTER 18

Organize better meetings

Yesterday I met Tatiana. She started off in the company as an assistant editor. She had worked hard over the years and had now been promoted to Deputy Managing Director. She looked tired. I asked her if her life was full of meetings and she replied, 'Yes.' It was clear that many of the meetings she attended were too long and lacked focus and so had dampened her former enthusiasm.

A significant amount of your time as manager may be taken up in meetings, but they can go on too long and not achieve anything significant, and colleagues can become unenthusiastic or even cynical. How can you improve them?

In this chapter we will look at:

- the purpose of meetings
- preparing for meetings
- chairing meetings
- participating in meetings and negotiating
- following up from meetings.

We will see that the key to a successful meeting lies in its preparation.

The purpose of meetings

Meetings are useful to:

- inform colleagues, e.g. to introduce new goals or give an update on progress
- discuss with colleagues, e.g. plan together the way ahead or evaluate a solution to a problem
- reach a decision and agree on the next steps to be taken.

Team meetings are also particularly useful to develop a sense of team identity as members interact with one another. As manager and team leader, you can use team meetings to encourage better teamwork and motivate your team.

'Time is money'

We sometimes say that 'time is money', but what does that mean? Suppose you earn £20,000 per year. If we divide this figure by the number of days you work productively, that is, omitting holidays and allowing for illness, this could give, say, 46 weeks per year. £20,000 ÷ 46 = £434.78 per week or £86.96 per day, assuming five days per week. If we then divide this figure by the time per day you spend on productive work, say two-thirds of seven hours (= 4.66 hours), we come to £18.66 per hour: this is the amount that you are paid per hour gross, that is, before tax and other deductions.

That is only half the story, however. Your actual cost to your company or organization is about twice that figure. This is to allow for overheads: the general business expenses, the taxes your company pays as an employer, the rent of an office building, heating, power, water and so on. So the cost to your company or organization is £18.66 × 2 = £37.32 per hour.

So, if a business meeting lasts seven hours and is attended by six colleagues, then the cost of that meeting to the company or organization is 7 × 6 × £37.32 = £1567.44, which is probably considerably more than you thought. It literally pays, then, to run a good meeting.

> The significance of this may help you decide how many people need attend your meetings and whether everyone needs to sit through the whole meeting or whether some colleagues need come only for the part that concerns them.

Preparing for meetings

 TIP *The key to a successful meeting lies in the preparation.*

The key to a successful meeting lies in the preparation. It is essential that you:

- **Know the purpose of the meeting.** Many meetings have no clear purpose and could easily be shortened or even cancelled. You need to be crystal clear about what you are trying to achieve.
- **Plan a venue and time** (start, finish) in advance. I have arrived at the stated venue for some meetings to find the meeting is in a different place.
- **Invite the key people** to participate in advance. If you want a director with a busy diary to be present, then it is no good inviting him or her the day before; you need to have invited them a long time before. It is also useful if you can discuss with key people in private in advance any agenda items that could be controversial.
- **Circulate an agenda in advance.** This means that you will have thought about the structure and purpose of the meeting beforehand. Also, circulate important papers with the agenda, not at the meeting itself. Ideally, the length of such papers should be no more than one page each.
- **Prepare the meeting room.** Plan the seating: chairs around a table invite discussion; a chairperson at the end of a long table with ten seats either side, less so. If a PowerPoint presentation is being given, ensure that a projector and connecting lead are set up. Check that the heating or air conditioning works.
- **Read reports in advance.** If reports have been circulated before a meeting, then read them. I have been in too many meetings

where we have sat during the meeting reading material, something which should have been undertaken in advance.
- **Ensure that you come up with accurate information.** For example, if the meeting is one to monitor progress, take all your latest data on progress with you.

Chairing meetings

The chair (chairman, chairwoman or chairperson) is the one who sets the tone for the meeting and guides the participants through the discussion. His/her tasks include:

- deciding the agenda in advance
- keeping to the agenda so that the meeting starts and finishes on time
- introducing and welcoming newcomers, or asking participants to introduce themselves
- reviewing progress on action points from previous meetings
- bringing in key individuals to contribute at appropriate points
- stating key aims and objectives
- summarizing progress of the points being discussed
- drawing together the points discussed, to reach agreement and draw conclusions and to make decisions; if a point has been controversial, the chair can express exactly what is to be minuted, to avoid possible misinterpretation later
- ensuring action points are clear, particularly who is responsible for following up particular points and by when. The action points should be SMART:

SMART and SMARTER

S Specific, not vague, e.g. not 'We want to increase profits', but 'We want to increase profits by £100,000'

M Measurable and quantifiable, e.g. with milestones along the way to assess progress

A Agreed by all present at the meeting

R Realistic or resourced, i.e. 'if you want me to complete this task, you need to provide me with the resources to

A good chair is a diplomatic and organized leader, someone whom the colleagues trust and someone who values, motivates and involves others, checking they understand the points discussed. Ideally, he/she will be able to quieten down those who talk too much and also draw out those who talk too little but can still make valuable contributions. A good chair will also sense when the time is right to bring a discussion to an end and be able to come to clear decisions.

> *'Any committee is only as good as the most knowledgeable, determined and vigorous person on it. There must be somebody who provides the flame.'*
>
> Claudia ('Lady Bird') Johnson (1912–2007), widow of former US president Lyndon B. Johnson

Good team meetings

Martha was a good team leader. The meetings she led were particularly good. She kept close to the agenda, which had been circulated before the meeting, and she followed up on the action points from the previous meeting. She prepared for the meetings well, thinking in advance how she might tackle objections to her ideas that colleagues might raise. She gave out overall information about how the company was performing and led fruitful discussions on how her unit could improve their efficiency even further. On confidential matters, she was diplomatic and as open as she could be. On difficult matters, she was able to identify the core issue and lead a discussion and evaluation of possible solutions before deciding on a particular course of action.

> She was particularly good at encouraging everyone to participate and express themselves. She always summarized the discussions and came to a clear decision about the next step. She made sure minutes of the meeting were circulated promptly after meetings so that colleagues were all clear about what they should do. The result was that colleagues in her team all felt inspired and wellmotivated.

Participating in meetings

Everyone has a part to play in a successful meeting. I have never understood how people can come out of a meeting asking 'What was the point of that?' when they themselves have not contributed anything. Each of us has a role to play by:

- listening well and concentrating. Switch phones and other electronic gadgets off; avoid sending text messages; don't interrupt when someone else is talking.
- asking for clarification if you are unsure about a point that has been made. It is highly likely that other colleagues will also want clarification but have been afraid to ask, perhaps for fear of looking ignorant.
- being constructive: having a positive attitude. Even if you disagree with what has been said, there are positive ways of expressing a difference of opinion by challenging an idea without angrily criticizing the person expressing it or publicly blaming an individual for a wrong action.
- confronting issues. Focus on the real issues; don't get sidetracked. Too many of our meetings avoid discussing 'the elephant in the room', the subject everyone is aware of but doesn't mention because it is too uncomfortable.
- being willing to change your mind. If you are listening and persuasive arguments have been offered then allow yourself to be convinced by them and change your opinion about an issue.

Negotiating: win–win situations

In negotiating, we are aiming for a win–win situation. A win–win situation can perhaps be well illustrated by an example. My son Ben has just moved to Asia and he wanted to sell his camera. His friend Rob wanted a camera to take photographs on his travels. Ben sold Rob his camera – both won. Both gained what they wanted: Ben money, Rob a camera.

In his book *The 7 Habits of Highly Effective People*, Stephen R. Covey points out that the basis for a win–win situation is our character:

'If you're high on courage and low on consideration, how will you think? Win–Lose. You'll be strong and ego-bound. You'll have the courage of your convictions, but you won't be very considerate of others. ... If you're high on consideration and low on courage, you'll think Lose–Win. You'll be so considerate of others' feelings that you won't have the courage to express your own. ... High courage and consideration are both essential to Win–Win. It's the balance of the two that is the mark of real maturity. If you have it, you can listen and you can empathically understand, but you can also courageously confront.'

The 7 Habits of Highly Effective People Personal Workbook, Stephen R. Covey
(Simon & Schuster, 2005), p. 91

A good negotiator of contracts

Danielle was respected as a good negotiator in contracts. The secret of her success lay in good planning. She spent a long time thinking through different business models and pricing levels so that, when it came to the negotiations, she knew exactly what approach to take. After both sides had presented their initial case, she was sometimes able to detect the weak points in the arguments of the other side and exploit them according to her own personality. When they came to the final bargaining she had clarified the critical issue (the price) in her mind and knew the less significant matters she could be flexible on; she didn't mind bringing delivery of the products forward by six weeks. She was assertive and firm on what was non-negotiable, however: the price. So she was able to settle and close deals well and arrange the next steps in business relationships between the two sides.

Videoconferencing

Videoconferencing means that you avoid spending travel costs and that you can link colleagues over the Internet. Here are some tips to help you plan a videoconference session:

- Make sure that the room in which the meeting takes place has good acoustics and also is tidy.
- Agree and circulate the agenda in advance to all participants. Appoint a chair who can introduce the participants. Email any special presentations (e.g. PowerPoint) in advance.
- Identify individuals using cards in front of them with their name on.
- Remind participants to look at the camera while they are talking. Ask other participants to listen while one person is speaking.

Follow-up from meetings

A meeting where decisions are made but after which no one acts on these decisions is a waste of time. If colleagues have action points to pursue, those colleagues should follow them up.

The minutes of a meeting are a record of what happened in a meeting, including its action points. The person taking the minutes does not need to write down everything that goes on, but significant decisions, especially the action points concerning dates, schedules and financial matters, must be noted specifically.

The sooner the minutes of a meeting are circulated to those present at the meeting and other key colleagues, the more likely it is that colleagues will follow up the action points asked of them.

A good manager will also follow through between meetings on the progress of the key action items; he/she will not leave it to the next meeting only to discover that action has not been taken and so valuable time has been lost.

Summary

In this chapter we have considered how to make your meetings more effective. I have particularly emphasized the need for careful preparation: think *why* you are holding the meeting (the reason needs to be something more than 'It's our normal monthly meeting'), *who* needs to be there, *what* you will consider, *when* it will start and finish and *where* it will take place. Plan and circulate the agenda in advance, together with any key documents. Make sure that proper minutes are circulated promptly and then also reviewed at the next meeting, to ensure that all the action points have been dealt with well.

Follow-up

1 Think about a meeting that you have attended recently. What were its good points? What were its bad points? What practical steps can you take to ensure that the bad points are not repeated in future?

2 If you are chairing meetings, what practical steps can you take to improve your leading of meetings?

3 If you are not chairing meetings, what practical steps can you take to improve your participation?

Fact-check (answers at the back)

1. My attitude to meetings is that:
   a) Occasionally they are productive ❏
   b) They are boring ❏
   c) They are a necessary evil ❏
   d) I want to make sure that they are better ❏

2. The key to a successful meeting lies in the:
   a) Room ❏
   b) Participants ❏
   c) Length of time it lasts ❏
   d) Preparation ❏

3. 'Every business meeting should have an agenda':
   a) False ❏
   b) True ❏
   c) Sometimes true ❏
   d) If you say so ❏

4. A good chairperson will:
   a) Summarize progress and make clear decisions ❏
   b) Wander away from the agenda ❏
   c) Let everyone have their say but never reach a decision ❏
   d) Expect all meetings to run smoothly ❏

5. When a decision is made, ensuring that someone is responsible for implementing that decision is:
   a) Nice to have ❏
   b) A luxury ❏
   c) Essential ❏
   d) We never make decisions ❏

6. In setting SMART action points, the S stands for:
   a) Silly ❏
   b) Specific ❏
   c) Special ❏
   d) Standard ❏

7. In setting SMART action points, the T stands for:
   a) Timed ❏
   b) Tough ❏
   c) Thought-through ❏
   d) Technical ❏

8. If I am not chairing the meeting:
   a) I can send text messages to friends ❏
   b) I can distract the colleagues sitting opposite ❏
   c) I am negative about my colleagues ❏
   d) I know I still have an important part to play ❏

9. If I am in a meeting and don't understand what is being discussed:
   a) I am silent ❏
   b) I want to go home ❏
   c) I ask, even though it may make me look ignorant ❏
   d) I wait for the chairman to explain it ❏

10. After a meeting, minutes should be circulated:
    a) What are 'minutes'? ❏
    b) Never ❏
    c) Promptly ❏
    d) If we are lucky ❏

CHAPTER 19

Give successful presentations

So far, we have looked at our aims, the importance of listening, writing documents and running better meetings. Now we come to another key aspect of your work as a manager that takes in all of the above: speaking, as you give a presentation.

You may never have given a presentation before and understandably you may be nervous, but you can relax, because the skills you need are the ones that you have been reading about and practising:

- Knowing your aims – who you are speaking to; what you know about them (you gather that from listening); what your key messages are and what response you want from your audience
- Planning what you want to say – you can build on the techniques you read about in Chapter 17 (for example, using a mind map to get your creativity going)
- Knowing your own special unique contribution to the meeting at which you are to speak.

As well as these key skills, we also discuss the use of visual aids, including PowerPoint, body language and feedback.

Lay a strong foundation

Look back at Chapter 15 and AIR (Audience, Intention, Response). Who is your audience: senior managers? colleagues? colleagues from outside your company, some of whom might be critical?

How many will be in your audience: five, 50, 500? How much do they already know about what you are going to say? Will you need to sketch in some background? What are their thoughts and feelings towards you, as speaker, likely to be? Discover as much as you can about your audience before you plan your presentation.

Sometimes, when I give a presentation, I actually think of one or two real individuals in the audience and, on the basis of my knowledge of them, prepare as if I am speaking only to them.

Think why you are giving the presentation. What is the background context in which you have been asked to give it? Is there a hidden agenda?

Try to summarize your message in 12 words. For example, if I were speaking about the context of this chapter in a presentation, the key message would be 'Prepare your presentation well'.

Remember practical points:

- Know how long you will speak for: 15 minutes? an hour? People will be grateful if you finish early (but not too early!) but will not appreciate it if you go on too long.
- Consider the layout of the seating. At one workshop I led with 15 delegates I complained that the suggested seating looked too much like that of a classroom, so we adjusted it to a 'horseshoe' or 'U' layout, which helped interaction between the participants. Don't forget the room's lighting, heating or air conditioning.
- Think about what you are going to say. Look back at Chapter 17 on using a mind map and answering the question words *why*, *how*, *what*, *who*, *when*, *where* and *how much*. You may think it unnecessary to do this but doing so is often fruitful, because you are putting down your key thoughts before you begin to organize and order them.

Before you organize your thoughts, I am going to add an additional stage to the ones I have already given. The keywords in your mind map are probably nouns (names of things); the aim here is to add a verb (doing word) to make a more powerful combination. For example, a draft for this chapter was:

Foundation		Yourself
Message	Presentation	Body language
Visual aids		Feedback

I then added verbs:

Lay a foundation		**Prepare** yourself
Refine your message	**Give** a presentation	**Be aware of** body language
Prepare visual aids		**Expect** feedback

And I even went on to a third stage and began to add adjectives (describing words):

Lay a **strong** foundation		Prepare yourself
Refine your message	Give an **effective** presentation	Be aware of body language
Prepare **useful** visual aids		Expect **positive and negative** feedback

Do you see? What I am trying to do is spread the load of the core meaning: rather than simply 'visual aids' I ended up with 'prepare useful visual aids'.

Use a thesaurus and/or a dictionary of collocations (word partners) to develop your words and phrases. Work on them, hone them, sculpture them so they clearly express what you want (*expect positive and negative* feedback; *refine* your message).

Organize your thoughts. You are now in a position to put your thoughts and basic messages in a certain order. You have worked out your key message 'Prepare your presentation well' and you can put the material in a certain order. Note that:

- you need to add an introduction and a conclusion; they are separate
- you should put your most important point first in the main part of your presentation.

The order of your draft may be different from the one you end up with. That is OK. It is only a draft. It is better to work on some order. For example, I know that 'Prepare useful visual aids' and 'Expect feedback' are important but they are not the basic, primary aspects of what I am trying to say, so they can go later in the presentation. So the final order of my draft is as follows (you can compare this with the final text):

	Give an effective presentation	
1 Lay a strong foundation		**6** Prepare yourself
2 Refine your message		**4** Be aware of body language
3 Prepare useful visual aids		**5** Expect positive and negative feedback

In the end, I put '6 Prepare yourself' as a short paragraph – not as a main point – under '4 Be aware of body language'.

Refine your message

- **Work out your key messages.** Be crystal clear on what you are trying to say. Keep your 'headlines' simple. Don't try to cram too much in – 'less is more'.
- **Break down your key points into subpoints.** Work on your words. Use short everyday words rather than longer ones. So use *try* rather than *endeavour*; *need*, not *necessitate*; *stop* or *end* rather than *terminate*; *harmful* rather than *detrimental*.
- **Say the same thing more than once.** If your key point is 'Prepare well' then say that and add something like 'You need to work hard at the planning to make your presentation effective'. This is *expanding* on 'Prepare well', saying it again in different

words. This is something you do more in speaking than in writing. You also do it in speaking when you see that your audience doesn't really understand what you are saying. This means that you should look at them when you are speaking, not at your notes. Hopefully, you are so familiar with what you want to say that you do not need to follow your script word for word.

- **Think about how you will communicate.** Ask questions. Give a specific case study (example) or tell a story to back up the point you are making. Include some well-chosen quotations or statistics. Be creative. Find a picture that will illustrate the key point of your talk (but make sure that you are not in breach of copyright if you use it).
- **Work on different parts of your presentation.** Work especially hard on the *beginning*, to capture your audience's attention with your introduction ('Did you know... ? I was reading in today's newspaper...') and the *end* ('So the next step is...') to round off your presentation, drawing together and reinforcing application of your key points.
- **Structure your main points in a logical sequence.** If you can structure them by making them all start with the same letter of the alphabet, or by 'ABC' (e.g. one of the talks I give on writing encourages writers to be *accurate, brief* and *concise*), then your points will be more memorable.
- **Check your message.** This is one of the key points for you to remember. Check facts and dates to make sure that they are accurate.
- **In your preparation, continue to think what the response of your audience is likely to be.** Interested? Bored? In need of persuasion? Sceptical? Anticipate likely reactions by dealing with them in your preparation and preparing answers to questions.
- **Write your presentation down.** Either write down (1) every word you plan to say or (2) notes that you can follow. If you do (1), then don't read it out word for word from your paper. Hopefully, your thoughts will have become part of your way of thinking. As you gain more experience, you will probably find you can work from notes. When I started giving presentations I wrote everything in pencil (so I could rub words out), then I typed them up (and enlarged the

printout so that I could read it). Now, with more experience, I write out the key points with important phrases or words highlighted. Do what you are comfortable with.

- **Be enthusiastic; be positive.** You have a message to declare. Go for it! Think about your own approach to your talk. You have your own unique personality, skills and experiences. Be natural; be yourself. It took me years to discover and work out my own style for giving presentations. I was amazed when a colleague contacted me after a space of five years to ask me to lead a workshop at his company and he said, 'I remember your style.'
- **Plan in a break.** If your presentation is going to last longer than 45 minutes, then schedule a break so that your audience can relax for a few minutes.

Unseen, but important, preparation

Hasheeb was wise. He had given a few presentations and was beginning to enjoy them, even though he was always nervous before he gave one. He realized that he would probably be giving presentations for a few years into the future, so he began to read more widely round the subject. He kept a hard-copy notebook and a computer file of useful ideas, stories, quotes and notes he came across. In this way, when he was asked to speak, he had a resource he could refer to, so that his interest and passion remained fresh. This unseen, but important, preparation work was one of the secrets of his effectiveness as a speaker.

Prepare useful visual aids

Will you give handouts of your presentation? How many will you need? Work out when you will give them out: before or at the end of the presentation? My personal preference is before, so that the audience knows where I am going. The disadvantage of that is that they do know where I am going, so always make sure that your notes are a skeleton (not the full text) of your presentation. Make enough copies of your handouts and some spare.

I made the mistake in one of my early presentations of preparing handouts that were in effect my full notes; so when a colleague said, 'We didn't really need to come, we could have just read your paper', I didn't have an answer.

Use tables and charts to support your points – but don't be so complex or technical that your audience can't understand what you are trying to say. Be as simple as you can be.

Use a flipchart if appropriate; I personally prefer a flipchart to a PowerPoint presentation as I find a flipchart more flexible than the rigidly ordered PowerPoint.

If you are using PowerPoint, then:

- Allow plenty of time to prepare the presentation, particularly if you are not familiar with the presentation software. To begin with, it is likely to take far longer than you think.
- Don't try to put too much information on the slides. Keep to your headings, not the complete outline of your talk.
- Keep to one main font. Use a large font size, ideally at least 28 points. Aim to have no more than six lines per slide (do you remember peering over people's heads trying to read tiny print on a slide?). In PowerPoint, a sans-serif font is easier to read than a serif one. Headings arranged left (not centre) are easier to read; capitals and lower-case letters are also easier to read than text in all capitals.
- Check the spelling of words on your slides.
- Work out which colours work well, for example red on grey, yellow on blue.
- Use tables and charts to support your message; bar charts, pie charts and flow charts that give the key information visually work well.
- Use illustrations that support your message, not ones that show off your (lack of!) design or animation skills.
- Don't put the key information at the bottom of slides; colleagues far away from the screen may not be able to see over other colleagues' heads.
- Rehearse the presentation with your notes/text in advance.
- Check whether you or a colleague will supply the projector, leads to connect the projector to your laptop and a screen. Arrive early to set everything up.

- Put your presentation on a memory stick (saved in earlier versions of PowerPoint for good measure) in case your laptop fails and you have to view it from someone else's laptop.
- Make sure that when you give your presentation your eye contact is with your audience, not with your laptop or the screen.
- Organize the room so that everyone can see the screen.

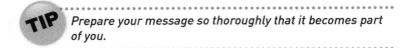

TIP *Prepare your message so thoroughly that it becomes part of you.*

A picture is worth a thousand words

Jason was looking for suitable illustrations to accompany a talk he was giving on encouragement. He was emphasizing the 'tough but tender' aspect of encouragement and had a picture of a father and son to illustrate tenderness. He found it more difficult to find one for the tough aspect, however, until he remembered one of the tableaux in the Bayeux Tapestry in which Bishop Odo was said to 'comfort' his troops by prodding them with a club. In modern colloquial English he was 'giving them a kick up the backside' to goad them into action. The picture Jason found was a good illustration of the point he was trying to make.

Be aware of body language

A friend once told me, 'They are not listening to a message; they are listening to a messenger', so be yourself. Look smart and then you are more likely to feel smart and more confident. Dress professionally. A colleague and I once met a publisher to try to persuade them to take up the idea of a book we were working on. I was appalled when my colleague turned up in a sweatshirt and jeans – that wasn't the professional image I was trying to express!

When giving your presentation, stand up straight and relax your shoulders. Don't hide behind the lectern (although I am aware that positioning yourself there can hide your nervousness); you could even move around the room a little.

Maintain good eye contact with your audience – for me that is the critical point. If you are using a flipchart or PowerPoint, don't look at that while you are speaking; look at your audience. But look across your whole audience, not just at those you like. Remember too that your whole posture will reveal a lot about yourself.

Use your voice well: speak sometimes loudly, sometimes softly; sometimes faster, sometimes more slowly. Don't mumble; speak out your words clearly. Be expressive: vary the tone in which you speak. Use hand gestures, according to your personality. Smile (in my early days of giving presentations I went so far as to write the word 'Smile' on every page of my notes). Pauses can be useful to help your audience digest what you have just said.

Prepare your message so thoroughly that it becomes part of you. Practise it by speaking it out loud. This will also help you time it.

Prepare your *self* as well as your *message*. The important point here is to be positive: you have been asked to give a presentation, so others have confidence in you. Be as enthusiastic as possible. Control your nerves. Take deep breaths. Drink water.

In your actual presentation, be authentic. Sometimes at the beginning of the workshops I lead, when I sense that participants and I are all nervous, I will say, 'How are you feeling about today?', adding 'I'm as nervous as you.' Such genuine self-deprecating comments can help defuse their tension.

A difficult but good experience

Harry was keen to improve his presentation skills, so his colleagues recorded a presentation that Harry gave. Harry realized that watching himself on video was a difficult but useful experience. He noticed what mannerisms he was unaware of (jangling his keys), words he kept on repeating (his recurrent one was 'OK?'). But it was worth it. The awkwardness and embarrassment he felt were a necessary part of his own learning experience. Becoming aware of his faults as others saw them was an important first step to his correcting them, as part of fulfilling his overall desire to become an even more effective presenter.

Expect positive and negative feedback

'Feedback' means questions from your audience – and you would be wise to prepare for them. These days I think a trend is to say at the beginning of a talk something like, 'I'll take any questions for clarification during the talk but please keep any more significant questions to the end.' If you say that, allow time, both for questions to aid your audience's understanding during the talk but also for the more significant questions at the end.

Here, as with so much of what you have read, the key lies in good preparation. Expect feedback. Expect a particular colleague to raise objections because that's what he/she always does. Expect them – and plan for them. Deal with their objections, and where possible return to the key messages you want to communicate. (I learned a trick here: when replying to an objector, don't keep eye contact only with that person, but let your eyes roam more widely through the room. If, while you give your answer, you look only at the person raising the objection, then he/she may take that as an opportunity to respond even further.)

If you don't know the answer to a question, be honest enough to say so. Often other colleagues in the room may be able to help you out. Conclude a question-and-answer session by again positively highlighting the key message(s) you want to communicate to round off the whole presentation.

After your presentation, evaluate it. You could also ask trusted colleagues to give their realistic assessment of your performance. What was the content like? Was your delivery/presentation too slow or too fast? Was it directed at the right level? Did the handouts/visual aids/PowerPoint detract from or add to your presentation? Recognize what worked well but don't be afraid to acknowledge what didn't work so well, so that you can learn lessons for the future. Remember, 'the person who never made mistakes never made anything'.

314

Summary

In this chapter we have looked at giving presentations. We have seen that to give an effective presentation means that you need to prepare well. You will:

- know who you are speaking to
- know what you are trying to achieve by your talk
- think about what you want to communicate
- plan and organize your thoughts
- work hard at the logical order and structure of your presentation
- work hard at your words
- work hard at your introduction and conclusion
- prepare any visual aids or PowerPoint slides but be as simple as possible; don't try to be too clever
- be aware of your body language as you deliver your talk. Be especially aware of keeping good eye contact with your whole audience.

Follow-up

Think about a presentation you have to give
in the next few weeks. Write out your
key message in 12 words.

Fact-check (answers at the back)

1. You have got to give a presentation in a week's time. Do you:
   a) Prepare well? ❏
   b) Panic? ❏
   c) Get so nervous that you don't prepare at all? ❏
   d) Not bother preparing, knowing you are good at improvising? ❏

2. What is the most important aspect about giving a presentation?
   a) Working out what PowerPoint slides you can use ❏
   b) Knowing how long you are to speak ❏
   c) Knowing what the weather is like ❏
   d) Knowing what your key message is ❏

3. When preparing what I am going to say:
   a) I jot down the first thing that comes into my mind ❏
   b) I take it slowly, thinking about my key message ❏
   c) I don't prepare; I just improvise on the day ❏
   d) I spend all my time thinking but never writing anything ❏

4. When giving a presentation, repeating what you say using different words is:
   a) Useless repetition ❏
   b) Useful to reinforce your message ❏
   c) Nice if you have a thesaurus ❏
   d) A waste of time ❏

5. When constructing my argument:
   a) I carefully order the points I want to make ❏
   b) I don't bother organizing my points ❏
   c) I improvise ❏
   d) I lose the train of thought in my whole talk ❏

6. When I think about my conclusion:
   a) I just repeat my six main points ❏
   b) conclusion – what's that? ❏
   c) I round off my presentation with the next steps I want my audience to take ❏
   d) I add two new points to liven up my talk ❏

7. I use PowerPoint:
   a) Always, as I want to show off my technical skills ❏
   b) Never; I hate technology ❏
   c) Usually, and put nearly all of my presentation on it ❏
   d) Wisely, to support the points I want to make ❏

8. When giving my presentation:
   a) I keep my eyes on my notes ❏
   b) I look only at my colleagues ❏
   c) I look at the attractive men/ women in the room ❏
   d) I look around widely at the audience ❏

9. When speaking:
a) I vary the speed and volume of what I say ❏
b) I always speak in one tone ❏
c) I think I am as bored as my audience ❏
d) I often use such words as *um* and *so* ❏

10. I expect feedback from my presentation:
a) Rarely ❏
b) Never ❏
c) Often ❏
d) If I am lucky ❏

CHAPTER 20

Build strong working relationships

In a section on business communication, you could assume that it would all be about finding the right formula to include in an email and choosing your words carefully in a presentation, but there is something underlying and deeper going on: developing good working relationships. Good working relationships are the glue that holds a company or organization together.

We can also express that positive idea negatively: bad working relationships – or the absence of good (or any) working relationships – will mean that the company or organization will not function well.

I chose the words in the title of this chapter very carefully. *Build*: we can take active steps to cultivate and work at relationships; *strong* working relationships are ones that are firmly established – which takes time – and are not easily broken.

So now we consider how we can cultivate such strong working relationships, and how they are seen in practice, including working in teams, in delegating work and in resolving conflict.

Develop better working relationships

I want this chapter to be practical. Establishing good rapport – a sense of mutual respect, trust and understanding – seems to come naturally and easily to some people, but not to others. My wife is much more naturally confident with people than I am, but she has taught me some skills that have helped me.

Here are some tips. I hesitate to call them 'techniques' because that can make them seem artificial and, if you try them, that could make them appear awkward.

- **See things from another person's point of view.** Listen to them – *really* listen to them (look back at Chapter 16 for more hints on listening).
- **Pay attention; be genuinely interested in other people.** I hesitate to write 'look interested' because that is all it could be – an appearance without a genuine interest. Smile; look at them; make eye contact with them.
- **Notice colleagues' body language.** Do you sense that they are awkward or relaxed? What expression do they have on their face? Does their tone of voice reveal their insecurity? However, be aware that you can misinterpret people's body language. A speaker was giving a talk and a colleague in the audience had her eyes closed. The speaker interpreted the closed eyes as a sign of lack of interest whereas in fact they helped the colleague concentrate on the speaker's message.
- **Adapt what you want to say to colleagues to suit them.** This, for me, is vital. For example, when I lead a two-day course on communications, I am aware that the time before the mid-morning break on the first day will be spent mainly *listening* to the participants – for example, how they are fed up with the politics of their company; how their bosses do not listen to them or value them. Once these colleagues have got these feelings off their chest, they are ready to

listen to what I have to say. If I were to start off with great enthusiasm and energy with *my* presentation and ignore the context of their frustration, they would not be ready to listen to me. I have to 'get on to their wavelength' – understand them first – and then adapt what I want to say to the reality of their situation as I have discovered it to be. In fact, I often explicitly say at the beginning of my courses, 'I am more interested in helping you than in getting through my material.'

● **Be flexible in your response.** If you are truly focused on the person you are talking to rather than on yourself, you will have a variety of responses available to you, for example 'One solution to this is...', 'Only you can decide' or even 'I'm not sure we're answering the right question. Isn't it more about...?'

● **Notice what colleagues are saying.** Pick up on their key thoughts and words. For example, I recall a meeting some years ago to discuss different departments' allocations of income in their budget. One head of department said he was 'firing a warning shot across the bows', that he was prepared to strongly oppose any attempts to reduce his department's budget. Knowing looks were exchanged by other colleagues and the chair of the meeting immediately withdrew his suggestion that his colleague's department should suffer a reduction in funding.

● **Engage in 'small talk',** conversation about ordinary things that are relatively unimportant from a strictly business point of view. When you meet someone for the first time, it's all right to talk about their travel to the venue, the weather, their family, the previous night's football results, holiday plans, and so on. Engaging in such conversation helps the actual business run more smoothly than if you did not have such conversation. Share a little of how you see life; ask questions, especially closed questions (ones that can be answered with a straight 'yes' or 'no') to begin with and then move on to some open questions (ones that may begin with *why, how, who, when, where, what* and get people talking), but don't make it seem as if you are interrogating the other person.

- **Be aware of roles.** When you meet someone for the first time and they tell you that they are, for example, a dentist, doctor, police officer or accountant, be aware that you will probably then put them into a category of that profession and that you will trust them accordingly.
- **Be aware of colleagues' status and power, but treat each person as a unique individual.** If you meet a headteacher for the first time, you may assume that he or she has a lot of authority and you may feel insecure because you have a lower status than they do. However, the problem may be more in your perception than in reality. If the headteacher genuinely says to you, 'I'm interested in what you can tell me about...', you may feel honoured that a person in such a position of authority has asked for your opinion. For me, what is important is valuing each person as unique. I recall a comment on a teacher friend years ago: 'He even talks to the cleaners.' Realize that you can crush someone's sense of identity by belittling them, constantly interrupting them or ignoring them. Treat each person as a unique individual.
- **Communicate what you are doing clearly and consistently and also why you are doing it.** This is particularly important in introducing change management; you will constantly need to state why you are doing things to counter the 'we've always done it this way' approach.
- Ensure, as far as it is up to you, that **the messages expressed by different departments in your company or organization are consistent,** that is, that they don't contradict one another.
- **Put the aims of your company or organization first** and make sure that you fulfil your own work to the best of your capabilities. In most organizations there will be office politics and you will find people you like and people you don't like. Part of doing your job professionally is rising above, as far as you can, any different outlooks that colleagues have and their diverse personalities. Always be polite; don't engage in gossip. You may need to stop complaining about your colleagues and make sure that you do your own work as professionally as possible.

Introducing changes gradually

Martha was promoted to team leader and had many good ideas on changing things, for example by introducing team statistics, rotas, new personal targets. However, her colleagues reacted badly to the speed of changes and her mentor had a quiet word with her ('Go for "evolution", not "revolution"'). So Martha slowed down and introduced the changes at a more measured pace, explaining to each colleague in informal one-to-ones why changes were necessary. The result was that her colleagues felt more valued and their self-confidence increased as they successfully navigated the changes.

A close working relationship

I have worked with Tony for over 30 years. We have worked on many long-term projects together: he as designer, I as writer/editor. We trust and respect each other for our different skills and experience. We have talked things through when we have had opposing views, to reach a positive solution. I phone him regularly when he is slightly behind schedule. We ask each other's opinion when we are unsure how to proceed. In 2011 we were awarded a prize for the work we and others had undertaken on *Collins Bible Companion* in a 'Reference Book of the Year' competition. When other colleagues have joined us in meetings, they have noted how we tend to think each other's thoughts and express them. Over our long period of collaboration, we have built up a close working relationship.

Develop stronger teamwork

A team is a group of diverse people who are working together towards a common goal. Team members bring a wide range of roles, which should *complement one another*: one person's weakness is balanced out by another person's strengths.

How can you build stronger working relationships in a team? One way is to be aware of different roles. A widely known set of roles was developed by Dr Meredith Belbin as he looked at how team members behaved. He distinguishes nine different team roles:

- **Plant**: creative, good at coming up with fresh ideas and solving difficult problems in unconventional ways
- **Resource investigator**: outgoing; good at communicating with outside agencies
- **Co-ordinator**: good as chairperson, focusing team members on the goals; a good delegator
- **Shaper**: dynamic action person who can drive a project forward through difficulties
- **Monitor/evaluator**: able to stand back and bring objective discernment
- **Team worker**: bringing harmony and diplomacy for good team spirit
- **Implementer**: dependable, efficient practical organizer
- **Completer/finisher**: able to follow through on details meticulously to complete a project
- **Specialist**: giving expert technical knowledge.

For further details and how to identify colleagues' different roles, see www.belbin.com.

This analysis is useful since it can reveal possible gaps – that is, your team may be lacking certain skills, which you can then seek to cover. For example, discussing these roles on one committee I was part of revealed we had no monitor/evaluator, someone who could stand back and objectively assess ideas. Identifying someone with those skills was therefore one of our aims.

Encourage better teamwork

As team leader, you are responsible for encouraging your team to work together successfully. To do that, you need to do the following:

- Communicate a vision. Where is the team going? What is its purpose? As leader, you need to present a strong and inspiring vision of your goals.

- Set your goals clearly. There is nothing like an abstract statement which is not earthed in reality to turn people off. It is hardly surprising that colleagues come out of a team meeting feeling cynical when only a vision has been cast but no practical implications have been drawn from that vision. A vision must be turned into practical steps.
- Ensure that your team values are agreed. Do team members trust and respect one another? Do individuals feel important and part of something bigger than themselves? Encourage team members to remain positive, to believe in the strength and unity of the team.
- Clarify responsibilities of each member of the team so that not only each individual knows their responsibilities but also the whole team knows what each member does. Different members of the team will bring different skills, so play to colleagues' strengths. For example, don't give the chairmanship of a meeting to someone who is unclear or indecisive.
- Ensure that lines of authority and responsibility are clear. Be clear about whether individual team members have authority to spend sums of money up to a certain amount or should direct all requests for purchases through you as team leader.
- Show that you value team members. Listen to them; provide opportunities for members of your team to approach you if they need help. You should not be aloof; be available for them to bring their concerns to you. Understand them. Try to find out 'what makes them tick'. Talk to them (not *at* them). Find out what interests them outside work.
- Show that you value their work. One worker worked in a factory for years producing a small part in a large machine without knowing what the large machine was for. He was amazed, and felt more fulfilled, when he knew the function of the large machine and where his work fitted into the overall picture.
- Ensure that their work is interesting and challenging. No one likes boring repetitive tasks. Make sure that your colleagues' work contains at least some interesting tasks that will stretch them.
- Be flexible about what is negotiable and different styles of working. Listen to suggestions from your colleagues. Be prepared to 'think outside the box' to find solutions to difficulties.

- Be fair and treat all your colleagues equally, even though you may like some more than others.
- Make sure that all team members work as hard as one other; everyone has to 'pull their weight'. You can't afford to carry 'passengers': those team members who work significantly less than others.
- Show enthusiasm in your work. Enthusiasm is infectious, and so is the lack of it. If you are half-hearted in your commitment, that will show in your tone of voice and body language, and colleagues will be aware that you may be saying all the right words but not believing them yourself.
- Encourage openness. As far as you can, involve members of the team in making decisions. Bring out those who are shy and use your skills of diplomacy to quieten those who talk too much.
- Encourage team members to use their initiative. They do not always need to come back to you to solve small difficulties but can be enterprising and resolve issues themselves.
- Encourage colleagues to look out for one another, so that, for example, when one colleague is struggling, a fellow team member can step in and help.
- Encourage uncooperative colleagues to try a new system if they are reluctant to follow it, or even ask them if they could suggest new ways of solving a problem.
- Focus on specific, measurable, agreed, realistic/resourced and timed goals (look back at Chapter 18 for SMART goals), not on vague ideas.
- Give feedback. You as team leader should give informal feedback to team members on whether they are doing well... or not so well. Be specific (e.g. 'I thought the tone of your email in response to the complaint was excellent') as far as possible.

Back to the shop floor

As Managing Director, Joe felt he needed to 'get back to the shop floor' and find out what his staff really thought of his organization. So he sat alongside members of staff for several days, listening to their concerns. They didn't feel their work was valued, and communications from 'them' (senior management) were thought to be very poor. At

the end of the week, Joe was able to take these valuable
lessons back to his role as MD and begin to change the
company's practices.

Delegate well

Delegate more rather than less. There are a few matters you
cannot delegate (e.g. managing the overall team, allocating
financial resources, dealing with confidential matters of
performance management and promotion), but you can and
should both delegate many of your actual work tasks and
some routine administrative activities. Here are some further
guidelines for good delegation:

- Be clear about the tasks you want to delegate. Don't give
  vague instructions (e.g. 'Could you write a short report on
  failings in security?') but be specific: 'I'd like a ten-page
  report giving examples of major security breaches together
  with possible reasons behind them and recommendations
  on how to avoid them in future.'
- Check that the person has understood the task you want
  him/her to undertake. Do this not by just asking, 'Have
  you understood what I want you to do?' but something
  like 'Could you summarize what you will be doing?' Their
  response will show how much they have understood your
  explanation.
- Give background details, so that the colleague knows why
  he/she is doing the task and how his/her task or activity fits
  into the overall scheme of things.
- Where necessary, follow up any spoken instructions in
  writing with a full brief, outlining the work.
- State the time by which you want your colleagues to complete
  the work. Remember that what may take you (with all your
  experience) a short time will probably take much longer for
  the colleague you are delegating to.
- Supervise their work properly: provide the necessary
  equipment and other resources that the colleague needs.

- Let the person to whom you are delegating the work decide the details of how he/she will undertake the work.
- Where problems arise, encourage the person to whom you are delegating to come to you not only with the difficulty, but also with thoughts on possible solutions.
- When your colleague has completed the task, thank the person, expressing your appreciation. Recognize him/her and the achievement.

Learning to trust

Oliver was usually fine at delegating tasks. He explained tasks well and let his team members get on with it, checking both informally – 'How's it going?'– as well as, less often, formally. However, with one colleague, Janet, he used to continually come and stand by her desk, moving about nervously, and constantly ask how she was getting on. This annoyed Janet so much that one day she lost her temper with Oliver and burst out, 'Why don't you trust me just to get on with the job?' Oliver had to learn to back off and gradually was able to trust Janet, enabling her to continue her work with less supervision.

A good salesman

Andy was a good salesman. Over the years, he had networked widely, earning his clients' trust and the right to be listened to... and to sell his products. He was known for his commitment, thoroughness and integrity.

He was also persuasive. He was an astute listener, empathizing with and respecting his clients, and so was aware of their needs, helping his customers to make an informed choice. He was able to match his products to his clients' requirements because he genuinely wanted to provide products that were of real value to them. He knew his subject well and was very passionate about it. He really did believe in his products. So no wonder he was the country's best salesman.

Resolve conflict

At times, you are bound to meet conflict. Trust breaks down. Personalities clash. Departments each want a bigger slice of the budget or to avoid the biggest cutbacks.

Deal with conflict quickly; tackle the issues. Don't be cautious and fearful about speaking directly and clearly about difficulties.

I have found the books *Difficult Conversations: How to Discuss What Matters Most* by Douglas Stone, Bruce Patton and Sheila Heen (Michael Joseph, 1999) and *The Peacemaker: A Biblical Guide to Resolving Personal Conflict* by Ken Sande (Baker, 1991) very useful. The following is based on what those authors helpfully suggest:

● **Distinguish the incident – what is happening/happened – from feelings about the incident.** Consider separately:
  – the incident – someone said something; someone is to blame. Try to focus on the real issue. Remain calm. Listen closely. Ask open questions. Understand other people's interests as well as your own.
  – feelings about the incident, for example anger, hurt
  – the identity of the person. Sometimes a person's identity, including their own self-worth, will feel threatened. Calmly affirm your respect for them.
● **Do what you can to resolve the issue and maintain the relationship if possible:** prepare and evaluate possible solutions to agree on the way forward.

Summary

In this chapter we have been concerned with cultivating stronger working relationships: establishing a better rapport between colleagues. Key to this is taking the time to understand your colleagues and develop even greater respect and trust and stronger teamwork.

Follow-up

1 Think about the colleagues in your company or organization. Think about the ones you like. Why do you enjoy working with them? Now think about the ones you don't get on so well with. What practical steps can you take to improve your working relationships with them?

2 Think about what you can do to rise above the petty aspects of office politics. What can you do (and what can you not do) to be even more professional in your work?

3 Think about an area of conflict at work. What can you do to listen to people's different viewpoints and distinguish the incident from feelings about the incident? What are the next steps for you to undertake?

Fact-check (answers at the back)

1. Having strong working relationships in an organization is:
   a) A luxury ❏
   b) Essential ❏
   c) A waste of time ❏
   d) Unimportant ❏

2. In trying to build better relationships, think more about:
   a) Yourself ❏
   b) Your boss ❏
   c) Your colleagues ❏
   d) Your holidays ❏

3. When you are in a discussion with colleagues:
   a) Make sure you that say what you have to, not thinking about your colleagues ❏
   b) Look at your notes and never make eye contact with them ❏
   c) Be embarrassed because you like them a lot ❏
   d) Listen and respond to what they are saying. ❏

4. I am aware of colleagues' body language, posture and tone of voice:
   a) Never ❏
   b) Always ❏
   c) Rarely ❏
   d) Often ❏

5. 'Small talk' is:
   a) A useful tool to establish rapport ❏
   b) A complete waste of time ❏
   c) More important than the actual business ❏
   d) Just about adequate ❏

6. When thinking about others' roles:
   a) I am awed by those with higher status ❏
   b) I am very bossy towards those with lower status ❏
   c) I have this at the back of my mind but don't let it control me ❏
   d) I don't think about others ❏

7. In our team, we are clear about having:
   a) Strictly defined roles that we discuss whenever we meet ❏
   b) Different roles that we use as a basis to help us ❏
   c) No set roles at all ❏
   d) All the same roles ❏

8. I would like to improve teamwork in my team:
   a) But it is already as good as it can be; I don't need to do anything more ❏
   b) And I am keen to take practical action to do so ❏
   c) But I am so aware of my failings as team leader ❏
   d) But I am too lazy to do anything about it ❏

9. When I delegate work, I do so:
   a) Clearly ❏
   b) What is delegation? ❏
   c) In a vague way, hoping the colleague will work out what I mean ❏
   d) In so much detail that I confuse everyone ❏

335

10. When resolving conflict, first of all I:

a) Go straight to the solution ❑
b) Put off dealing with it ❑
c) Ignore everyone ❑
d) Listen closely to what both
   sides have to say ❑

CHAPTER 21

Engage effectively online

We conclude this Part by looking at how you can develop an online presence and engage in business online, from the point of view of communication. Much of what we discuss builds on what you have read earlier: this chapter pulls together a number of themes that we have already discussed, such as writing with a particular audience in mind, writing clearly and developing effective business relationships.

Websites have become an essential part of business life and it is difficult to imagine how we ever managed without them. Yet we are also aware that some websites are easier to navigate than others and information is more accessible on some than on others. So now we will consider:

- knowing your aims and planning your website carefully, so that the information is organized in a way that is accessible to the users you want to target
- writing text for your website, with tips on design and layout of your words
- exploiting the importance of social media in business.

Your company website

Know your aims

As for all forms of communication, it is essential that you clarify the exact aims of your website.

You may say that your company's or organization's website is your 'shop window', but what exactly do you mean by that? Your website will show the location of your office or store, and your opening hours. The website may show your goods or services, but do you want customers to buy direct from you or through a retailer or other intermediary? How do you want interested users of your website to respond to you? If you are offering a service, and if users want to complain, do you want to make it easy or more difficult for them to do so? You may want to promote an author or a rock band. You may want to inspire users by your choice of photographs, stories or poems. You may want to inform or educate users about a particular need or hobby and maybe ask them to give money towards your cause.

Plan your website

Work out your users' needs. We are back to AIR (Audience; Intention; Response), which we looked at in Chapter 15.

What are your users' needs? To know the aims of your company or organization? To be persuaded that they need to buy your product or service or ought to donate money? One way of beginning to think about this is to write a brief mission statement. You can fill this out with longer explanatory paragraphs and case studies (real-life examples) of your company or organization at work.

Think hard about how and when your users will use your website and what information they want. For example, we are currently renovating our bathroom and have accessed different companies' websites for details of the tiles, baths, basins, and so on they offer. Some companies give prices on the website, some in a separate downloadable brochure; some don't give prices at all!

Some users will view your website for only a few moments; others want to read what you have to say and respond positively, for example by buying a product or finding the information they want. Do you want users to download further files (e.g. in PDF)? How do you want users to contact you? Think all this through practically and realistically.

Organize your website

Here are some tips:

- Plan a hierarchy of information, that is, how you want users to go from one page to the next.
- Remember that people will navigate your site in a variety of ways.
- Separate your information into major – but manageable – parts. Group such parts into categories.
- Plan from 'the bottom up'; start with your most detailed pages and work backwards to your home page.
- Allow for flexibility. For example, if you are selling ebooks in various formats, allow for further tabs on your website alongside your existing ones to anticipate future changes in technology.
- Imagine a user accessing your website and work through how he/she will navigate your site. Make sure that the choices you are offering are the ones you want to offer. Some websites are built on the 'three-click' principle: give users the information they want within three clicks from the home page or they will go elsewhere. But the truth is, in reality, if users are interested – and determined – enough, they will explore your website more deeply.
- Have a balanced combination of words and images. Some websites seem to contain only words; some only images. I think an effective website will contain both.
- Plan how you will maintain your website. It is fine to work very hard on your website now, making it live by a certain date, but you also need to plan how you will keep it up to date. Too many websites have a section with 'latest news' that give stories that happened a year ago or more. Having out-of-date information does not communicate an image that your company or organization is successful now. So the rule is: plan to keep your website fresh.

- Consider specifically search engine optimization (SEO): how you will reach your target audience most effectively through the use of keywords, tags and so on.

> ## A new concept
>
> Ray, one of the directors of the plumbers Smithson & Son, asked Jo, a website consultant, to design and build their company's website. When Jo first met Ray, she explained that a website was different from the normal printed pages of a book, in that a website does not really have a finishing point; it is much more flexible than the traditional printed page. Pages are more like photographs: they provide a visual snapshot for users. This interactive nature of the website was an entirely new concept to Ray. Previously, he thought that he could just put his company's existing leaflets on the website and that was it. Jo helped Ray see that the company's website could open up a whole new world, enabling customers to see what the company offered.

Write your website

Here are some useful tips:

- Keep in mind your users' needs. You are writing for them, not for yourself. Writing for a website is like having a conversation, except you cannot see the person you are talking to.
- Make sure that your home page says:
  - who you are and your basic aims
  - the goods and/or services you offer
  - how users may obtain your goods and/or services.
- Make your text easy to read. The following points are good practice:
  - Don't put text right across the whole width of the screen; if you do so, the text will not be legible. It is better to use up to half the width of the screen.
  - The best position for text is towards the top of the screen and towards the left.

- Text that is centred on the page is difficult to read, so align your text – including headings – to the left, but keep the right-hand side 'ragged' (unjustified).
- A sans-serif font is more legible than a serif one on a computer screen.
- You should keep the colours of your text and background different, but don't use too many colours.
- Give each page its own title.
- Divide your text into paragraphs and write a clear heading above the paragraph. Keep paragraphs to no more than 100 words.
- Have white space around your text; this creates an impression of openness.
- Put the most important information first in each paragraph.
- Use everyday words that you would say in a normal conversation, e.g. *explain*, not *elucidate*; *more* or *extra*, not *supplementary*.
- Keep your sentences short: a maximum of 15–20 words.
- Make sure that your text is clear. Draft the text and then revise it, asking yourself what the paragraph is about. For example, some friends were writing about fishing for their website but had assumed that their readers knew all about that particular kind of fishing. When we discussed this, it became clear that what was missing was an opening definition of the particular kind of fishing they were writing about.
- Add hyperlinks to other pages on your website and/or back to your home page, for example: 'Click here to find out more or contact us.' (When users click on the underlined words they will be taken to a new page or a form.) Excessive use of hyperlinks can, however, make the page look too detailed.
- Make sure that your spelling is correct. 'Stephenson' or 'Stevenson'? 'Philips' or 'Phillips'? Be consistent (e.g. use *-ise* or *-ize* throughout).
- Keep punctuation to a minimum; full stops at the ends of bullet points can make a website look fussy.
- Avoid abbreviations that are not generally known and jargon and slang.
- Put information in lists, which work well on websites.
- Make sure that your text is accurate. Check dates and financial information so that they are correct.

Look back at editing documents in Chapter 17 for further guidelines.

Business and social media

In recent years, as the pace of innovation in the Internet age has quickened, use of social media sites such as Facebook has become an important part of many people's lives. The impact of these sites is still being assessed but undoubtedly digital formats will remain immensely significant for the foreseeable future.

- Professional networking sites such as LinkedIn allow you to keep informed about trends in your area of business, network with colleagues around the world, discuss matters of common interest and see what business opportunities may arise.
- Blogs and Twitter help you to develop an online community by connecting with potential and existing clients, sharing links to interesting articles, exchanging pictures, information and specific insights, discussing ideas and asking – and responding to – questions.

Summary

In this chapter we have looked at engaging effectively online by first of all considering your website: how to know your aims and move on from those to planning and organizing your website so that it fulfils those aims. We then looked at different aspects of writing for your website to make sure that your message is communicated successfully.

As an effective manager, you will also want to engage with your potential and existing customers using online social media. It can be very useful to think which online media networks will be most profitable both in the short term (spreading the message now) and also in the medium and long terms (maintaining good business relationships).

Follow-up

1 Summarize the aim of your website in 12 words.

2 Now think about your website and think how much it fulfils that aim.

3 How will you change and maintain your website to make sure it stays up to date?

4 How effective to your business are the social media sites that you use?

Fact-check (answers at the back)

1. Your website is:
   a) A luxury ☐
   b) A waste of time and money ☐
   c) Essential ☐
   d) Nice to have when you can afford it ☐

2. Your website is your organization's:
   a) Shop window ☐
   b) Rubbish tip ☐
   c) Set of printed leaflets ☐
   d) IT department's responsibility ☐

3. The first thing to do when planning a website is:
   a) Start writing as soon as possible ☐
   b) Organize the pages ☐
   c) Be flexible ☐
   d) Know your aims ☐

4. When designing web pages, put text in:
   a) Whatever the committee we will set up decides ☐
   b) Less than half the width of the screen ☐
   c) The whole width of the screen ☐
   d) More than the width of the screen ☐

5. Working out how users will navigate the website is:
   a) A luxury ☐
   b) Essential ☐
   c) A waste of time ☐
   d) Important if you have the money ☐

6. When designing web pages:
   a) Use a sans-serif font and lots of headings ☐
   b) Use a serif font and lots of headings ☐
   c) Use a serif font and no headings ☐
   d) Use a sans-serif font and no headings ☐

7. Giving each page a title is:
   a) Unnecessary; users can see what it's about ☐
   b) A nice idea if you are creative ☐
   c) Important – do it! ☐
   d) Extravagant – it takes up too much space ☐

8. You need to update your website:
   a) Regularly ☐
   b) Never ☐
   c) We haven't got a website to update ☐
   d) I will have to ask, as I'm not sure ☐

9. After writing text for the website:
   a) The website goes live immediately ☐
   b) If I have time, a colleague may check it ☐
   c) The website goes down; what did I do wrong? ☐
   d) Check the text to make sure that it is clear and accurate ☐

10. I use social media in my work:
   a) For a laugh ☐
   b) Never ☐
   c) To interact with potential and existing clients ☐
   d) As the only means of business communication ☐

7 × 7

1 Seven steps to sharpen your writing

- Plan! Think about what you want to write, why you are writing, what you hope to achieve and what response you want from your audience. Drawing a pattern diagram is a great first step.

- Identify your key messages and your audience – what will be the most effective way to impart this information?

- Structure your text; consider presenting arguments in order of importance (most important first), as a comparison of advantages and disadvantages, chronologically, or broken down by theme.

- Write a first draft; the blank page won't write itself! Focus on providing an introduction, the key data and a conclusion.

- Edit your draft; check accuracy of facts, spelling and punctuation, length (whether you are aiming for short and snappy or lengthy and detailed), and whether your overall message is clear.

- Reread your text after editing. Check it against your original plan – have you achieved what you wanted to achieve? If so, move to the next step; if not, loop back to another round of editing.

- Press 'send'! All too often, people use just two of these steps: 'Write a first draft' and 'Press "send"'; follow all seven steps to make your writing stand out.

2 Seven reasons to listen up

- Listening helps you to understand where the other person is coming from, and what they are trying to communicate.

- Listening encourages you to ask the right questions; as you focus on the other person, you will want to know more.

- Listening allows you to read between the lines; or, more correctly, hear between the lines – what's the underlying message?

- Listening helps you to understand your colleagues better: what's important to them, what concerns them, how they think, and how they are feeling.

- Listening gives you the opportunity to distinguish between fact and opinion.

- Listening builds trust between colleagues: value them and they will value you.

- Listening can resolve conflict: hearing and understanding – if not agreeing – are the first steps to resolution.

3 Seven ways to improve your business reading

- Decide what your aim is before starting to read: what do you want to get out of this?

- Vary your speed: spend more time on the important parts of the text, and be prepared to skim the waffle.

- Focus on key words and key phrases to identify the most significant sections of the text.

- Read more widely: reading is good! The more you read – whether relating to business or not – the more you will learn new words, phrases and ideas, and be better placed to apply them to your work.

- Try not to mouth words as you read them – this slows you down and also forces you to focus on the words rather than the sentiment.

- Think about the author's argument – do you agree with him/her, and, if not, why?

- If you find it helpful, take notes as you read. Summarizing the author's argument in your own words can be a powerful learning tool.

4 Seven tips for organizing meetings

- Know the purpose of the meeting.
- Plan a venue and time.
- Invite the key people.
- Circulate an agenda in advance.
- Prepare the meeting room.
- Read reports in advance.
- Ensure that you come up with accurate information.

5 Seven tips for chairing meetings

- Stick to the agenda and ensure that the meeting starts and ends on time.
- Introduce and welcome newcomers, or ask people to introduce themselves.
- State the meeting's key aims and objectives.
- Review progress on action points from previous meetings.
- Bring in key speakers to contribute at appropriate points.
- Summarize the points being discussed.
- Draw conclusions and make decisions: ensure that action points are clear and state who is responsible for following up on particular points (and by when).

6 Seven ways to polish presentations

- Try to summarize your message in 12 words or fewer. This is your key message to deliver: keep your headline simple.
- Know how long you will speak for. It's fine to finish a little early, but people start to fidget when they realize that you are overrunning.

- Think about what you are going to say! Check out the 'Seven steps to sharpen your writing'.
- Write your presentation down: either write word-for-word what you're going to say, or create a list of key points to guide you – whichever method works best for you.
- Deploy useful visual aids: yes, you cut a fine figure of a gentleman or lady, but give your audience something else to look at from time to time!
- If your presentation lasts for more than 45 minutes, plan a short comfort break for the audience.
- Be enthusiastic! Be positive and sell your message; your audience wants to hear your views, so share them gladly.

7 Seven things to avoid

- Confusing jargon and unknown terminology. Industry-specific language is fine, but avoid buzzwords and over-complication.
- Poor timing: whether asking for an immediate response or delivering bad news last thing on a Friday afternoon, timing is an incredibly important communication tool. Think about when will achieve the greatest impact.
- Voice says one thing, body says another: ensure that your body language is sending the same message as your wording.
- Unfocused, vague presentation: instead, be clear, precise and prepared.
- Wandering off the point.
- Providing too little information: everyone likes snappy communication, but assess your audience to better decide the best information to give.
- Providing too much information: see above, but in reverse! Once again, know your audience to judge exactly what to communicate.

PART 4
Your Decision Making Masterclass

Introduction

You make decisions all the time in everyday life: what to eat, what clothes to wear, with whom you spend your leisure time and how you spend your money. In your business life you are also constantly making decisions, and this decision-making process is the subject of this Part: the different activities you – and your business colleagues – need to carry out in order to arrive at a sound decision.

At work, you are deciding how to spend your time, which emails to answer, what subjects to raise at a meeting, when is the best time for your company to launch a new product, what companies you should invest in, what you are not willing to compromise on in negotiations, what policies to develop and how best to market your products and services. Some of these decisions may have already been made for you by other colleagues, usually those above you in your company or organization, and your task is merely to implement them. In other matters, however, you can exercise some control over the actual decision-making process.

CHAPTER 22

Know your aims clearly

'Ready, fire, aim.' This anonymous quotation describes how we, all too often, set about things. The right way round is, of course, 'Ready, aim, fire': prepare yourself, know exactly what your target is and then act. Time spent in planning and preparation is time well spent.

In this chapter we lay foundations for making good decisions at work. We begin by asking what it is exactly that a decision needs to be made about. We then move on to consider the following questions:

- What kind of person are you?
  - How would you describe your values, motivation and working style? These will affect the decisions you make at work.
- Do you know your own style?
  - Are you by personality decisive or indecisive? Perhaps the reason you are reading this book is that you are indecisive: you need to realize that by not making a decision you are also in fact making a decision!
- Are you more logical or more creative?
  - What is your own preferred learning style?

Knowing the answers to these questions will help prepare the way for you to make good decisions.

What is the real decision?

Suppose your company wants to refresh its website. The original website was put together hurriedly a few years ago when everyone suddenly discovered the Internet and realized that they needed a web presence. One of the managers in your company at that time knew that the husband of one of the secretaries understood a little about the web and asked him to build a website. The result is acceptable but the website is ordinary and unimaginative and now looks dated. The subject of refreshing the website has recently come up at meeting after meeting. Frankly, you're a little tired of that, so you decide that you will act on it. After all, you know a couple of friends who could do with the cash and could do a good job.

So you chat with your friends ... and then one of them asks you, 'What is your website for?' This makes you think and you suddenly realize that you don't really know. There's been no discussion, let alone agreement, on the aims of your company's website.

You may say that your company's or organization's website is your 'shop window', but what exactly do you mean by that? Your website may show the location of your offices, with information about your goods or services, but what else do you want it to do? An essential first step is that you clarify the exact aims of your website. You will therefore need to ask yourself some questions, such as:

- Will customers buy direct from us or via a retailer or other intermediary?
- How do we want interested users of our website to respond to us?
- If users want to complain about our service, do we want to make it easy or difficult for them to do so?
- Do we want to promote something – such as an author or a rock band – or inspire users by our choice of photographs, stories or poems?
- Do we want to inform or educate users about a particular need or hobby?
- Do we want to ask users to give money towards our cause?

The first rule in decision making is to ask yourself what exactly you are making a decision about. You need to identify as clearly and precisely as you can what your goal is: what are you trying to decide?

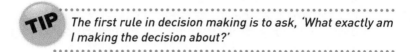

TIP *The first rule in decision making is to ask, 'What exactly am I making the decision about?'*

Defining exactly what you need to make a decision about will not come easily. You will need to discuss this with your colleagues. When I say discuss, I mean talk – not email! We need to hear and see the challenge from others as we talk about a subject. Gradually, and over time, you will hone – sharpen, make more focused – what exactly the decision is. In the above example, the primary decision wasn't about 'Who should we ask to refresh our website?' but 'What is our website for?'

> **'Nothing is more difficult, and therefore more precious, than to be able to decide.'**
>
> Napoleon Bonaparte, military and political leader (1769–1821)

Other factors in the decision

As you begin to focus on the core issue of the decision, other factors will begin to emerge, for example:

● What is the **budget?**
● What is the **timescale?**
  – See if you can break down the time factor. Does a decision need to be made quickly? Often the answer is yes, but you need to consider the long-term implications of a rushed decision, especially if it turns out to be the wrong one.
  – If you are introducing change management, you will be faced by cries of resistance: 'We've done it this way for

years; why do we need to change?' You need to explain why changes are being made and why this is a good time to begin to make such changes.

- As you may have only one opportunity to make a decision, you need to ensure that it is the right one and that it is made properly. For example, a Member of Parliament once told me that they have many policies they could pursue but that an important part of their party's thinking was to discern what would be most acceptable at any given time.
- You may need to ask for more facts.
- In determining an ultimate goal, you will identify milestones along the way. For example, my son Ben wanted to live in Japan, so this meant that he wanted to learn Japanese. Such a goal was realized practically as a Japanese friend of my wife's gave him lessons every Thursday evening for two years. Visualizing his goal constantly kept him going even during the times when learning the language was demanding and laborious.
- You may need to ask for more time in order for you to reach a decision. In negotiations, you can say, 'I need a little time to think about that.'

● What **secondary matters** can you resolve at the same time?
  - For example, if you are redesigning your website, can you also redesign the company logo at the same time? It is important, however, to keep such secondary matters separate from the main focus of your decision making.

At this stage, don't discount any aim or thought because it is limited. Here, you are 'dreaming dreams' and 'thinking outside the box'. You are looking at creative ways of solving problems and, indeed, of turning problems into opportunities.

If you want to solve a problem, you need to get to the root of it:

1 Think; discuss it with other colleagues; analyse the problem by separating it into its parts to help you define it more closely and understand it more fully.
2 Concentrate on the causes of the problem, not on its symptoms or effects. If someone's work is below standard, for example, don't keep moaning about it by giving examples, but try to find out why. Ask whether they need training or whether they would be more suitable for a different kind of work.
3 Keep on asking questions, especially the question 'Why?' so that you gain a complete understanding of the real issue. At this stage, it's more about asking the right questions than finding the right answers.

As you begin to list various factors in the decision, you will begin to realize what the decision is *not* primarily about. Again, to use the example above, the decision about a website was not primarily about who was to make the changes but what the purpose of the website was.

Know what kind of person you are

It is good to stand back, as you begin to consider the foundations of decision making, and analyse what kind of person you are in terms of your:

- morals and principles
- standards of work
- motivation and attitude
- working style.

Answer the following questions to help you find out.

Morals and principles	• How honest and responsible are you? • Do you do what you know is right? • Do you always act fairly towards others, respecting them, or do you take unfair advantage of them? • What other values do you and your company or organization hold that you seek to follow in your working life? • Would you make a decision that is wrong for the sake of making a short-term gain? • Are your procedures honest and open to scrutiny?
Standards of work	• Do you always do your work consistently well or are you often satisfied with a task that you know you have not completed properly? • Do you persevere with a task or do you give up quickly? • Are you committed to excellence?
Motivation and attitude	• Are you enthusiastic or half-hearted? • Are you diligent or lazy?
Working style	• Are you content with simply working efficiently, not wasting resources of time and money, or are you also concerned to work effectively, to do the right thing to the best of your ability? • Do you work well with others or are there often areas of conflict? • Do you set priorities and stick to them or are you constantly dealing with crises so that you don't get round to doing what you really should be doing?

Doing what is right

Oliver's first job was in an agricultural business, where he soon found that he had a natural flair for sales. Customers would often arrive with a worn-out item such as a lawnmower and expect a generous trade-in allowance against a new one.

The farming customers consistently drove a hard bargain, and none more so than Sam. Sam had the ability to get what he wanted and would almost intimidate staff to secure the best possible price ... and Oliver was to be no exception.

Sam arrived late one day (when all Oliver's senior colleagues had gone home) with a worthless trade-in. After demanding an inflated trade-in allowance, Sam set about seeking generous discount levels. Oliver did his best to hold out and, when the price was finally agreed, he was relieved to have done a deal without making a loss.

Later, when going over the figures, Oliver noticed that he had made a mistake: he had supplied Sam with a basic model mower but charged him for a more expensive one with more features. The result was a reasonable profit and so natural justice seemed to have been done.

However, that night Oliver's conscience set to work as he went over the day's events. He tried to justify what he had done ('unscrupulous customer', 'reasonable profit', 'best for the company', 'too late to change it' and so on) but, whichever way he looked at things, he still knew it was wrong to have overcharged Sam. He wondered what would happen if he owned up to the boss; would he be punished? He worried about his boss's reaction, and thought he might just keep quiet; after all, no one would ever know and so no harm would be done.

Still troubled, however, Oliver owned up the next day, and his boss's argument was simple: 'Do what's right. Credit the customer and don't worry about the profit. The company's reputation is too important.' Humbled and relieved, Oliver had learned a lesson. He phoned the customer, who appeared a little stunned, but Oliver's conscience was clear ... and Sam always seemed a little more amenable after that.

In the above case study, what if Oliver had kept silent? What if his boss had pressurized him into doing wrong? Whether it's big business or a family firm, there is always a cost to doing what you know is right and a temptation to do well for the company in a way that is in fact wrong. You should do what you know is right, even when it is difficult and even costly for the company you work for.

Know your own style

'We know what happens to people who stay in the middle of the road. They get run over.'

Aneurin Bevan, British statesman (1897–1960)

Think about your own ability to make decisions.

- Are you cautious?
  You may be unwilling to take risks and so put off making a decision, perhaps hoping that the need to make a decision will go away.
- Are you rash?
  If you make decisions quickly, you may not spend time examining all the various factors and risks, so your decisions often turn out to be wrong.
- Do you take a long time to make decisions?
  If you take the time to consider carefully all the various factors and consequences, they often turn out well.
- Do you often 'go round in circles'?
  If you waste a lot of time thinking about all the different aspects of an issue, you may never actually arrive at a point where you come to a decision.

Know how your brain works

Being aware of how your brain works can help you make more effective decisions. Generally, we can say that the left-hand side of the brain is the more logical side and the right-hand side of the brain is the more creative.

Being indecisive

Being indecisive is illustrated by the philosophical position known as Buridan's ass. In the example, a hungry donkey stands an equal distance between two identical bales of hay. He starves to death, however, because there is no reason why he should choose to eat one bale rather than the other. The dilemma is said to

> show the indecisiveness of the will when faced with two equal alternatives. The philosophical example is associated with the French philosopher Jean Buridan (c.1295–1356), although it was first found in the philosophy of Aristotle.

In some people, one side of the brain is more dominant than the other.

- People whose logical (left side) is more dominant deal with information in a linear sequence, tend to be organized and are able to analyse and process words, numbers, facts and other detailed information comparatively easily.
- People whose creative (right side) is more dominant are relatively artistic and imaginative and are used to thinking more visually, intuitively and spatially.

This is a good reason to ensure that you have a mix of both logical and creative thinkers in your decision-making team.

In decision making you may need to adapt your natural way of thinking. If naturally your logical (left side) is more dominant, it can be helpful to work at being more creative, imaginative and intuitive and consider being less cautious and take more risks in decision making. Similarly, if your natural tendency is for your creative (right side) to be more dominant, then it can be helpful to work at being more detailed, analytical and organized, and undertake more long-term planning.

Know your learning style

Each of us learns differently. Three main types of learner have been identified:

- **visual learners:** those who 'see' things more in pictures, images, diagrams and written text
- **auditory learners:** those who learn by listening and discussing with others
- **kinaesthetic learners:** those who learn by doing, for example through role play, and who are 'in touch with' their feelings.

Again, it can be very useful to make sure you have colleagues with a variety of different learning styles to help you make decisions. Similarly, if you are used to one learning style, it can be helpful to identify that and see whether you can extend your own range to include a greater diversity.

Skills in decision making

'I'll give you a definite maybe.'

Attributed to Sam Goldwyn, film producer (1879–1974)

Finally, we open up the dynamics of the skills included in decision making: analysing, synthesizing and evaluating.

- **Analysing**

  This means breaking a task or process down into its constituent parts, often in a logical order. For example, to analyse what the real matter is that needs to be decided means asking and answering the basic question words *who, why, where, when, how, what*. Of these, 'Why ...?' is the most significant one to ask – as in the example earlier: 'Why do we need a website?' Those whose left (logical) side of the brain is more dominant will find this aspect relatively easy.

- **Synthesizing**

  This is putting the bits back together after you have analysed them (broken them up), or even not analysing them in the first place but seeing things as wholes. This way of thinking sees ideas not as things that need analysing but more like seeds that grow. Those whose right (creative) side of the brain is more dominant will find this aspect relatively easy.

- **Evaluating**

  This is weighing up the significance of different options, putting a value on something. This can be subjective but it also means that you will probably draw on the specialist technical experience of experts who know the subject matter better than you and who can advise you.

Summary

In this chapter you learned what questions to ask to help you make good decisions, and about the factors that affect the decision-making process. You need to be able to identify the real issue that you need to make a decision about, along with the secondary issues. You also need to consider the timescale for making the decision and whether it is realistic and, if it is not, how to work out a strategy to seek more time. The kind of person you are is also a factor in decision making, especially in terms of your values and what motivates you at work and the way you work. You'll need to take account of aspects of your personality and what your learning style is, because they also affect the way you make decisions.

Follow-up

Think about a decision you need to make in the next few weeks.

1 What is the real issue and what are the secondary issues?
2 List five values that you seek to hold that will help inform your decision.
3 Are you by personality cautious or rash; do you want to change such a trait?

Fact-check [answers at the back]

1. How important is knowing the core issue that you need to make a decision about?
   a) Nice to have ❏
   b) A luxury ❏
   c) A waste of time ❏
   d) Essential ❏

2. When preparing to make a decision, how often should you spend time working out the core issue you need to decide, as distinct from secondary issues?
   a) Occasionally ❏
   b) If I feel like it ❏
   c) If I remember ❏
   d) Always ❏

3. In preparing to make a decision, what do you also need to think about?
   a) Lunch and going to the bank ❏
   b) My annual appraisal ❏
   c) The timescale and budget ❏
   d) Evaluating the decision ❏

4. What should you think about when calculating the time needed to implement a decision?
   a) Doodling to pass the time away ❏
   b) Identifying intermediate milestones ❏
   c) Being promoted ❏
   d) Evaluating the decision ❏

5. When should you take risks in making decisions that you know may get you into trouble?
   a) When I think I can get away with it ❏
   b) Sometimes ❏
   c) Often ❏
   d) Never ❏

6. What is the purpose of the values you hold in life?
   a) To support and provide a firm basis for my actions ❏
   b) I've never even thought about them ❏
   c) To spend my time thinking about them but not doing anything with them ❏
   d) What do you mean by 'values'? ❏

7. When should you try to uphold the values of your company or organization?
   a) When I feel like it ❏
   b) When it's convenient ❏
   c) Constantly ❏
   d) What are our values? ❏

8. How should you use your natural tendency in making decisions, e.g. being cautious or rash?
   a) Always act like that ❏
   b) Try to do the opposite ❏
   c) Be willing to consider changing that way ❏
   d) Not bother changing ❏

9. How should you involve colleagues in the decision-making process?
a) Only on Mondays ❏
b) Often, to gain balanced views ❏
c) When I feel like it ❏
d) Never ❏

10. What's the best way to make a decision?
a) Just make it ❏
b) Separate the tasks of analysing the core issue and of evaluating the options ❏
c) Ask other people to make it ❏
d) Analyse the different options but let someone else make the decision ❏

CHAPTER 23

Collect relevant information

In the previous chapter we began to establish some ground rules for the whole decision-making process. Now we move on to consider the gathering of relevant information. This is an essential step that will enable you to identify and later evaluate different options to help you come to an informed decision.

We will look at:

- understanding the context by asking questions: for example, why the decision needs to be made; who needs to make the decision; who will implement the decision; who will be affected by the decision; and by when the decision needs to be made
- gathering different kinds of relevant information, including consulting experts and undertaking research from a wide range of sources
- working on your costs: knowing how much your time costs and how long tasks take, and drawing up a budget
- reading and understanding statistics.

Understand the context

Every important decision you make has its own context: it is set in a particular situation. Considering as many of these background factors as possible is an important first step in gathering information.

One good way of helping you start thinking about the context of a decision is to draw a pattern diagram (also known as a 'mind map'). Take a blank piece of A4 paper. Arrange it in landscape position and write in the middle the core issue that you identified in Chapter 22. (Write a word or phrase, but not a whole sentence.) You may find it helpful to work in pencil so that you can rub out what you write if necessary.

Now write around your central word(s) the different key aspects that come to your mind. You do not need to list ideas in order of importance; simply write them down. To begin with, you do not need to join the ideas up with lines linking connected items.

If you get stuck at any point, ask yourself the question words *why, how, what, who, when, where*, and *how much*. These may well set you thinking.

When I do this, two things often amaze me:

1 how easy the task is; it doesn't feel like work! The ideas and concepts seem to flow naturally and spontaneously. I think this is partly because at this stage I am not trying to put the ideas in any order.
2 how valuable that piece of paper is. I have captured all (or at least some or many) of the key points. I don't want to lose that piece of paper!

Suppose you need to make a decision about installing a new computer system at work. Your diagram might look like the one below. You are not trying to make a decision at this point, and you should avoid the temptation to do so. You are simply listing different aspects of the issue that could be relevant factors.

The example shown is a general one, and you could add a lot more detail under each point. For instance, the bullet point under **Time available** is 'Should be ready for 1 January' and you could expand this to include various milestones related to time and schedule, such as:

Gather data	June–August
Identify options	by 15 September
Shortlist the three most likely solutions	by 1 October
Agree best solution	by 15 October
Approach top company	by 1 November

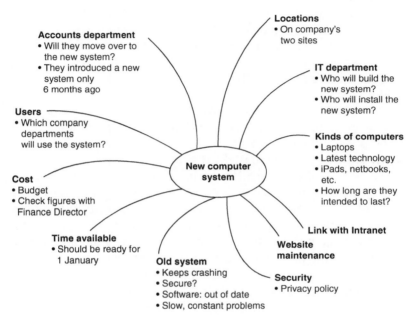

To pursue this further, here are some questions you could ask to get you thinking.

- **Why** does the decision need to be made?
- **Who** are the key people involved?
- **Who** are the best colleagues to implement the decision?
- **Who** will make the decision?
- **Who** will be affected by the decision?
  Will colleagues – or you – need to be trained in new skills? If you are dealing with a professional business matter, think about how that affects your personal life outside work. For example, if you are being asked to relocate or undertake a

job that involves being away from home for four nights every week, think about how this will affect your home life.

- **What** are the different competitive products?
  It's useful to compare different items, for example different solutions or types of new computer software to replace your existing ones.
- **How** does the problem express itself?
  You could draw a flow chart to show the various different stages that led to the problem, how the problem is expressed (its symptoms) and the connections between the problem's causes and effects.
- **How** will you measure the success of the results of your decision?
  Be as objective as you can. Will the new system be less disruptive to business? Will it produce fewer computer crashes and fewer calls to helplines?
- **When** will you need to make the decision?
  You will need to determine the intermediate stages you must complete to reach this point and the dates by when they need to be completed. For example, if you are recruiting new staff, work out a timetable for the various different elements of the task, beginning at the end, that is, the ideal date when you want the person to start employment. Work backwards from that date to now, including the following stages: agreeing the job description, person specification and method of application; advertising the post; allowing time for applications; working out how to deal with references; shortlisting; interviews; offer of job and acceptance of offer; and issuing contract.
- **Where** are the relevant factors located?
  Is space an issue? Would buying and installing certain software need you to change offices or even rent new offices?

Now is the time to question assumptions, for example about the perceived limitations of your role or about a possible new direction for your company. Think big! Do you need to think differently about how you will market your company and let the 'outside world' know of your existence?

374

PESTLE and SWOT analyses

PESTLE and SWOT are two acronyms for techniques to help you understand the context of the decision you have to make by examining a range of factors.

PESTLE analysis

Political changes	Changes in government, e.g. consideration of the effects of war
Economic changes	Is the economy in a recession or is it growing? Is your market expanding? What is the level of your potential customers' disposable income?
Sociological changes	Is the birth rate increasing? What changes in lifestyles are there? How socially mobile are your potential customers?
Technological changes	The latest innovations in the digital market, e.g. smartphones, tablets
Legal changes	Changes in the law, in regulatory bodies or in regulations, e.g. health & safety
Environmental changes	The effects on your carbon footprint

Considering these external influences on your business will help you put your decision in a wider context.

SWOT analysis

Strengths	What are you better at than your competitors? What is your USP (unique selling point)?
Weaknesses	What do your competitors perceive as your weaknesses? Is morale low? Is your leadership committed? Are there gaps in the skills of your colleagues?
Opportunities	What changes in the market or changes in lifestyle can you exploit to maximize your profits?
Threats	Is the market for your product declining? Are key colleagues on the verge of leaving? Is your financial backing stable?

Conducting a SWOT analysis to analyse where your company/ organization is now will help you make the decision before you.

Gather relevant information

By looking at the context of a decision, you are beginning to gather relevant information. You can build on what you have thought so far by undertaking research in several ways.

You can carry out some initial research by asking questions. Build on the information you have collected in your pattern diagram. Go back to the question words we discussed earlier: *why, how, what, who, when, where* and *how much*.

You will already have some of the information you need, but you should now conduct research to gather enough information to enable you to make an informed decision.

Make a list of the following details:

1 the information you need
2 the sources of such information, such as:
   – colleagues
   – former colleagues with a good working knowledge of the field
   – friends
   – the Internet, via a search engine
   – specialist magazines or periodicals
   – books – don't ignore these; not everything in the history of the world is available digitally
   – industry-specific data and information
   – experts – a search on the Internet may well reveal experts' websites and a well-worded email may elicit some help
   – a coach or mentor to offer more general guidance
3 the timescale by which you need to have gathered this information.

You could put this in table form, as shown here. This is based on today being 1 May.

Information-gathering timescale

Information needed	Source of information	Timescale to have information by
Range of new software: positive and negative features	Colleagues, former colleagues and friends	end May
	Internet	end May
	Specialist periodicals	end June
	Books	end June
	Industry-specific data	end June
	Experts	end June
	Coach/mentor	at monthly meeting: 15 May

It can be helpful to gather as much relevant objective data as possible, for example the number of computer crashes in a given period or the number of calls made to a computer helpdesk. Such data can support your choice of a certain type of computer software as a replacement.

Available or relevant?

A lot of information will be available. In fact, since the advent of the Internet, you probably have access to too much information. What comes with experience is knowing which information is relevant, closely connected to the matter you need to make a decision on.

Gather information about the extent of a problem. For example, if the quality of a product is failing, does this affect 1 in 1,000 products or 900 in 1,000?

Work on your costs

Sooner or later, money comes into your decision making.

On many of the courses I lead, the words 'money', 'figures' or 'math[s]' evoke a reaction in some participants of 'I don't do math[s]' or 'I'm no good with figures'. A few delegates are skilled in this area and enjoy figures, relishing their ability to do mental arithmetic in their head, but many colleagues are not. But the hard truth is that you've got to have some grasp of math[s] to make business decisions. Decisions nearly always include the money factor, so you need to get used to that fact sooner rather than later.

Fortunately, we can break down what you need to understand into some basics: knowing your own costs, knowing how much time tasks take, and drawing up a budget.

TIP *Now is the time to get a grip on the figures.*

Know your own costs

What we want to work out here is how much you cost your company or organization. This is different from how much you are paid, as we shall see.

Suppose you earn £20,000 per year. If we divide this figure by the number of days you work productively, i.e. omitting holidays and allowing for illness, this could give, say, 46 weeks per year. £20,000 ÷ 46 = £434.78 per week or £86.96 per day, assuming five days per week. If we then divide this figure by the time per day you spend on productive work, say two-thirds of seven hours (= 4.66 hours), we come to £18.66 per hour: this is the amount that you are paid per hour gross, i.e. before tax and other deductions.

That is only half the story, however. Your actual cost to your company or organization is about twice that figure. This is to allow for the overheads of the company, which include the general business expenses, the taxes it pays as an employer, the rent of offices, and heating, power and water. So the cost to your company or organization of employing you is £18.66 × 2 = £37.32 per hour.

On this basis, if a business meeting lasts seven hours and is attended by six colleagues, the cost of that meeting to the company or organization is 7 × 6 × £37.32 = £1,567.44, which is probably considerably more than you thought.

Know how much time tasks take

As mentioned above, the time you spend doing productive work is only a proportion of the total time you spend at work. This productive work comprises the main tasks that your job involves, especially those tasks that produce actual income. Saying that some work is productive implies at least three things:

1 Some of your time is productive and some is unproductive.
2 You know the difference between your productive time and your unproductive time.
3 You know how much time you are spending productively and unproductively.

Today, for example, my tasks are:

● write this chapter – I know from experience that writing each chapter of this book takes about two good mornings' work (I know I work better in the morning so I reserve mornings for productive work)
● read back through the draft of my previous chapter and make some changes (productive work)
● make some phone calls to chase colleagues; prepare for courses and meetings later this week (unproductive work).

The first two (productive) tasks will probably take me four to five hours. The last (unproductive) task will perhaps take me about two hours. In other words, I have some grip on my time: I am managing it.

Interruptions will probably come: a delivery of stationery is due this morning; I will check and answer emails at certain times through the day. Overall, however, I exercise some control over my time. I keep a log of both my productive and my unproductive time so I know how much time writing projects take. I can then work out the hourly rate I need to charge my customers.

If you don't know how long tasks take, don't just pluck a figure out of the air. Try a sample first. For example, you might think that checking 100 items in a list will take you four hours. You try it for half an hour and discover to your horror that you only check two items. Don't be tempted to say that the figure will improve significantly because you will know what you are doing when you come to the actual task. The rate at which you work may improve slightly, but even if you finished checking three items in half an hour, checking 100 will take 16.7 hours (30 minutes divided by 3 = 10 minutes each; 100 × 10 minutes = 1,000 minutes = 16.7 hours), which is more than four times longer than you originally thought.

Admin takes far longer than you think

Your admin tasks ('unproductive' work) – such as putting in an expense claim, arranging a future meeting with colleagues and making phone calls – are all important but they may not be part of your productive work. You still need to do these tasks, however, to keep your company or organization running smoothly, and it's important to realize that the time they take is probably far longer than you think.

Draw up a budget

As part of the decision-making process, you will often need to plan a budget. Your aims here are:

1 to list the range of different items of expenditure and income
2 to make the figures as accurate as possible.

I often work on these on a spreadsheet, with columns for 'projected' and 'actual' expenditure and income.

All that you have read above, on costing your time and knowing how much of your time is productive, is significant here. Your aim is not to write down just any figure without thinking about it, but to make sure that the figures you put down are as accurate as possible.

You are in business to make a profit. Even if your company or organization is not for profit, you do not want to make a loss, so you need at least to cover costs. Probably you need to make a profit.

Here is an example of a budget for a training course. The budget is made up of the projected figures under two main headings: costs (expenditure) and income.

A budget for a training course

Costs	Income	£
Speaker		4,000
Venue		6,000
Marketing		3,000
Administration		5,000
Office		2,000
Subtotal		**20,000**
Contingency		2,000
Total costs		**22,000**
	Delegates' fees	24,000
Profit		**2,000**

1 Administration costs of £5,000 are for 125 hours at £40 per hour. (This is what the admin personnel costs the company, not what they are paid!)
2 Contingency is the amount included for unforeseen events: about 10 per cent of the total figure is widely used.
3 Income is the amount you need to receive to at least cover your costs.

You need to gather all this information to enable you to make a decision about the price you will charge each delegate.

You can work out the 'break-even' point, the point at which the money you receive covers your costs. The break-even point here is £22,000, so if delegates' fees are £400 each, you will need 55 delegates (55 × £400 = £22,000) to cover costs. If you have more than 55 delegates (in the example shown the income is £24,000, i.e. 60 delegates at £400 each), a profit is made. If you have fewer than 55 delegates, you will make a loss.

Return on investment (ROI)

Return on investment is the percentage return you make over a certain time as a result of undertaking the project. It is calculated according to the formula:

ROI = (profits [or benefits] ÷ investment [your costs]) × 100

One way of considering return on investment is to work out the *payback* period, the time taken for the profits or benefits to cover the cost of your investment.

Example

A project to train all your staff in report-writing skills might cost £50,000, including the tutor's fee, materials and administration. Its benefits could be measured in terms of savings of work time and productivity increases of £60,000 over one year, so the return on investment is:

$$(60,000 ÷ 50,000 [= 1.2]) × 100 = 120\%.$$

Reading statistics

If you are gathering statistical data, check the figures. Use an alternative way from the main way the figures were compiled to verify the data.

Here are some tips on reading and understanding numbers presented in tables.

- **Check the basics:** the dates covered, the sources used, the scale used and the context of the figures. For example, if the figures represent a sample, how large is that sample? Are the assumptions reasonable? Are certain figures omitted? Why? Check the definitions of terms used. Are they sound? If percentages are shown, percentages of what?
- **Understand the data:** take one row or column and think through its content and implications to make sure you understand it.
- **Compare figures:** look at the columns and see if you can discern patterns in the data. Consider any trends: do the numbers show a consistent pattern that increases or

decreases? For example, is actual expenditure consistently higher than budgeted?

- **Consider averages:** calculate the average for a particular row or column and see what variations and exceptions there are. Try to work out reasons for such differences, such as variations because of higher or lower income or differing levels of employment.
- **Read the text that accompanies the data:** check that you agree with it and be particularly wary of such words as 'significant' and phrases like 'these figures of course show'.
- **Beware of making assumptions:** be careful about putting too much confidence in making extrapolations of data that assume a trend will continue.

Summary

In this chapter we discussed the need to collect relevant information. We have thought about the importance of understanding the context of the decision you need to make and of asking questions to help you understand the different factors that make up your decision. We then looked at ways to gather information and at the importance of knowing your costs so that you can draw up an accurate budget.

Follow-up

Think of a particular decision you need to make.

1 Draw a diagram to show the different aspects of what you need to make the decision about.

2 If any fresh ideas occurred to you as you drew this up, add them.

3 List the sources of information you need to consult and the dates by which you need to consult those sources.

4 List the different stages you need to complete to make the decision and the dates for completing those stages.

5 Undertake a SWOT analysis of your company or organization.

6 Work out how much you cost your company or organization.

Fact-check [answers at the back]

1. How important is it to understand the context of what you need to make a decision about?
   a) A waste of time: I want to make the decision now ❑
   b) A luxury ❑
   c) Nice to have ❑
   d) Essential ❑

2. From what sources should you gather data?
   a) Only the Internet ❑
   b) A range of sources including colleagues, friends, periodicals and books ❑
   c) So many different sources that I've lost track ❑
   d) The few sources I always trust ❑

3. What do the letters in PESTLE stand for?
   a) Products, experience, service, targets, loyalty, energy ❑
   b) Profits, ethics, selling, teamwork, leadership, empowerment ❑
   c) Political, economic, sociological, technological, legal, environmental ❑
   d) Political, economic, structure, technology, literacy, employees ❑

4. What do the letters in SWOT stand for?
   a) Structure, what if, organizing, thinking ❑
   b) Strengths, weaknesses, opportunities, threats ❑
   c) Strategy, wealth, objectives, trust ❑
   d) Sales, win–win, operations, teamworking ❑

5. What is the best way to undertake research?
   a) When I feel like it ❑
   b) It's not that important ❑
   c) Carelessly ❑
   d) Methodically ❑

6. How should you keep track of time spent on different aspects of your work?
   a) When I remember ❑
   b) Constantly ❑
   c) Never ❑
   d) So often it's hard to do my work ❑

7. What is a key aspect of preparing a budget?
   a) To estimate all the costs and hope they are realistic ❑
   b) To finish it as quickly as possible ❑
   c) To make the figures as accurate as possible ❑
   d) Spending so much time on it that I miss the deadline ❑

8. How important is a contingency in a budget?
a) Essential ❑
b) Nice to have ❑
c) What is contingency? ❑
d) A luxury ❑

9. What is ROI in the context of costing?
a) Republic of Ireland ❑
b) Ratio of interest ❑
c) Return on investment ❑
d) Resources of interaction ❑

10. What is the payback period, in the context of costing?
a) The time taken for the profits or benefits to cover the cost of my investment ❑
b) My product's costs ❑
c) The pay I am owed ❑
d) An act of revenge ❑

CHAPTER 24

Identify different options

You have now learned about two key aspects of the decision-making process. You know exactly what you need to make a decision about and you've started collecting information. Now you can begin to identify the different options that are opening up before you. If you are unclear about the best option to choose and don't know which way to turn, you will be shown different ways to generate alternatives that you could use in your decision making.

In this chapter we shall look at ways to:

- widen your thinking
- challenge assumptions
- concentrate your resources where they will be most effective
- be imaginative, using the SCAMPER technique to help you be more creative
- consider timing
- give your subconscious mind and your intuition the opportunity to do their work and allow fresh ideas to emerge
- move beyond confusion.

Widen your thinking

You can widen your thinking in various ways. One good way is to meet with colleagues and discuss ideas freely. When discussing ideas, don't be too critical of any idea. Don't limit yourselves. Think of as many different options as possible; build on others' ideas. Explore unlikely – even random – possibilities.

Here are some don'ts to follow as you discuss various possible options.

- Don't pretend you still have to make a decision when you have already made up your mind.
- Don't stick with what you are used to. For example, don't always go with your favourite supplier: see whether other suppliers can offer a better service.
- Don't choose the first option that offers itself. For example, if you move to a new area and are looking for a dentist for your regular check-up, a colleague may recommend theirs. You may then choose that one, even though you haven't undertaken wide research.
- Don't ignore the obvious. The obvious might just be the best option.
- Don't get stuck in the past. Move on to the decision you need to make now. For example, you may already have spent £1,000 replacing the steering wheel on your car and then you have another bill for £1,500. It is important not to let the £1,000 you have already incurred (the 'sunk cost', a cost that you have already spent and which you cannot recover) weigh too heavily in your decision to spend a further £1,500.
- Don't be hopelessly optimistic. You are not a gambler, hoping that roll of the dice must eventually fall in your favour. Don't discern patterns where there aren't any. Don't indulge in wishful thinking but be realistic.
- Don't focus on the wrong issue. A few months ago I decided I needed to sort out all the paper I had amassed during ten years of leading training courses. I kept putting off this task until the pile got unwieldy and I was losing valuable time trying to find papers. When I stopped to think, the core

issue wasn't time but having enough space to lay out all the papers while I sorted them out. So I planned a time when my wife was at work and I could spread out all the papers, sort them and throw many away.

- Don't be too cautious. I am naturally quite cautious. I remember leaving my house many years ago to go to a publishing meeting. A little voice inside me said, 'Why are you going? You know nothing will happen.' I made myself go, however, and at the meeting agreed to compile a book that later sold more than 80,000 copies. What if I had listened to my natural cautious self and had not been adventurous? You can be so cautious that you never do anything. What have you always wanted to try? Is now the time to do it? If not now, then when? For example, suppose you want to delegate a task to a colleague. If you wait for that colleague to be absolutely ready to fulfil that task, you might wait for ever. Delegate to colleagues who are nearly ready. After all, were you fully ready when work was first delegated to you?
- Don't delay too long in making a decision. Often, prices for flights, trains, etc., increase as the time for their departure draws near. You will remain more in control – and pay less! – if you decide sooner rather than later.

Challenge assumptions

When you are generating ideas and coming up with estimates or forecasts, challenge the assumptions you make. For example, yesterday I worked on a schedule for a new project that I am about to start. I thought I knew how long a particular task would take and had estimated it to be about ten hours. It was only when I worked through a sample text that I found far more errors than I thought there would be. I originally thought that the task would take me 15 hours. I then recalculated that the task would probably take about 40 hours, considerably more than my original estimate.

Try to gain definite facts. If you haven't got access to definite facts or statistics, separate the process that you are considering into its constituent parts and test each part to identify what assumptions you are making to see if they are true. The SCAMPER technique described below may be useful here.

- Be prepared to think differently, e.g. be explicit if your present strategy is failing. Face up to the 'elephant in the room', the subject everyone is aware of but that is not discussed because it is too uncomfortable.
- Are you keeping up with (if not in advance of) trends in your industry?
- Don't be afraid to take risks.

Never be tempted just to guess a number; when estimating and forecasting, remember that your final figures are likely to be nearer the trick of 'think of a number and double it'.

Concentrate on what will be most effective

The 80:20 rule, also known as the Pareto principle (or law), is seen, for example, in company sales: 80 per cent of the sales may come from 20 per cent of the customers. The expression derives from the name of the Italian economist and sociologist Vilfredo Pareto (1848–1923).

Pareto worked as a director of Italian railways and a superintendent of mines before becoming a professor of economics in 1892. His studies led him to analyse consumer demand and to formulate a law of the distribution of income within a society.

Pareto's observations, later formulated as the 80:20 rule, have also been applied to spheres outside economics and business; for example, 80 per cent of crime may be committed by 20 per cent of criminals. This has significance: if you want to see a meaningful reduction in crime, you target the 20 per cent of criminals. You concentrate your efforts on where they will really make a difference and have the most effect.

Be imaginative

Too much of our thinking is often based solely on data and 'information'. Ways to be more imaginative including using the SCAMPER technique and other methods of improving creativity.

The SCAMPER technique

The SCAMPER technique, first developed by Alex Osborn in his book *Applied Imagination* (1953), offers a set of questions to help you come up with new ideas. It is a useful way to help you produce fresh thoughts about an issue. SCAMPER is an acronym that stands for a series of actions, as shown in the following table.

Letter	Action	Question	Example
S	**Substitute**	Can you look for someone or something as a substitute for a person, product or process?	What happens if we substitute 3.20 p.m. for 3 p.m. as a meeting time? (Perhaps colleagues would arrive at the meeting more promptly.)
C	**Combine**	Can you combine two or more parts to fulfil something different?	Can I combine two different forms that are filled in by two different colleagues into one, to save time?
A	**Adapt**	How could you adapt the functions or appearance of a product?	What would happen if I changed the ketchup container from a glass jar to a plastic bottle?
M	**Modify**	Can you make a significant change to a situation, perhaps in an exaggerated way?	How can I add extra value to my product?
P	**Put** to other use	How can you apply your product elsewhere, or is there an external idea that you can apply to the opportunity you are considering?	What different markets could I sell my product in?

E	Eliminate	Can you remove anything superfluous in the product or process?	Can I omit the footnotes in the report I am writing?
R	Reverse	Can you swap the order of elements in your process?	What would happen if I began with the needs of my consumer rather than the advantages that I see in my products?

Be creative

An example of creative thinking is shown in the 1956 film *The Man Who Never Was*, based on the book of the same name by Ewen Montagu (to whom I am distantly related). Montagu had the idea of deceiving the German forces during the Second World War by planting false information on a dead body that was washed up on the coast of Spain. His plan ('Operation Mincemeat') was effective.

Here are some tips to help increase your creativity.

- **Visualize situations.**
  For example, here is a brief extract from a diary I wrote following a recent visit to China: 'It's Saturday morning ... 25 degrees ... we walk through the park sipping kumquat and lime juice: older folks dancing, a lady balancing several layers of wine glasses on her nose (later, the lady had gone and in her place clowns were performing in front of children), groups of deaf people signing to one another, many people walking, others exercising or doing t'ai chi ... this was our experience a few days ago.'
- **Evoke the senses.**
  When I am stressed, I try to think of one of two situations: hearing the gentle lapping of water on a shore of a lake in Austria or sipping cola in a restaurant in France. Both these situations are memorable because they evoke the senses.
- **Think of television advertisements that stick in your mind.**
  What makes them successful? What are the elements of story?
- **Change your mind; don't stay with your fixed opinions.**

Alongside all the objective criteria, be prepared to think of the unexpected and to be original, innovative, inventive and adventurous. You could begin by drawing a situation or actively playing it out.

> *'Genius is 10 per cent inspiration and 90 per cent perspiration.'*
> Thomas Edison, American inventor (1847–1931)

My creativity paid off

I remember it now. Our daughter was still in a cot in our old house. I was thinking about words beginning with the letter G. A few were interesting: *galore* (plenty) is an example of an adjective that follows the noun it refers to (*whisky galore!*); *galvanize* (stir into action) is an example of a word named after a person (the 18th-century Italian scientist Luigi Galvani).

I suddenly had a brainwave – what if on every page of a dictionary we could highlight a few words that were remarkable in a distinctive way? Thus the idea came about for a book that I later worked on with my friend and colleague Nigel Turton. It was originally published by Penguin as the *Wordmaster Dictionary* and sold well. It is an 'ordinary' dictionary except that on nearly every page alongside the main entries we highlighted in a boxed panel a particular word with an interesting history, idiom, grammatical feature or point of usage. My creativity paid off!

Consider timing

Certain events have to come before others. A friend of mine is currently renovating a house. At the start, he thought it would be relatively easy: call a plumber to fix the bathroom, redecorate a few rooms. Then he realized he had to pursue matters in a certain order: hire an architect to produce plans, cost different options, rewire the house ... in fact, the redecorating is one of the last things he has to do.

Timing has to do with the *order* of events. It is obviously also critical when deciding to launch a new product. For example, it would be foolish to begin to think about launching a new toy on to the Christmas market in September. That is far too late because you will want to be selling it in the shops from October/November. You should have begun far earlier.

Are there recurrent seasons in your industry? After a few years as a freelance editor, I noted that May is a significant month in the year for publishers: this is when they turn their attention to the following year's books. Work on their list for publication in September/October is relatively complete by then and they have time to consider the following year. So I have found that publishers are receptive to fresh thinking in May.

A further significant point about timing is to distinguish the short term from the medium and long term. Is your aim to plan only for a short-term success or do you want to build a long-term success for a new product?

Don't ignore your intuition

'I just know', 'I felt that was right', 'I had a hunch that ...' and 'The thought just came to me.' How often do you use or hear such phrases? Intuition has a role to play in the decision-making process.

Intuition can be defined as 'the power of knowing something without evident reasoning'. There may be no logical explanation for something; you discern the truth about a person or situation and you just know it is right. For me, intuition is important, but it is only one factor in the decision-making process. If I am tired or stressed, my emotions can play havoc with my thinking processes, so I have to be careful.

Intuition is linked to your 'depth mind', your subconscious. It seems that your depth mind digests myriad thoughts – analysing, synthesizing and evaluating them – resulting in an intuitive thought coming to your consciousness.

That is why it is useful to 'sleep on it': sleep for a night before making a significant decision. Sometimes this is plain common sense. I have an informal rule for myself that I do not send out a costing for a project without sleeping on it. A while back I costed a project one day and, when I checked my figures the next day, I realized I had for some inexplicable reason calculated the figure to be only half the correct total, so there is ordinary wisdom as well as intuitive reason behind the need to 'sleep on it'.

Don't ignore the thoughts that occur to you when you are taking a shower or driving home from work and are not thinking about a problem. Allow your subconscious mind the opportunity to do its work and let fresh ideas emerge when you are not thinking about making the decision.

Something wasn't quite right

From the first meeting, Harry had a gut feeling that something wasn't quite right with the outside supplier, Special Solutions Ltd. Harry's company had accepted the lowest bid and Harry had reservations about that, but he was left to manage the project. When he met regularly with colleagues from Special Solutions, they were pleasant enough – in fact, at times they were too pleasant: it was as if their superficial pleasantness was hiding something below the surface. Sure enough, matters came to a head at the second of their monthly review meetings, when it became clear that Special Solutions had not met their targets for manufacturing and were waiting on one of their suppliers to deliver machines.

The whole matter left Harry with a bad taste in his mouth. Not only did his company have to negotiate a withdrawal from their contract with Special Solutions but they also had to put the contract out for tender again and several months' valuable time was lost. Never again would his company accept a bid simply because it offered the lowest price. In future, Harry knew he would make sure not only that he would consider the objective facts and figures but also that he would listen to his own niggling thoughts, his own intuitive sense.

Move beyond confusion

Have you ever felt confused in the decision-making process? It is a good sign – it means that you have immersed yourself in the relevant factors well. You may even feel as if you are drowning. From having not enough information you may suddenly feel overwhelmed by having too much information to think about.

Some of the information may conflict with other information: one expert may be strongly in favour of choosing a certain brand of software, whereas reviews on the Internet describe it as weak and underperforming.

You may not know which way to turn – but this is all part of the decision-making process. In fact, you may even think life seemed far simpler before you began having to make this decision! You may want to go back to that time when everything seemed safe and secure.

But you are beginning to change. As you have thought through different approaches, you have begun to wonder. For example, at the same time as installing new computer software to deal with accounts, you may find some software that can also help you as a good project-management tool, so you come up with the idea of achieving two goals at the same time.

 At times you may catch a glimpse of how things might fit together. Capture it by pursuing it before you lose it.

Summary

In this chapter we've looked at a range of techniques to help identify different options in your decision making. You have learned how to widen your thinking so that you don't stick with what you are used to or choose the first option that offers itself. You can challenge assumptions, concentrate on what will be most effective, and take timing into account. You have also understood the importance of your imagination and intuition in decision making, and recognized that allowing yourself some confusion can also lead to new ideas and approaches.

Follow-up

Think of a particular decision you need to make.

1 Be imaginative. Think of different ways of creatively expressing your decision and the options you can choose from. Discuss ideas with colleagues.

2 What is the most imaginative idea you can think of?

3 What assumptions are your options based on?

4 Where does the 80:20 rule apply in your company or organization?

5 How important to you is your intuition?

Fact-check [answers at the back]

1. How often should you identify different options?
   a) Nearly always ❑
   b) Occasionally ❑
   c) Never; I choose according to my gut instinct ❑
   d) Never; I always choose what I've chosen before ❑

2. When you have to decide between something you've chosen up to now and something new, what should you do?
   a) Always choose what I've chosen before ❑
   b) Always choose something new ❑
   c) Toss a coin ❑
   d) Consider choosing what I've not chosen before ❑

3. When making a decision, what should you do?
   a) Consider my personality ❑
   b) Ignore my personality ❑
   c) Toss a coin ❑
   d) Go home early ❑

4. How often do you challenge your assumptions?
   a) Regularly ❑
   b) Occasionally ❑
   c) Never ❑
   d) Always and awkwardly ❑

5. What does the 80:20 rule tell you?
   a) To lose 20 per cent of my body weight ❑
   b) To target my resources so they will be most effective ❑
   c) To have lunch ❑
   d) To exhaust my resources ❑

6. How often should you consider fresh ways of looking at an issue you need to decide?
   a) What's wrong with how I've thought about it before? ❑
   b) Occasionally ❑
   c) Often ❑
   d) Never ❑

7. What do the letters in the SCAMPER technique stand for?
   a) Strategy, communication, alternatives, management, problem solving, emotion, responsibility ❑
   b) Sales, costs, aspirations, marketing, profits, employees, risk ❑
   c) Stakeholders, competition, adaptability, motivation, products, environment, resources ❑
   d) Substitute, combine, adapt, modify, put to other use, eliminate, reverse ❑

8. How would you improve your ability to be imaginative?
a) What's 'imaginative?' ❏
b) I don't bother because I don't need it ❏
c) By persevering until I find I am innovative ❏
d) By wondering how much money I could make ❏

9. How important is timing in making a decision?
a) The only matter to think about ❏
b) One significant factor among others ❏
c) Totally irrelevant ❏
d) My boss's problem, not mine ❏

10. How important are intuitive thoughts about a decision?
a) The most important factor ❏
b) One factor to bear in mind ❏
c) An infallible guide ❏
d) A complete waste of time ❏

CHAPTER 25

Work effectively as a team

Who makes the decisions in your company or organization? Is it only the managers themselves, or do the managers involve others in the decision-making process?

In this chapter we stand back from the detail of identifying and evaluating options to discuss the making of decisions in teams. We know that when we begin to talk through the different aspects of a matter the real issues become clearer, so now I am going to suggest that it is better if decisions are made by groups.

When a decision is made that affects colleagues, the more they are included in the decision-making process the stronger their motivation will be. When decisions are made by the whole team, there needs to be a balance of different roles within the group, so we will consider different team roles.

Finally we will look at the forum in which we make decisions – the meeting. We'll consider the need to make good preparations for meetings and how to run them well in order to facilitate the making of good decisions.

Who makes the decisions in your organization?

What is the dominant style of decision making in your company or organization?

1 **Decisions are made by the leader.**
   - Advantage: considered to be quick and efficient
   - Disadvantage: could be considered ruthless; some colleagues may disagree or not feel valued because their opinion was not sought
2 **Decisions are made by the majority.**
   - Advantage: considered to be fair
   - Disadvantage: could be divisive among colleagues; a minority may not agree and so they may not be willing to give their support to implementing the decision
3 **Decisions are made by general agreement (consensus).**
   - Advantage: as the way forward about a decision becomes apparent from discussion, colleagues will feel valued and will 'own' their involvement in implementing the decisions
   - Disadvantage: can take a long time

As you can see, each way has its own advantages and disadvantages. My opinion is that the third way, in which a decision is made by consensus, is probably generally the best as it is most likely to lead to colleagues' commitment to the decision and its implementation.

In particular, a decision that is discussed and arrived at by a group has distinct advantages over a decision made by one individual, for the following reasons.

- Each of us has our own weaknesses, activities or areas of thinking that we consider particularly important ('hobbyhorses') or particularly unimportant ('blind spots'). It takes a group to balance out and widen our own perspective.
- The decision itself will need to be implemented by other people and the more they have been involved in making the decision as well as agreeing with it, the more likely they are to be fully committed to it and support its implementation to others.

> *Try to reach a collective decision: at least if the decision is wrong, blame will come to the whole group and not just one person. If necessary, discuss a delicate issue with a colleague in private rather than in a group, as 'political' matters may come into play in the wider group.*

Acknowledge your weaknesses ... and your strengths

Now is a good opportunity to emphasize the point just made. Each one of us has our weaknesses and strengths. While we all want to emphasize our strengths, which we consider particularly important and will mention whenever we can, we often ignore the things about ourselves that we don't consider particularly important because they are in fact weaknesses and we want to avoid doing things that we find difficult or unpleasant.

Are you aware of your own weaknesses and strengths? Think back to school reports or ask friends – some aspects may be obvious to them but not to you!

My own weaknesses are:

- lack of creativity
- being too organized
- being poor at physical activity, e.g. sports and DIY around the house.

My strengths are:

- the ability to listen
- the ability to ask insightful questions
- my (usually!) personable nature
- being methodical.

Notice that a strength can also be a weakness: one of my strengths (being methodical) is also one of my weaknesses (being too organized). I expect everyone around me (colleagues, friends and family members) to be as organized and methodical as I am and I have learned (or, more correctly, am still learning!) not to be too disappointed when they are not.

Because we each have different weaknesses and strengths, we need to balance them out with the different qualities that other colleagues possess to be able to make balanced decisions. This means that a team ideally needs a range of types of people who can take on different roles.

Team roles

The members of a team should together bring a valuable and wide range of roles. These different roles complement one another: one person's weakness is balanced out by another person's strengths. What are the different roles?

A widely known set of different roles was developed by Dr Meredith Belbin as he looked at how members of teams behaved. He distinguishes nine different team roles, as shown in Chapter 20.

This analysis is useful since it can reveal that there may be gaps in your team. If you find that your team is lacking certain skills, you can then actively seek to cover them.

Teambuilding in action

I led an awayday for a group I'm connected with, as we were beginning to work together as a team. Using the Belbin model, I ended up (re-)discovering that I had skills in co-ordinating/chairing, so I was formally asked to chair meetings. Some people offered more than one role: for example, our resource investigator, who is good at communicating with many outside contacts, is also an excellent team worker who brings tact and a good spirit to team meetings. A discussion between our team members then revealed that we had no monitor/evaluator, one who could stand back and objectively assess ideas. Identifying someone with those skills was therefore one of our aims.

As well as the different roles that people play, team members should be just that: team members who are willing to work alongside others. The term *synergy* is often used to describe what happens in a successful team. It is often defined as 2 + 2 = 5, meaning that when two groups of two people work together, the result is greater than simply the sum of their individual skills. Something extra happens: the combined effect is greater.

A simpler concept was developed by Robert Dilts, known for his work in neurolinguistic programming (NLP). He distinguishes three team roles:

1 **dreamer:** a visionary with creative ideas
2 **realist:** a colleague who puts the ideas into practice and makes them happen
3 **critic:** a colleague who gives constructive criticism as he/she tests and evaluates the thoughts of the dreamer and the realist.

Whichever model you adopt or adapt, they both show that you need a range of abilities and skills in your decision-making group in order for it to be able to make balanced decisions.

Not everyone needs to be involved in every decision

Despite the importance of having a range of different people in a decision-making group, not everyone needs to be involved in every decision.

The so-called RACI analysis helps distinguish certain colleagues:

- **R** – colleagues, e.g. directors and executives, who are **responsible** for making a decision
- **A** – colleagues, e.g. directors, who are ultimately **accountable** for a decision
- **C** – colleagues, e.g. consultants or experts, or suppliers or trades unions, who are **consulted** about decisions but who do not actually make the decisions themselves
- **I** – colleagues, e.g. assistants, who are **informed** about decisions that have been made but who need not be consulted.

The importance of meetings

The meeting is the forum at which decisions are made, so we need to be clear about:

- the purpose of meetings
- preparing for meetings
- participating in meetings
- follow-up from meetings.

The purpose of meetings

Meetings are useful to:

- inform colleagues, e.g. to introduce new goals or give an update on progress
- discuss with colleagues, e.g. plan together the way ahead or evaluate different options to solve a problem
- reach a decision and agree the next steps to be taken to implement the decision
- develop a sense of identity as members interact with one another and as you motivate your team.

Preparing for meetings

The key to a successful meeting lies in the preparation and the following preparation is essential.

- **Know the purpose of the meeting.**
- **Plan a venue and time** (start and finish) in advance.
- **Invite the key people** to participate in advance.
- **Circulate an agenda in advance.** This means that you will have thought about the structure and purpose of the meeting beforehand. Also, circulate important papers with the agenda, not at the meeting itself. Ideally, the length of such papers should be no more than one page each.
- **Prepare the meeting room.** Plan the seating: chairs around a table invite discussion.
- **Read reports in advance.** If reports have been circulated before a meeting, then read them. I have been in too many meetings where we have sat during the meeting reading material that should have been read in advance.

● **Ensure that you come with accurate information.** If the meeting is to monitor progress, for example, make sure you take all your latest data on progress with you.

The role of the chair

A good chair is a diplomatic and organized leader, someone whom the colleagues trust and someone who values, motivates and involves others, checking that they understand the points discussed. Ideally, he or she will be able to quieten down those who talk too much and also draw out those who talk too little but who can still make valuable contributions. The chair will state the key aims and objectives of items being discussed, summarize progress and bring together the points raised, to reach agreement and draw conclusions. If a point has been controversial, the chair can express exactly what is to be minuted, to avoid possible misinterpretation later. A good chair will also sense when the time is right to bring a discussion to an end and be able to come to clear decisions.

Rescuing a failing project

Imran was called in to troubleshoot on a failing project. The existing project manager was beginning not to cope with the growing responsibilities of the project. Fortunately, Imran had a good working relationship with him.

Imran quickly noticed that basic points were missing: meetings were poorly structured with the barest agenda. During the meetings, discussions rambled on for a long time, often without decisions being made. Even when key action points were agreed, they were not noted, followed through or even reviewed at the next meeting. No wonder the project was in a mess!

As Imran had good relationships with all the colleagues, he was quickly able to put in place well-structured meetings that he chaired effectively with good decision-making skills, action points and reviews at the next meeting, so the project got back on track.

Presenting an argument in a meeting

When presenting an argument in a meeting, it is essential to bear in mind the following dos and don'ts.

Do:

- present facts clearly
- put forward arguments logically
- support your arguments with relevant quotations, easily comprehensible facts and examples (case studies)
- give reasons for and against a course of action
- keep to the main point at issue
- challenge yourself and others, and question assumptions
- play the 'devil's advocate' – put forward an argument that is completely different from your own to test the strength of your own argument

Don't:

- think of plausible but untrue reasons to justify a course of action
- just guess; always give reasons for your choices
- only think of reasons that support the option you want to choose
- give in to peer pressure to conform to everyone else's opinion. Stand up for what you believe is right and express your own opinion. (A committee should not simply consist of people who will always unquestioningly agree with the chair's opinions.)
- disagree with someone else's opinion in an awkward or nasty way, but show respect for others.

A good negotiator of contracts

Danielle was respected as a good negotiator of contracts. The secret of her success lay in good planning. She spent a long time thinking through different business models and pricing levels so that, when it came to the negotiations, she knew exactly what approach to take.

When they came to the final bargaining, she had clarified the critical issue (the price) in her mind and knew that she could be flexible on the less significant matters – for example, she didn't mind bringing delivery of the products forward by six weeks. She was assertive and firm on what was non-negotiable, however: the price. So she was able to settle and close deals well and arrange the next steps in the business relationship between the two sides.

SMART decisions

At a meeting it is vital to ensure that action points are clear, and in particular who is responsible for following up the specific points and by when. The action points should be SMART, as discussed in Chapter 18 and shown in the following table.

Letter	Meaning	Example
S	Specific, not vague	Not: 'We want to increase profits', but 'We want to increase profits by £100,000.'
M	Measurable and quantifiable	You have included milestones along the way to assess progress.
A	Agreed	All present at the meeting are in accord with next steps.
R	Realistic/ Resourced	'If you want me to complete this task, you need to provide me with the resources to enable me to do so.'
T	Timed	What date are actions to be completed by?
Some colleagues also add –ER to give SMARTER:		
E	Evaluated	At a later meeting, progress is assessed.
R	Reported	The evaluation is recorded at the next meeting.

Summary

In this chapter we asked the question, 'Who makes decisions in your company or organization?' and considered teams making decisions, team roles and the importance of meetings.

Follow-up

Think of a major decision that your company or organization has made recently.

1 How much were colleagues involved in the decision-making process? What was the relationship between their involvement and their motivation to implement the decision?

2 List three strengths and three weaknesses that you have. Check your responses with colleagues and/or friends.

3 Look at your answer to 2. How many of your weaknesses are balanced out by the strengths of other members of your team?

4 Think about the meetings you hold. How could you make them more effective? Be as practical as possible.

5 Consider the actions of the last meeting you attended. Were they SMART? If not, what will you do about it?

Fact-check [answers at the back]

1. As team leader, why should you share the decision-making process with others?
   a) To avoid taking full responsibility ❏
   b) To compensate for my own insecurity ❏
   c) To increase their motivation ❏
   d) To increase their pay ❏

2. What does 'consensus' mean?
   a) Counting how many people are present ❏
   b) General agreement by people ❏
   c) Agreeing to have different views ❏
   d) Many people waiting for a bus ❏

3. What should an effective team consist of?
   a) All similar kinds of people so that decisions are made as slowly as possible ❏
   b) A group so large that you don't know everyone's name ❏
   c) All similar kinds of people so that decisions are made as quickly as possible ❏
   d) A range of different kinds of people so that different approaches can be considered ❏

4. What is synergy?
   a) The result of people working together being more successful than when they each work separately ❏
   b) The result of people working separately being more effective than when they work together ❏
   c) Energy produced by all the colleagues in the room ❏
   d) The wrong things colleagues have done in the past ❏

5. What does RACI stand for?
   a) Relationships, accountability, consultation, intention ❏
   b) Resources, assessments, choice, implementation ❏
   c) Respect, authority, competition, integrity ❏
   d) Responsible, accountable, consulted, informed ❏

6. What is the key to a successful meeting?
   a) The refreshments ❏
   b) The room ❏
   c) The length of time it lasts ❏
   d) The preparation ❏

7. How should you put forward an argument?
a) Present only the advantages of each of the options ❑
b) Present the advantages and disadvantages of each of the options ❑
c) Don't bother with advantages or disadvantages ❑
d) Present only the disadvantages of all the options I discount ❑

8. What attitude should you show if you disagree with the boss?
a) Respect ❑
b) Humour ❑
c) Sarcasm ❑
d) Awkwardness ❑

9. What does the acronym SMART stand for?
a) Schedules, markets, assumptions, recruitment/risk, trends ❑
b) Strategy, marketing, assets, regulation/resources, trust ❑
c) Specific, measurable, agreed, realistic/resourced, timed ❑
d) Shareholders, management, authority, respect/roles, training ❑

10. As a manager chairing a meeting, what should you seek to do?
a) Pay more attention to the colleagues I like ❑
b) Involve all the colleagues on my team ❑
c) Wander from the subject as much as possible to avoid taking a decision ❑
d) Ignore everyone else and talk all the time ❑

CHAPTER 26

Evaluate different options

You now know your aims and have collected relevant information and identified different options. Working effectively in a team, your next task is to evaluate these different options so that you can come to a decision.

Your aim here is to reduce the number of options available, to enable you to make the right decision. It is sometimes easier to say that you don't want to choose a particular option (and why you don't want to) than to say what you do want.

In this chapter we will look at:

- distinguishing different aspects of the decision
- setting objective criteria against which you can then assess each of your different options
- considering the consequences of each option
- listing the advantages and disadvantages and/or essential and desirable qualities of each option
- the need to compromise: probably no option is perfect
- costing the different options open to you
- assessing risks: knowing how and when things could go wrong and therefore being prepared for them.

Distinguish different aspects of the decision

Many people have found Edward de Bono's 'six thinking hats' helpful. He distinguishes:

- **the white hat:** an analytical and objective consideration of facts and information
- **the red hat:** looking at a subject from an emotional point of view. What do colleagues feel about it?
- **the black hat:** looking at a subject from a critical point of view, considering its negative aspects, risks and disadvantages. What is the worst possible scenario?
- **the yellow hat:** looking at a subject from a positive, optimistic and visionary viewpoint, considering its advantages
- **the green hat:** looking at a subject from a creative viewpoint, examining any fresh constructive ideas
- **the blue hat:** looking at a subject in a structured way and coming to a decision.

Applying 'the six hats' means that you value different thoughts but you can separate objective facts from subjective feelings, advantages from disadvantages, and creative from structured viewpoints. We will now examine these different ways of evaluating options in the decision-making process.

Set objective criteria

This is the 'white hat' way of thinking. Years ago, my wife and I needed to buy a new house. We had one child and wanted a larger family. I needed office space: working from the dining-room table was all right in the short term but not suitable for the long run. We drew up a shortlist of the criteria we wanted for a house:

1 at least three bedrooms
2 at least two rooms downstairs, one of which could be used as an office
3 a more modern house than our current one (built in 1901)

4 within walking distance of the town centre (at that time my wife couldn't drive)

5 within our price range.

Eventually we settled on one that fulfilled all the criteria. The first two criteria were relatively easy to fulfil – most of the houses we looked at matched these. (In fact, the house we bought had only one large room downstairs but we converted the integral garage into an office.) Number 4 was the critical one – the new house had to be within 15 minutes or so of the town centre – and to achieve it we had to ignore some of the nicer houses in category 5.

What were the steps we took in this part of the decision-making process?

1 We analysed the situation.

2 We established certain objective criteria.

3 We looked at a wide range of options (houses) to see which fulfilled our criteria.

4 We narrowed down the choice to two or three houses that satisfied our criteria.

Using our criteria, we were able to reject perhaps 90 per cent of the properties for which we received details without needing to view them. Many houses were possible, but far fewer were realistic, for the reasons we had identified – as old as our previous house; too far away from the town centre; too expensive – so we quickly eliminated those from our thinking.

TIP *When examining different options, eliminate those that are possible but unrealistic.*

Alongside these steps we also used 'red hat' thinking, the intuitive sense of 'Yes, we can live in this house,' that we felt on viewing the house we eventually chose.

> When I go to a restaurant, sometimes I find it easy to know which dish to choose: an Indian curry! If no Indian curries are on the menu, I set some criteria and go through the choices, eliminating the dishes I don't want and then settling for the one I don't want least.

Distinguish essential and desirable qualities

When setting criteria to inform your decision, you will need to distinguish between those that are essential and those that are desirable. For example, when recruiting new staff, you will need to define the skills, qualifications and experience that the person you are looking for will have. You do this in a **person specification**. Some of these qualities will be essential, others desirable.

For example, previous experience of a similar role is usually considered essential: to be a team leader of staff at a customer services help desk, for instance, it is essential that the person has previous experience of working in customer services. Depending on the position you want to fill, you might be looking for a good team player or for a 'lone ranger' who is better at working by themselves, for someone who can plan ahead or someone who works well with spreadsheets. Some of these qualities may be desirable rather than essential.

You can list the fulfilling of criteria objectively by setting up a chart like this one for prospective candidates.

	Previous experience in customer services?	Team player (T) or lone ranger (L)?	Organized
Jo	No	T	Yes
Louise	Yes	T	Yes
Henry	Yes	L	?

Using these criteria, you offer Louise the job because she has previous experience in customer services, is a good team player and is organized.

If the choice within each category is not a definite yes or no, you can give a numerical value to each, e.g. on a scale of 1 to 5, with minus numbers indicating disadvantages (– 5 most disadvantageous) and plus numbers indicating advantages (+ 5 most advantageous). You can then add up the scores to see which option will be more advantageous overall, as in the following example.

	Previous experience in customer services?	Team player (+) or lone ranger (-)	Organized	Total
Jo	− 1	+ 3	+ 4	6
Louise	+ 4	+ 5	+ 5	14
Henry	+ 3	− 3	+ 1	1

Such a numerical analysis highlights even more strongly that Louise is the best candidate.

Consider the consequences

Every decision has consequences, and your task as manager is to:

● be aware of the risks of choosing different options
● evaluate the risks of choosing different options
● minimize the risks of choosing different options.

To do this, you need to do more than imagine you *might* choose a particular option: you need to think about what would happen if you *did* choose it. Be both subjective (e.g. what would it feel like?) and objective (e.g. what would be the profit or loss?). Use criteria that are in line with the values that you and/or your company or organization hold. It would feel nice to have £1,000,000, but the only way of getting that much money – by robbing a bank – does not align with my values!
     Here, you deliberately think of some 'what ifs'.

● What would happen if you did nothing? Sometimes this is a valid option. Sometimes – but not always – the response to a crisis can be to continue as if nothing has happened because the crisis will exhaust itself and fade away.
● What would happen if the decision were not made now? Can you delay it?
● What would happen if the decision were not made by you? Is it your decision to make – or is it the responsibility of you and others?
● What would happen if you adopted each one of the options that emerge? You need to think about this before you make your choice. For example, when preparing for negotiations,

consider whether agreeing to deliver the products within three months is a realistic schedule for you. If it is not, don't offer it in the first place.

● What possible future situations could develop?

Avoiding adverse consequences

Max was great at his engineering job. His technical knowledge of the company's products was outstanding. He knew the background to each kind of wheel and all the different specifications and measurements for each nut and bolt. However, he was poor at building good working relationships. No one was quite sure how he came to be shortlisted in the interviews for a new sales rep for the company.

Fortunately, the sales director who interviewed him realized that he would be a disastrous choice, and a colleague with slightly less technical knowledge but far better people skills was appointed. The sales director had considered the adverse consequences of appointing Max to be their new sales rep.

TIP *When considering the consequences of a decision, imagine yourself in the situation, experiment and then consider the advantages and disadvantages of each option. In this way you are more likely to avoid adverse consequences.*

List the advantages and disadvantages

Weighing up different options by considering their advantages and disadvantages is best illustrated by an example, as follows.

Disadvantages of keeping old computer system	Advantages of installing new computer system A	Advantages of installing new computer system B
The existing system: ● keeps breaking down ● is too complex to handle present needs ● is not compatible with the department's processes ● cannot handle the production of reports that Head Office now demands.	This new system: ● is compatible with most other departments' systems ● can handle the production of reports that Head Office now demands ● will save time in that it is far easier to operate than the existing system.	This new system: ● is compatible with only one department's systems ● cannot handle the production of reports that Head Office now demands ● will save time in that it is far easier to operate than the existing system ● is half the price of system A.

The conclusions you might draw from the example include the following.

● It is possible that we could keep the existing system but it is inefficient.
● While the initial costs of installing a new computer system are high, the benefits to the company in time saved will come within a few months of installation.
● System A is more expensive than B but A can do more of what we need so, although the initial cost is higher, it will save time and therefore money in the medium term.

Realize the need to compromise

As you weigh up the various alternatives before you, you will probably need to compromise. We need to realize that we do not live in an ideal world and therefore no one option is likely to fulfil all the essential and desirable features. For example, you may be running late on a project and have to outsource a particular part of it. You find suitable colleagues who can undertake that part of the project well, but the disadvantage is the cost of paying such staff, which significantly exceeds your budget. Nonetheless, you decide to go ahead and outsource that part of the project because you consider that the advantage –

that the project will be delivered on time and you will retain your client – far outweighs the disadvantage of the higher bill. (You learn from your mistake, and next time you will be better at planning both the schedules and the costs.)

The term *trade-off* is used to refer to a compromise: you obtain an advantage but have to make some sacrifice, as with the trade-off between individual freedom and public security.

Cost your different options

Think about the resources you need to fulfil each of your different options. There are four different aspects to consider.

1 **Budget** – prepare a budget for each option and see which produces the greatest profit (or the lowest loss).
2 **ROI** – calculate the return on investment and consider which option produces the greatest.
3 **Risks** – calculate the costs of dealing with possible risks.
4 **Business category** – consider which category the aspect of business falls into according to 'the growth–share matrix' developed by the Boston Consulting Group (BCG) in the 1970s.

The BCG's founder Bruce Henderson observed that a company's business units or products could be considered as belonging to one of four categories. The categories are based on relative market share and market growth.

- **Cash cows**
  These are products that generate high income relative to the low cost of retaining their large market share. Such products are 'milked' – producing profits easily and continuously.
- **Dogs**
  These products have a low market share and a low rate of growth. They remain in production mainly for sentimental reasons, but they are not profitable and are therefore likely to be sold off.

- **Question marks** (also called **problem children** or **wildcats**)
  These products have a low market share but a high rate of growth. Their future profitability is uncertain but they might become stars.

- **Stars**

  These are profitable products with a high market share and a high rate of growth, and they are likely to be invested in strongly.

The Boston growth–share matrix

	Relative market share: high	Relative market share: low
Market growth: high	Stars	Question marks
Market growth: low	Cash cows	Dogs

It's not just about cost

For a forthcoming business trip to Germany, do I choose a more expensive international hotel or a cheaper local one? I have found a good local one on the Internet, but it does not provide evening meals, which of course the international one does. However, thinking about it, I've realized that I will not want an evening meal except for on the first evening, as I may well have a good lunch in the restaurant at the university where I will be lecturing. Perhaps my lurking fear is that I will be stranded and starving on a Sunday evening in a large German city – hardly realistic!

The lessons I am learning are to explore every option in detail so that I am as fully informed as possible about the decision I am making. Cost may not be the most significant factor.

Assess the risks of each option

Risk assessment is **knowing how and when things could go wrong and dealing with them**. It is important to manage risks so that the threats of possible risks are minimized. For example, if you are making decisions about managing a project, risks are the uncertain events that could happen which could prevent your project from being carried out successfully.

Questions to ask yourself might include the following.

- Is the schedule realistic?
- Have sufficient financial resources been made available?
- Are roles and responsibilities clear?
- Are you measuring the quality of what you are producing objectively enough?

Risks need to be identified, assessed and then dealt with. The one key point to remember is that you will not survive in business without encountering certain risks, so it is better to plan to deal with them than be surprised when they unexpectedly arise.

You should prepare a risk-assessment document that lists potential risks, their probability of occurrence, the extent of their effect on your project objectives and your responses to them. The following example shows a risk assessment for a holiday booking company.

Risk	Probability	Effect	Response
Publicity inadequate	Low	Medium	Revise publicity; go to a new supplier
Computer software breaks down	Medium	High	Ensure technicians are available 24/7
Too many bookings	Medium	High	Identify other accommodation
Poor weather	Medium	High	Include holidays with indoor activities

You could even add a further column to indicate the likely cost of implementing the response. Here, do not pluck figures out of the air, but undertake research to ensure that they are fair estimates.

When it comes to decision making, you need to act at least on those options that have a medium probability. Time spent preparing for unforeseen events is not wasted: if they should occur, you will be ready.

'Hope for the best; plan for the worst.'

Anon.

Summary

In this chapter we've looked at evaluating different options, weighing up your choices by distinguishing different aspects of the decision-making process (de Bono's six thinking hats). We have looked at setting objective criteria, considering the consequences, listing advantages and disadvantages and distinguishing essential and desirable qualities. We also explained the importance of compromise. Finally, we looked at ways of costing options and assessing risks.

Follow-up

Take Edward de Bono's six thinking hats and apply them to a decision you need to make.

1 The white hat: what are the objective facts?
2 The red hat: what do colleagues feel about the issues?
3 The black hat: what disadvantages do the various options have?
4 The yellow hat: what advantages and benefits do the various options bring?
5 The green hat: what fresh creative alternatives and ideas can you think of?
6 The blue hat: where are you up to in the structure of making the decision?

Fact-check [answers at the back]

1. When evaluating different options, what should your aim be?
   a) To draw pretty pictures ❏
   b) To increase the number of options available ❏
   c) To draw complex charts ❏
   d) To reduce the number of options available ❏

2. In de Bono's 'six thinking hats', what do the white and red hats represent?
   a) The white hat represents facts and the red hat feelings ❏
   b) The white hat represents feelings and the red hat facts ❏
   c) The white hat represents purity and the red hat love ❏
   d) The white hat represents light and the red hat joy ❏

3. What criteria should you use when evaluating options?
   a) Subjective ❏
   b) Objective ❏
   c) What are 'criteria'? ❏
   d) Different ones, depending on the options ❏

4. How often should you consider the advantages and disadvantages of different options?
   a) Occasionally ❏
   b) Never ❏
   c) Always ❏
   d) When I feel like it ❏

5. When drafting a person specification, what should you distinguish?
   a) Subjective and objective qualities ❏
   b) Essential and desirable qualities ❏
   c) Whether I like the person or not ❏
   d) Management and leadership qualities ❏

6. How should you consider the consequences of each option?
   a) Informally in my mind ❏
   b) As if they actually happened ❏
   c) Never ❏
   d) In so much detail that I never make a decision ❏

7. What does trade-off mean?
   a) A business that is sold ❏
   b) A compromise: you obtain an advantage but have to make some sacrifice ❏
   c) The profit you gain from selling a product ❏
   d) An arrangement in which you give a used article (e.g. an old car) as part payment for a new product (e.g. a new car) ❏

8. What are cash cows?
   a) Milk, cheese and other dairy products for sale at a supermarket ❏
   b) Products that generate high income relative to the low cost of retaining their large market share ❏
   c) Products with a low market share and low market growth ❏
   d) Products with a high market share and high market growth ❏

9. How should you cost different options?
   a) As infrequently as possible ❏
   b) I don't; I hope for the best ❏
   c) Objectively and methodically ❏
   d) Imaginatively, by plucking figures out of the air ❏

10. What is a risk?
    a) An event that will definitely happen and have a good effect on your decision ❏
    b) An uncertain event that could affect the success of an option ❏
    c) An event that will definitely happen and have a bad effect on your decision ❏
    d) A game you play ❏

CHAPTER 27

Make an informed decision

Now you're finally at the point of coming to a decision. You know the core issues, you've gathered information, and you've identified and evaluated the various options. You're about to make the decision. How do you feel? Are you still uncertain or do you now consider yourself to be in control of the situation?

In this chapter we will look at the emotions you may experience as you draw closer to the point of making your decision and also at how you feel after having made the decision.

We will also consider:

- arriving at the actual decision
- implementing your decision: the next steps
- communicating your decision
- planning for change.

We will see that, after the decision has been made, you will need leadership qualities and interpersonal skills to implement it, especially in communicating it and working through both the 'big picture' and the details.

Factors against making a decision

Many factors may stand in the way of you making your final decision.

- **Do you feel confused?**
  You may have too much information even after evaluating all the options.
- **Do you want to continue to analyse the issues,** identifying and evaluating future options?
  Act; don't over-analyse. By temperament, I'm an analyser. Fortunately, my wife is an action person – that's why we make a good team. At the end of the day, you need to stop analysing and make a decision.
- **Do you think that you still do not have enough information?**
  Often, you will have to make decisions without knowing the full picture. Recently, on one of my courses, a colleague was being asked to make decisions but it was as if she was being asked to assemble a jigsaw of which not only the picture was lost but also half the pieces were missing.
- **Do you feel too tense to make a decision?**
  In this case, try trusted ways to relax and/or seek the advice of trusted colleagues or friends. When my mother died suddenly and unexpectedly just after the 9/11 terrorist attacks in 2001, she was on holiday in Australia and the rest of the family was in the UK. In the immediate aftermath of 9/11, it seemed unclear whether insurers were insuring planes to fly. As a family, we had to decide which of us three children in the UK (plus spouses), if any, would fly out. It was a hard decision to make, but close friends were very helpful at this point: '*You* must go,' my friend Michael told me. It would after all have been unthinkable for me not to attend my own mother's funeral, so I went. Friends pushed me to go when I was unable to make the decision for myself.
- **Do you feel afraid of making the wrong decision?**
  What if you choose that option and it fails? If you're afraid of making mistakes, you may well end up doing nothing. Remember, the person who never made mistakes never made anything. The key is to learn from your mistakes.

> *'The person who never made mistakes never made anything.'*
>
> Theodore Roosevelt, US president (1858–1919)

Arriving at a decision

The moment has come to make the decision. But what does that mean? In many situations, the best decision will often emerge as you weigh up the various options. As you go through the stages that lead up to reaching the decision, an option may well just feel right: you have identified and evaluated the various options open to you and you choose the one that seems objectively right.

What then? What do you do after making the decision?

Implement your decision: the next steps

I remember it well. My colleague and I had taken our proposal to Penguin Books, and they had decided to publish our dictionary (as referred to in Chapter 24). I got the phone call saying, 'Yes!' But I wasn't prepared, and I didn't know what to do next. This was because I hadn't planned it. Fortunately, I lost only a few hours' worth of work and I used those hours to think and work out the next steps that I had to pursue.

There are always things to do to implement a decision, such as:

- sign contracts, legal papers or other documents
- make phone calls to inform relevant people of the decision
- compose emails and letters that confirm in writing precisely what you are committing yourself to
- arrange to see people (perhaps phoning them first and then following up with an email)
- plan later stages, which might include:
  - establishing priorities and a list of tasks: draw up a spreadsheet or Gantt chart to show the tasks, schedules and personnel responsible for different tasks

- planning the overall view: set out the milestones of progress to be fulfilled within the overall task
- planning the detail of each stage: list the order in which certain items need to be undertaken
- integrating your decision into your normal cycle of planning: for example, if you are increasing your mortgage, add that to your list of bank standing orders.

Be realistic. As the proverb puts it, 'Rome wasn't built in a day.' It takes a long time and much effort to achieve great things and you will need patience and perseverance to see the whole decision implemented.

Be courageous. As a manager, you are called on to provide leadership. You are the captain of the ship: you need to face up to the challenges, have the courage of your convictions and pursue what you know to be the right course of action. I used to think that courage is the opposite of fear, but it isn't: courage is an inner strength to decide to do something difficult or dangerous, even if the fears are present: 'Feel the fear and do it anyway.'

> *'Each indecision brings its own delays and days are lost lamenting over lost days ... What you can do or think you can do, begin it. For boldness has magic, power and genius in it.'*

Johann Wolfgang Von Goethe, German poet, scientist and writer (1749–1832)

The point of no return

The point of no return is the moment in a journey or project at which the person has to continue: it is now too late to turn back or reverse the decision.

Communicate your decision

Among the next steps we need to take, outlined above, one of the most important is to consider the 'people' aspect of the

434

decision and how you will communicate your decision to them. You will need to decide (!) exactly what to communicate and what you want to achieve. This means communicating not just that the decision has been made (the 'big picture') but also what this means for individual members of staff and others involved (the detail). For example, 'Good news! We've just won a major contract to supply ... with ... and that means the further project will provide work for us through to the end of next year. Over the next few days, we'll let you know what this means for all the different teams.'

It will be important to clarify roles and responsibilities and make sure that colleagues have the resources they need to fulfil the agreed tasks. Such an approach will help secure buy-in from a wide circle of colleagues.

Take into account the following.

1 Think *who* the best person is to communicate the decision. This may not be the same person as the one who made the decision. Who is best at communicating with colleagues? If the news is bad, who has developed the most trusted working relationships and would be best suited to breaking such news?
2 Think *how* to communicate the decision.
   Should this be face to face or by email or by phone? Email is not good for every form of business communication, particularly if the matter is delicate (see below), when face to face is better.
3 Explain not only *what* you are doing but also *why* you are doing it. This is especially important when communicating an unwelcome change, for example, 'Profits are down, so we need to re-assign certain members of staff to different areas of work.'

Dealing with a sensitive matter

If the matter is sensitive, always seek a personal meeting, rather than communicating your decision by text, email or phone or in public.

● Where possible, alert the person to whom you have to make known the decision in advance. This can be done subtly – 'I've been wondering about ...' – or more explicitly: 'Could we have a chat about ...'

- Prepare for the meeting, both what you will say and how you will respond to the other person's potential reactions.
- At the personal meeting, be clear and honest, affirming your respect for the other person.
- Listen to the other person's response: seek to understand their interests as well as your own.
- Seek to end the meeting on a positive note.

Resolving conflict

At times you are bound to meet conflict. Seek to deal with conflict quickly by tackling the issues. Don't be cautious and fearful about speaking directly and clearly about difficulties.

Two useful books on the subject of conflict resolution are:

- Douglas Stone et al., *Difficult conversations: How to Discuss What Matters Most* (Michael Joseph, 1999)
- Ken Sande, *The Peacemaker: A Biblical Guide to Resolving Personal Conflict* (Baker, 1991).

The following is based on what those authors helpfully suggest.

1 Distinguish the incident – what is happening/happened – from feelings about the incident. Consider separately the following:
  - the incident – someone said something; someone is to blame. Try to focus on the real issue. Remain calm. Listen closely. Ask open questions. Understand other people's interests as well as your own.
  - feelings about the incident – these may include anger or hurt.
  - the identity of the person – sometimes a person's identity, including their own self-worth, will feel threatened, so calmly affirm your respect for them.
2 Do what you can to resolve the issue and maintain the relationship:
  - prepare and evaluate possible solutions
  - agree on the way forward.

After you have made the decision

After you have made the decision, how do you feel? Do you have niggling doubts as to whether you have made the right decision? In marketing terms, this feeling is known as 'buyer's remorse'. How do you deal with such feelings?

1 Know yourself. If you know you are likely to have such feelings, then accept them when they come.
2 Realize that the feelings will probably go away as you get used to the changes that the decision brings.
3 Go through in your mind all the objective steps that you have taken to reach the decision. Repeat to yourself the various steps you followed: for example, you examined the different options open to you and considered the consequences of choosing each one and their advantages and disadvantages.
4 Look at the positive side of things.
5 Above all, follow through on your next steps to implement the decision.

Plan for change

You have made your decision and have begun to implement it. However, the rest of the world will not remain static. Your decision may also affect other people's decisions. For example, if you start making a few people redundant, other colleagues may then start looking for other jobs. Ideally, therefore, part of your decision-making process should have considered the 'what-if' situations. In other words, you need to plan for changes so that you are prepared for them and not surprised when they do occur.

You will need to put in place procedures that monitor and control major items such as time and cost. If you are running a project, check constantly that:

- you are on schedule
- your costs are as planned
- the quality of what you are producing or delivering reaches the agreed standard.

If any of these is not following your original intentions, then discuss and agree with others how you will adjust matters so that you get back to making the progress you want.

Be flexible and creative in solving problems that may arise. For example, on one project I was involved with, we were running late on a delivery of books from China. The books were needed for an exhibition and there wasn't enough time to send them by ship, so we made the decision to airfreight them. The cost was greater than planned but the customer was satisfied and later came back for a repeat order, when we could work on a more realistic schedule.

The committee's finances were in a mess

The committee's finances were in a mess and the treasurer had resigned. There was, everyone thought, just about enough money to pay the three full-time staff, but the trustees knew it would be difficult. The trustees met and called on experienced colleagues to offer their expertise. This revealed that the committee would run out of funds in a few months unless drastic action was taken.

An urgent call for financial help was issued and, fortunately, the request was heeded. The extra funds gave the trustees an opportunity to put the running of the committee on a firmer financial basis. They now put in place proper monitoring controls that measured actual income and expenditure regularly and rigorously. Permission for expenditure on items over £200 had to be specially sought. By establishing such thorough controls, the trustees were able not only to survive difficult times but also to gather sound information that they could use as a basis to make wise decisions in the future.

Summary

In this chapter we looked at the issues around making the actual decision. We have considered the emotional side of decision making, both before and after you have made it. We have also been concerned with implementing the decision and the need to do this carefully, planning what you want to achieve. It involves creating the schedule and milestones along the way, and knowing the costs and quality of what you are delivering.

We also discussed the need to plan how you will communicate the decision to everyone affected by it, to tell them what you will do and why you are doing it.

Follow-up

Think of a decision you made recently.

1 How important were your emotions in the immediate steps both before and after making the decision? Discuss this with a trusted friend or colleague.

2 How good were you at communicating the decision? Again, discuss your answer with the friend or colleague.

3 How flexible are you now in adjusting to the changes required since making the decision?

Fact-check [answers at the back]

1. How much information do you gather before making a decision?
   a) None ❏
   b) Enough to make an informed decision ❏
   c) So much that it's difficult to make the right decision ❏
   d) Never enough, so I never make any decisions ❏

2. When you are afraid of making the wrong decision, what should you do?
   a) Still do my best to make the right decision ❏
   b) Not make any decisions ❏
   c) Spend more time analysing all the factors again ❏
   d) Toss a coin and hope for the best ❏

3. What is the point of no return?
   a) The name of a pub down the road ❏
   b) A situation in which I have not made a return on my investment ❏
   c) The point in a project when I want to start again ❏
   d) The moment in a project at which I have to continue: it is now too late to turn back or reverse the decision ❏

4. What should you do when you have made a decision?
   a) Look again at the other options ❏
   b) Move on to the next decision ❏
   c) Carefully implement the decision ❏
   d) Sit back and do nothing ❏

5. How important is it to communicate your decision?
   a) Essential ❏
   b) A waste of time ❏
   c) A luxury ❏
   d) Nice to do if you have the time ❏

6. If a subject is sensitive or delicate, how should you discuss it?
   a) I don't discuss it; it's too sensitive ❏
   b) In public ❏
   c) In private ❏
   d) Within earshot of the department ❏

7. How should you decide how to communicate a decision?
   a) Always text the decision ❏
   b) Seek to find the best way, e.g. face to face or by email or phone ❏
   c) Never communicate anyway ❏
   d) Always use email ❏

8. Who should you communicate with about a change that affects a large number of colleagues?
a) Only close friends ❏
b) The colleagues in the office next to me ❏
c) Everyone in the company ❏
d) All those with an involvement or interest to ensure their buy-in ❏

9. How should you respond when changes occur after you have made a decision?
a) With surprise ❏
b) With resignation ❏
c) By doing nothing ❏
d) Calmly; I planned for at least some of them and so am prepared ❏

10. What should you put in place to make sure your decision is implemented well?
a) My resignation letter ❏
b) A new long-term plan ❏
c) A marketing plan ❏
d) Monitoring and control procedures ❏

CHAPTER 28

Review the decision carefully

Congratulations! You have made your decision and are putting it into action. You have worked successfully through all the different stages of the decision-making process.

Is this the end? No: now is an excellent time to review how you have managed the whole decision-making process. So in this final chapter we will look at evaluating the process by going through the main stages:

- defining your aims clearly
- collecting the relevant information
- identifying different options
- evaluating the different options
- looking at what has gone well and also learning from your mistakes.

We will complete the Part by considering the qualities of a good decision maker.

Evaluate the decision-making process

Let's review by going back through the stages of the process and checking that you have covered everything.

Defining your aims clearly

Did you identify:

- what the real issue was that you needed to make a decision about and what the secondary issues were?
- the time when the decision had to be made by? Was that timescale realistic? If not, did you work out a strategy to seek more time?
- what kind of person you are, especially in terms of your values and what motivates you at work and the way in which you work?
- your personality regarding decision making: are you naturally decisive or indecisive, cautious or rash, for example?
- who in your company or organization makes the decisions – is it only you as manager or do you involve others?
- who will implement the decision?
- what your learning style is and how this affects the way you make decisions?

 When a decision is made that affects others, the more involved the people affected are in the decision-making process the stronger their motivation will be.

Collecting relevant information

Regarding the decision you made, did you:

- understand the context?
- gather relevant information, including consulting experts, as necessary?
- work on your costs?

Identifying different options

When you considered a range of techniques to help you identify different options in your decision making, did you:

- consider imaginative alternatives, widening your thinking so that you didn't stick with what you are used to and you didn't choose the first alternative that offered itself?
- challenge assumptions?
- consider where you can concentrate your resources so that they are used most effectively?
- consider the timing, working out which events come before others?

What role did intuition (your gut feelings) play?

Evaluating the different options

Did you:

- reduce the number of options available, to enable you to make a decision?
- establish certain objective criteria against which you then assessed each of your different options?
- consider the consequences of each option and their advantages and disadvantages?
- make a compromise?
- list the resources needed to fulfil each option?
- cost the different options that were open to you?
- assess risks, knowing how and when things could go wrong and therefore being prepared for them?

Making and implementing the decision

You eventually arrived at the point of coming to a decision. Did you:

- define the core issues?
- gather information?
- identify and evaluate the various options, weighing up each of the options in your mind and dealing with your emotions?

How are you now getting on with implementing your decision and communicating it to all the relevant colleagues? Have you set in place good monitoring controls to help you track progress?

Learn from your mistakes

What if you have made the wrong decision? Realize that making the wrong decision is different from having doubts when you have made the right decision. If events have turned out completely differently from what you planned and they have become confused, complicated, or unsatisfactory compared with what you had envisaged before you made the decision, then you may need to rethink your plan.

All was not lost

A publishing company outsourced the compilation of a new medical reference text to Harry. The project sponsor decided that Harry would be the best person to lead the project as Managing Editor, and Harry duly organized a team of consultants, compilers and subeditors for the project. Only once the project was under way did it become apparent that Harry lacked sufficient specialist medical knowledge to brief the subeditors and compilers fully. All was not lost, however. The project sponsor decided to appoint a general editor with excellent knowledge of the medical field, to work alongside Harry. Funds were agreed to finance such a role. Unfortunately, the work had to be put on hold for several months until a suitable general editor was found. However, once one was found, the project was relaunched successfully.

The result of Harry working with the general editor and all the other colleagues was an excellent reference tool. Although initially a wrong decision was made, the project sponsor used that as a basis to correct the course and turn the difficulty into a success.

Depending on the nature of the mistake, you will need to go back to the beginning again and take the following steps.

1 Plan a new series of actions that you need to undertake to reach your desired goal, using the point you have reached under the wrong decision as a basis for the new course you will now follow.
2 Deal with issues that have arisen from the wrong decision.
3 Start again.

Reversing a decision

Organizations sometimes make a wrong decision on a grand scale. In 1985, for example, the Coca-Cola company tried to reverse the decline in its sales by reformulating the popular soft drink and launching it as 'new Coke'. The company had thought that the original Coca-Cola needed replacing to boost sales but they had underestimated the goodwill towards the brand and its iconic image in the US psyche. The launch of the new drink provoked a massive public outcry as people remembered why they loved the 'old' Coca-Cola, and new Coke was withdrawn after a mere 79 days. The company then reintroduced the original Coke, which was later rebranded as Coke Classic.

Learn from failure

We all make mistakes in life. The other day I took my wife to a restaurant ten minutes' walk from our house. She enjoyed the meal but would have preferred to have travelled by car as her foot was painful. I made the mistake of only partly looking after her.

You may well know the story about the inventor Thomas Edison: when asked how he felt about failing to design a working light bulb, he is said to have replied, 'I have not failed. I've just found 10,000 ways that won't work.'

We often fail in life, but we can view our mistakes as opportunities to learn and become stronger people.

Jack changed his mind

When Jack first became a manager, he found himself in charge of people who had previously been on the same level as him. Once one of them, he now was senior to them. When he became team leader, he thought he would introduce new daily briefings and new performance targets and, rather than implementing these changes gradually, he decided to introduce them all at once. He did this to try to project a confident image and to show his colleagues that he was in control.

Unfortunately, the team did not cope well with this and their attitude became negative towards him. So Jack changed his mind: he decided to try a different way. He decided to have one-to-ones with each colleague to find out their own suggestions and comments on the changes. Such sessions proved to be opportunities for them to understand that the changes were for the good of the team, and gradually Jack was able to introduce all the changes successfully.

What makes a good decision maker?

Finally we consider the qualities that make a good decision maker. They are:

- **integrity:** being honest and sincere; being open and transparent and not deceitful; being upright and doing what you believe to be the right thing; and dealing with all staff fairly
- **strategic thinking:** able to see the big picture and plan ahead well; proactive
- **vision:** able to see beyond the immediate situation to the ultimate goal; purposeful
- **wisdom:** having good business sense and experience
- **balance:** able to weigh up alternatives, avoiding both personal weaknesses and extravagances

- **decisiveness:** not one to put off decisions; not hesitant or dithering but firm
- **courage:** having an inner strength that can firmly face up to difficult situations, even if you are afraid
- **insight:** able to discern what is significant among complex or difficult issues
- **determination:** energetic and patient in seeing a decision through; committed and persistent to complete tasks reliably
- **creativity:** able to find fresh solutions to difficult issues; resourceful and innovative; adaptable; able to deal with people well and solve problems imaginatively
- **authority:** gaining the respect of others; influential
- **being a good motivator:** one who values, encourages and inspires others
- **diplomacy:** one who can bring together people with different opinions; able to conduct negotiations that respect others' rights; tactful; avoiding giving unnecessary offence and knowing how to deal with sensitive situations
- **being a good communicator:** able to explain a vision positively and clearly; knowing how to use words well; gracious; an encourager
- **executive ability:** good at implementing projects; good at developing others
- **being good at listening:** not too talkative but one who takes time to understand others first
- **being a good delegator:** able effectively to assign tasks to members of your team.

TIP *Sometimes you will not have all the facts, or your colleagues may hesitate, but you still need to have the ability to make the decision.*

Summary

In our final chapter we have looked back at the whole of the decision-making process and tried to evaluate the different steps. How have you got on?

I have tried to show you that, even when you make mistakes, all is not lost: you can view them in a positive light and consider them as experiences from which you can learn valuable lessons.

Finally we considered the range of qualities that make a good decision maker.

Follow-up

Look back on a recent decision you made.

1 Did you examine the context, identify the key issues and collect relevant information?
2 Did you identify and evaluate different options?
3 Did you work as a team, implementing and communicating the decision well?
4 What did you do well and what less well?
5 What will you learn for next time and how will you make decisions differently in the future?
6 Looking back at the qualities of a good decision maker, which qualities do you already have and which do you need to cultivate more?

Fact-check [answers at the back]

1. How important is it to evaluate the decision-making process?
   a) Not at all important ❏
   b) Slightly important ❏
   c) Very important for seeing what went well and to learn from mistakes ❏
   d) Useful but only if there is time ❏

2. What will you do when you make a decision in future?
   a) Make a snap decision ❏
   b) Identify and follow through on the different steps I need to take ❏
   c) Muddle through without a formal plan ❏
   d) Do what I've always done ❏

3. What should you be aware of in your role as a decision maker?
   a) My strengths and weaknesses ❏
   b) My strengths ❏
   c) My weaknesses ❏
   d) My strengths and weaknesses in order to tackle my weaknesses ❏

4. What should you do when you make a mistake?
   a) Try to learn from it ❏
   b) Make the same mistake again ❏
   c) Get upset but do nothing ❏
   d) Ignore it ❏

5. What is one key quality of a good decision maker?
   a) Being happy ❏
   b) Decisiveness ❏
   c) Carelessness ❏
   d) Fearfulness ❏

6. If as a manager and decision maker you get absorbed in details, what should you also do?
   a) Stop making progress ❏
   b) Share the ones that fascinate me ❏
   c) I never look at the details ❏
   d) Make sure I also see the big picture ❏

7. What is one of the roles of a manager and decision maker?
   a) To spend more time on social networking websites ❏
   b) To take longer lunch breaks ❏
   c) To communicate a decision clearly ❏
   d) To ignore the needs of colleagues ❏

8. What else does a manager and decision maker need to be?
   a) More punctual at work ❏
   b) Awkward and heavy-handed ❏
   c) Lazy and careless ❏
   d) Discerning and courageous ❏

9. What is the best way to make a difficult decision?
a) Delay making it till the following day, so that I can think it through ('sleep on it') ❑
b) Make it immediately, hoping for the best ❑
c) Delay making it until it's too late ❑
d) Avoid making it ❑

10. As a decision maker, what should your aim be?
a) To stay the same ❑
b) To make my own rules about decision making ❑
c) To be the best decision maker I can be, using this book for reference ❑
d) To remain an average decision maker ❑

7 × 7

1 Seven key questions to ask yourself

- What am I actually making a decision about?
- In truth, have I already made up my mind or is there a decision to make?
- What are the most influential factors affecting my decision?
- What are the secondary factors affecting my decision?
- Do I have a preferred or an expected outcome?
- What will happen if I make a mistake?
- Do I have all the relevant details to make my decision?

2 Seven things to do today

- **Check back:** Remind yourself why you need to make a decision in the first place: think about the context.
- **Get reading:** Immerse yourself in the subject matter as thoroughly as possible, by reading online, in professional journals or books, and by discussing the issues with colleagues.
- **Follow up:** Review the outstanding actions from your last meeting – do you have the latest details, and are there actions still to take before you can reach your conclusion?
- **Risk-assess**: Run through the likely outcomes based on different decisions you might make, and analyse how they would affect your goal.
- **Clear your mind of clutter**: Focus on the decision in hand rather than trying to resolve countless issues all at once.
- **Carry out background research:** Find out what competitors have tried, and why they succeeded or failed.
- **Remember the steps to take:** Start SCAMPERING around and being SMARTER.

3 Seven things to avoid

- **Appeasement:** Make the right decision because it is the *right* decision, not because it avoids confrontation or extra work.

- **Pig-headedness:** Don't be afraid to change your mind if you're presented with a persuasive and well-judged argument.

- **Data overload:** Detail is great, but don't drown in it. Assess what level of data you need to make an informed decision and focus on that.

- **Issue evasion:** Be direct and tackle issues head on; skirting around them means you will not resolve them.

- **Personal bias:** Yes, red may be your favourite colour, but is it *really* suitable for your business's new toothpaste?

- **Procrastination:** Dithering will get you nowhere... if you're taking your time to make a decision, be sure that you're using that time wisely.

- **Wearing too many hats:** Delegate tasks to those who are best at them, and use their feedback to inform your final decision. You can't be butcher, baker, and candlestick-maker all at once without becoming a knave.

4 Seven SMARTER steps to success

- **Specific** – not vague detail
- **Measurable** and quantifiable targets
- **Agreed** decisions with other stakeholders
- **Realistic** and resourced to meet success
- **Timed** actions – no drifting
- **Evaluated** progress and project analysis
- **Reported** progress to all stakeholders

5 Seven great qualities for decision makers

- **Balance:** Being able to see multiple angles and assessing them without bias makes you a stronger decision maker.
- **Courage:** Summon your inner strength to follow the path that you've decided upon, even when this is intimidating.
- **Determination:** Don't give up after one small mistake or wrong decision – use it as a learning opportunity.
- **Integrity:** Honesty, transparency and following your principles mean that, no matter what the outcome, you'll earn respect for your approach to decision making.
- **Listening:** One of the greatest tools of communication is the human ear: use it when planning your decision.
- **Strategy:** Seeing the big picture and targeting it without being sidetracked by unnecessary detail can sometimes make even the toughest decision seem simpler.
- **Vision:** Looking beyond your current situation to envisage the best outcome allows you to act with purpose.

6 Seven steps to SCAMPER

- **Substitute:** Can you look to swap out a person or process?
- **Combine:** Can you combine two or more parts into one more efficient part?
- **Adapt:** Can you adapt what you already have without reinventing the wheel?
- **Modify:** Can you implement a significant change to your product or process?
- **Put to other use:** Can you use your idea in a completely different way or repurpose it?
- **Eliminate:** Can you trim any excess fat to bring efficiency?
- **Reverse:** Can you swap the order of your processes to make a change for the better?

7 Seven inspiring business decisions

- Automobile magnate Henry Ford decided to double the wages of his workforce, enabling him to attract the quality of employee he desired and raising workforce engagement – his employees could afford to buy the cars they were working on.

- Ursula Burns secured the future of Xerox when competitors such as Kodak were falling by the wayside, by moving beyond – or eliminating – traditional products and branching out into hi-tech business solutions for the digital era.

- Apple's board decided to bring Steve Jobs back to the company, a decade after firing him... leading to a stunning change in fortune through innovative products such as the iPod and iPhone.

- Bill Allen persuaded the Boeing board to invest $16 million in developing the Boeing 707, transforming US transatlantic commercial flight from propeller technology to the jet age.

- Never one to be pigeonholed into a single area of commerce, Richard Branson revolutionized the mobile phone sector by introducing prepaid mobiles, listening to the needs of customers rather than following the conventions of his rivals.

- Sport is big business these days, and one of the shrewdest decisions in the modern era of football was made by Lisbon's famous football club, Benfica, which gave virtually unknown former translator José Mourinho his big break in management: he has gone on to countless big leagues and cups, and has won the UEFA Champion's League twice (but, sadly, not with Benfica).

- *Your* next big decision; you have the tools and ability to make the right call, so go for it!

Answers

Part 1: Your Leadership Masterclass

Chapter 1: 1c; 2d; 3b; 4a; 5b; 6c; 7a; 8b; 9d; 10a.

Chapter 2: 1a; 2c; 3b; 4d; 5b; 6a; 7c; 8b; 9d; 10a.

Chapter 3: 1a; 2d; 3c; 4d; 5a; 6b; 7c; 8b; 9d; 10a.

Chapter 4: 1b; 2a; 3b; 4d; 5c; 6a; 7d; 8b; 9c; 10a.

Chapter 5: 1a; 2b; 3d; 4a; 5c; 6b; 7d; 8c; 9a; 10c.

Chapter 6: 1c; 2c; 3a; 4b; 5a; 6d; 7b; 8d; 9a; 10d.

Chapter 7: 1b; 2d; 3c; 4a; 5c; 6b; 7d; 8c; 9a; 10c.

Part 2: Your Motivating People Masterclass

Chapter 8: 1b; 2a; 3d; 4c; 5b; 6c; 7d; 8a; 9b; 10a

Chapter 9: 1a; 2c; 3d; 4a; 5a; 6b; 7b; 8d; 9a; 10b

Chapter 10: 1a; 2d; 3c; 4c; 5c; 6a; 7d; 8d; 9b; 10b

Chapter 11: 1b; 2d; 3a; 4c; 5d; 6d; 7a; 8b; 9a; 10c

Chapter 12: 1b; 2c; 3c; 4a; 5d; 6c; 7d; 8a; 9a; 10b & c

Chapter 13: 1d; 2a; 3b; 4d; 5a; 6a; 7c; 8d; 9b; 10d

Chapter 14: 1b; 2a; 3d; 4b; 5d; 6a; 7b; 8d; 9c; 10b

Part 3: Your Business Communication Masterclass

Chapter 15: 1c; 2d; 3c; 4a; 5b; 6b; 7a; 8b; 9c; 10d

Chapter 16: 1c; 2d; 3b; 4a; 5b; 6c; 7d; 8c; 9c; 10a

Chapter 17: 1b; 2c; 3d; 4a; 5d; 6d; 7c; 8b; 9a; 10b

Chapter 18: 1d; 2d; 3b; 4a; 5c; 6b; 7a; 8d; 9c; 10c

Chapter 19: 1a; 2d; 3b; 4b; 5a; 6c; 7d; 8d; 9a; 10c

Chapter 20: 1b; 2c; 3d; 4d; 5a; 6c; 7b; 8b; 9a; 10d

Chapter 21: 1c; 2a; 3d; 4b; 5b; 6a; 7c; 8a; 9d; 10c

Part 4: Your Decision Making Masterclass

Chapter 22: 1d; 2d; 3c; 4b; 5d; 6a; 7c; 8c; 9b; 10b.

Chapter 23: 1d; 2b; 3c; 4b; 5d; 6b; 7c; 8a; 9c; 10a.

Chapter 24: 1a; 2d; 3a; 4a; 5b; 6c; 7d; 8c; 9b; 10b.

Chapter 25: 1c; 2b; 3d; 4a; 5d; 6d; 7b; 8a; 9c; 10b.

Chapter 26: 1d; 2a; 3b; 4c; 5b; 6b; 7b; 8b; 9c; 10b.

Chapter 27: 1b; 2a; 3d; 4c; 5a; 6c; 7b; 8d; 9d; 10b.

Chapter 28: 1c; 2b; 3d; 4a; 5b; 6d; 7c; 8d; 9a; 10c.

Notes